THE FAMILY
MEDICAL HERBAL

THE FAMILY MEDICAL HERBAL

KITTY CAMPION

BARNES
& NOBLE
B O O K S
NEW YORK

This edition published by
Barnes & Noble Inc. by arrangement
with Random House UK Ltd.

1996 Barnes & Noble Books

First published in Great Britain in 1988

Text copyright © 1988 Kitty Campion

Library of Congress Cataloging data
available on request.

M 10 9 8 7 6 5 4 3 2 1

ISBN 0760703914

Printed and bound in Great Britain by
Mackays of Chatham

ACKNOWLEDGEMENTS

I am happy to be working once again with Jill Norman, my Editor. She is, as always, eagle-eyed and immensely practical. She certainly handles this author's fragile ego with tact, delicacy and humour. My literary agent, June Hall, who has served me so well with my other books continues to do so, making sure that, at least as far as my literary efforts are concerned, I don't have to worry about anything, large or small.

Gail Buckland typed my manuscript with speed and alacrity. My patients forgave me when I deserted my clinic for two months to write this book and Roslyn Smith took over its running. She was sorely missed on her return to Australia. Roger Thomas gave me lots of loving and moral support and uncrossed my eyes at the end of many a weary day. Thank you all.

I would also like to thank James Colton for the use of his British Chart for Clinical Iris Diagnosis on page 49.

For Jan de Vries: *who loves unstintingly, inspires with his courage and who has taught me the art of persistence and endurance.*

CONTENTS

INTRODUCTION

Every human body harbours an energy which science is unable to quantify or explain. Herbalists call it the vital force which inspires the body to life and is chiefly concerned with ensuring its equilibrium. If this dynamic balance, this homeostasis, is encouraged the whole person will enjoy good health. If it is disturbed disease results. Herbalists will use the least intrusive treatment to encourage the body to make its own corrective processes. The remedies they use are individually tailored to the patient's needs, so that two patients with the same disease may be treated with quite different advice and prescriptions, simply because the underlying causes of the disease may be quite different in each individual.

All the factors which make up disease need to be taken into account. Besides the physical side, environmental and emotional factors need to be considered. I have had patients refuse to get well because they have an emotional investment in staying ill. An arthritic who had progressed from wheelchair to walking stick under my care refused to continue her treatment because she feared if she got any better her husband might leave her. I often find it very difficult in these circumstances to get the patients to recognize that they are participating however consciously or unconsciously in the development of their illness and so should also be able to participate in their healing process. They generally refuse to consider the idea, associating it with blame or moral judgement, but the development of illness involves a continual interplay between mental and physical processes that reinforce each other through a complexity of feedback links. Disease patterns are often layered on psychosomatic processes that also need to be dealt with. In other words you are what you think. Acceptance of individual responsibility is crucial to any system of wholistic healing. I appreciate that individual responsibility can often be severely curtailed by social or cultural conditions as well as by economic, political and environmental factors. Some of these we can change if we act collectively, others may need more individual protest.

I recall a case where the symptoms of headache and nausea suffered by a VDU operator vanished once she had taken my advice and changed her job. The cause of her illness only emerged after close questioning about environmental factors which in this instance were directly responsible for her illness. More than 50% of every illness is caused by conditions which are *not* physical. Modern medicine tends to concentrate on anatomy and symptoms and the non-physical side of illness, if it is taken into account at all, comes a very poor third.

Some would argue that doctors cannot be expected to shoulder the heavy burden of a counsellor, teacher, priest, social worker and environmentalist. But this is not a new problem. More than 2000 years ago Plato insisted:

The cure of the part should not be attempted without treatment of the whole and also no attempt should be made to cure the body without the soul, and therefore if the head and body are to be well you must begin by curing the mind: that is the first thing.
Chronicles 156ᵉ

Hippocrates knew that fresh air and water, and appropriate exercise is central to good health and that study of the patient's environment is a vital part of correct diagnosis. He instructed that:

> *Who ever would study medicine aright must learn of the following subjects. First he must consider the effect of each of the seasons of the year. Secondly he must study the warm and cold winds . . . then think of the soil . . . lastly consider the life of inhabitants themselves; are they heavy drinkers and eaters and consquently unable to stand fatigue or being fond of work and exercise, eat wisely but drink sparely?*

Indeed the Hippocratic School with breathtaking simplicity went further and suggested environmental and emotional factors were often the *only* conditions that needed correcting if a patient was to get well.

I am often amused by how surprised patients are that the treatment I suggest to them is so simple. It is not uncommon for some of my patients to dump a carrier bag full of allopathic medicines on my desk when I ask to see what they are taking. For example, I see a large number of patients who have been on drugs for high blood pressure for some 10 or 20 years and these are surely not correcting or healing the condition. Such dependency is the result of years of ignoring or improperly treating the initial signs of high blood pressure or the malfunctioning organ that induces the blood pressure to rise in the first place. If caught early, most cases of high blood pressure can be cured without drugs. Time and time again I see acute illnesses that have been handled badly and as a result they degenerate into chronic disease for which drugs are administered in an endless stream.

Patients cannot be standardized, nor can their medicines, if they are to be truly effective. This presents the pharmaceutical industry with an enormous problem, even supposing it were not antipathetic to herbal medicine as currently it is. The nature of the beast dictates that it produce drugs in huge quantities, but the problem is that the recipients of such drugs remain, thank goodness, stubbornly individual and this has led, over the years, to widespread disillusionment with modern drug therapy. One man's aspirin is another man's stomach ulcer.

Even doctors are becoming increasingly worried about the number of patients being exposed to such irrefutably useful drugs as antibiotics. They are often prescribed for the mildest bacterial infection and occasionally for viral ones as well, where they are absolutely useless. Where allopathic antibiotics are required, and their use justified by a serious life-threatening illness their effectiveness is frequently diminished because the patient has become antibiotic resistant. This is the result of taking too many courses of antibiotics as well as eating hidden antibiotics in animal produce. The after-effects of fungal and bacterial infection induced by antibiotics is also well documented. In Italy all patients taking antibiotics are urged to eat a cup of live yoghurt with each dose to stop them destroying the beneficial bacteria in the body. There are some within the medical establishment who are worrying about the day when antibiotics are remembered only as a 'temporary and historical' form of treatment. It seems we are now only some three years ahead on drug research and development in this area. Too small a lead for comfort. Yet there are some effective herbal antibiotics which have been used for centuries (see p.28) and these do not have the side effects of conventional antibiotics.

The overall problem with a surgical or drug-based approach to illness is that it concentrates on symptoms as they arise and must necessarily wait until the patient is at the furthest reach of the disease pattern before decisions as to how to treat it can be made. But most diseases begin years before such radical intervention is required. I am always amused by patients who tell me that they have just got arthritis or been diagnosed with diabetes. These are classic examples of diseases that take many years to build up in the body before manifesting their symptoms. By ignoring or suppressing acute diseases as they manifest themselves from babyhood on we are pushing the body towards catastrophe, and in my experience serious health problems are hitting people earlier and earlier. I have treated diverticulitis in 10 year olds, been presented with juvenile diabetes in a 7 year old and polyarthritis in teenagers.

Natural medicine is very simple and practical. You won't find any unintelligible Latinized medical terminology here. I am not hoodwinked by the mystique allopathic medicine cloaks itself with. The original meaning of the word doctor stems from the Latin 'docere' which means to teach. I have always believed my first duty to people who decide to work with me is to teach them about the nature and meaning of their illness, and about the possibilities of changing the patterns in their life that have contributed to their illness.

So in order to make the book easily comprehensible I have divided it into body systems and put the small number of entries that simply do not fit into any body system in a miscellaneous section. I must add that it is foreign for me to name a disease. I prefer to acknowledge conditions, by which I mean I prefer to look at a person wholistically and not just treat a sore arm or a bloated stomach. However, for ease of reference and general understanding I have used terms like 'arthritis', while trying to keep my approach as wholistic as possible, given the restraints of a reference book like this and the fact that I am not personally acquainted with the patient. So if your problem strikes you as an emergency look up the section under first aid and if you can't find it there think which system or systems of the body it affects and take that route instead.

Knowing is one thing. Doing quite another. It is essential you read the section about herbal preparations with care before attempting to make any formulations. The Appendix listing suppliers will prove invaluable here.

The first chapter of this book is concerned with prevenattive medicine. I am a great believer in nipping disease in the bud. When I was in China in 1983 I was told that in some parts of the country doctors were paid only when their patients were well. All payment ceased if they became ill. This is a truly preventative approach and would certainly revolutionize the current health systems in the Western World!

Finally if in doubt don't diagnose yourself. Even the best GPs are only about 50% accurate with diagnosis without access to pathology laboratories. Even if your own intuition is highly tuned your chances of accuracy are not likely to be much better. So if in doubt seek out an iridologist and ask for an iridology test. I have explained about this exact diagnostic science (see p.48) and further details of the whereabouts of registered practitioners are available in the Appendix. There are also other means of diagnosis and I have briefly described these at the end of Chapter 1.

If in doubt about any aspect of your health seek the advice of a qualified practitioner as listed in the Appendix. Indeed you might go further and consider a general check-up before you encounter any health problems. By the time people come to see me they are often at their wits' end, having dragged themselves to every specialist and often through several surgical theatres before being spat out and rejected as incurable. Too often, allopathic practitioners are only concerned with a narrow bio-medical approach to the treatment of disease and this results in fragmented treatment that has become highly ineffective and appallingly inflationary.

To change the direction of current medical thinking we will need a quiet revolution requiring a different social and economic system. I firmly believe we will not be able to maintain, let alone increase, our well being unless we adopt profound changes in our value system and our social organization. Meanwhile, I will have to content myself by holding my particular candle and hoping it will eventually kindle enough unlit ones to create an illuminating blaze. Glimmers of light are beginning to dawn. The United States has stopped jailing its herbalists, though my own teacher Dr Christopher, a leading herbalist in the United States, went to jail many times in defence of his profession. Germany now sends its hard-pressed executives for recuperation to registered naturopathic clinics. Herbal medicine is available in most French and some Italian pharmacies and Czechoslovakia boasts some of the best spas in Europe. Witch doctors hold conferences in Zimbabwe and are considered quite respectable. China, continues to revere its 'barefoot doctors' as among the most skilful diagnosticians in its medical network. The World Health Organization is now positively encouraging the Third World to use the herbal medicines they have used for centuries. If we keep forging on with a multi-dimensional approach we will emerge with a standard of health care which has hitherto been only a dream.

CHAPTER 1
HEALTH MAINTENANCE

The World Health Organization's definition of health is, not 'the mere absence of disease, but total physical, mental and social well-being'. In other words health at its best should have a positivity which cannot be separated from spiritual, moral, political and social nuances. We have obviously taken the wrong track with a system of medicine which merely responds, reacts, tries to mend the broken pieces and concerns itself only with illness. Typical of this approach is that in the UK approximately £½ million is spent explaining the health dangers of alcohol while the alcohol industry spends £36 million on advertising. Yet alcoholism is the third biggest killer in the UK next to heart disease and cancer.

If we are seriously to improve the health of the nation we must begin with our children, before birth, at birth and in their developing years. Indeed I would go much further and suggest we start with pre-conception. We pass on our genetic blueprints to our children, and sadly they tend to get scruffier as they go down the line. So if you come from a family with a history of allergies, hay fever or asthma, it is much more likely that your children will suffer from the same problem. If your children had to wear glasses or have a mouthful of fillings in spite of a reasonable diet, the chances are that you, your parents and even your grandparents have all been lacking in adequate nutrition and the problem has been exacerbated generation by generation. It is possible to change this dismally predictable pattern by looking at your own state of health *well before* you attempt to conceive. Far better to prepare and prevent than repair and repent!

If you have a particular health problem and you are planning a family for some time in the future, resolve now to put all your energies into eliminating or at least alleviating it as far as you can. You may need to seek professional advice to do this, but if you have or have had in the past an unhealthy life-style (perhaps involving a junk food diet, smoking, heavy drinking, drugs, obesity, or lack of exercise) it is possible to do something about this yourself. Allow at least a year to prepare for a really healthy conception.

You can go a step further and contribute to the health of future generations by bringing up your own children with a clear understanding of the philosophy behind your diet and life-style. This is probably the greatest and most durable gift you can ever pass on to your children. Be persistent and make it fun, so that good health and all that its maintenance entails becomes second nature to your children and not just one of 'mum or dad's little quirks'.

My goddaughter is a perfect example of this. She has been raised by a mother who is also a very talented herablist and will willingly eat even the bitterest of herbal tablets because she has never been given any allopathic medication and has consumed very little sugar. She actually asks for her favourite herbal tea.

Remember too that allopathic drugs can be stored in the body for years, usually in the long suffering liver, and can be passed on to the foetus via the placenta or in breast milk, so use natural remedies for all your ailments as far as you possibly can.

DIET, THE BASIS OF ALL GOOD HEALTH

When I see the amazing rewards all of my patients reap from alterations in their diets I do not need convincing that a good diet is the indispensible bedrock of all preventive and corrective medicine. Dr Roger Williams, the noted biochemist, comes straight to the point.

> *If in doubt try nutrition first ... The most basic weapons in the fight against disease are those most ignored by modern medicine: the numerous nutrients that the cells of our bodies need ... Faulty cellular nutrition of one type or another may be the most basic cause of the non-infective diseases – diseases that are at present poorly controlled by medical science.**

It is important to understand that no one diet suits everyone. Our nutritional needs are as different and as individual as our fingerprints. They will vary according to life-style and stage of life, and are affected by such factors as stress, illness, puberty, pregnancy and lactation, the menopause and old age. What is less clearly understood is that structural and enzymic differences, which are partially determined by genetics, will determine how you will absorb any nutrients. For example, it is possible that you may be continually urinating away nutrients simply because your renal threshold for it is very low, or you may have insufficient intestinal bacteria to ensure the absorption or manufacture of a certain nutrient.

Worldwide research proves that our eating habits are linked to many of the major and most common British diseases including coronary heart disease, heart attacks, strokes, cancer, gall stones, severe disorders of the intestine as well as tooth decay and obesity.

In the last century the average British diet has changed enormously. In general we eat far less bread, potatoes, vegetables and cereals and far more meat, dairy foods, sugar, white flour, refined cereals, fats and oils and we certainly drink more alcohol. The food industry may have produced more variety and convenience in foods but they have also encouraged food preferences which are unhealthy. The centre of our problem is now not only too much of the wrong food, especially rich foods, but often too much food of any kind.

My own views on diet are detailed in *Kitty Campion's Handbook of Herbal Health* and I have subsequently listed the nutritional contents of scores of foods, together with recipes and appropriate advice about their background and selection in *Kitty Campion's Vegetarian Encyclopaedia* so there is no need to cover this basic ground again here. However, there are a

---

* *Biochemical Individuality* by Roger Williams, University of Texas Press, 1979.

few points that you may not have thought of, which I have not covered elsewhere and which do need emphasizing.

WATER

In most Western countries fluoride is banned because it is believed to be a slow-acting poison but in this country local authorities are continuing to fluoridate water in spite of vociferous opposition. Once it is artificially in the water it can only be removed by distillation or ion exchange.

There are four major pollutants causing particular concern: nitrates from fertilizers, lead, aluminium and pesticides. All of these can be filtered out by special nitrate water filters (see Appendix). There are other water filters which are popular and readily available on the market but which do not filter out nitrates. Bear in mind that it is impossible to filter out fluoride by whatever means if you live in a fluoridated water area (and you can determine this by contacting your local water authority and asking). The only alternative is to drink bottled mineral water. One word of warning, Perrier is slightly acidic so it should not be drunk while you are fasting and trying to alkalize your bloodstream.

MEAT

Factory-farming methods generally lead many animals to become less resistant to disease and drugs are liberally administered so animal feedstuffs often contain antibiotics. Hormones are also used to stimulate growth and fatten animals faster. The synthetic protein many of them are fed is often the by-product of industrial processes such as refining oil (such food is not the sort we would want to eat ourselves) but we eat it indirectly through meat and fish. As yet no one knows the long-term health effects of synthetic proteins.

A high protein diet can be ageing. Farmers giving their livestock processed protein pellets found that this accelerated their development making them grow bigger and faster but this hastened ageing, and it would do the same to humans. Digesting protein puts a strain on the body. Protein is broken down into amino acids which then enter the bloodstream until they are picked up by the cells that need them. When more protein is eaten than is currently needed spare amino acids are converted into energy. Uric acid and urea form as a byproduct of this and are a strain on the kidneys trying to excrete them. An accumulation of these in the body can aggravate rheumatic joints and cause gout.

A lion which is designed by nature to eat meat has a gut which is only 10 ft long whereas a human has a digestive tract which is 26 ft long. Meat in the human digestive tract quite literally putrifies resulting in yet more waste substances that have to be processed through the liver and neutralized into harmless substances being excreted – thus straining the liver.

One of the major health objections to meat is the large amount of fat it contains. It should be remembered that in animals fat is a dumping ground for many waste products that are not eliminated through the normal channels. Drug residues and other impurities find their way into the fat stores and bearing in mind the amount of antibiotics and hormones used in animal farming today the thought of eating them in this second-hand form is most unattractive.

It is true that feed for mature animals does not include antibiotics because this would interfere with the animal's digestion which relies on bacteria but other additives are reserved for mature animals to modify the digestive process and reduce the amount of methane produced, so saving on energy which can then be diverted to put on body weight.

Hormones and anabolic steroids were also used in animal feed to encourage growth. By juggling with the amount of thyroid hormones thyroxine and sexual hormones such as oestrogen and progesterone the animal's body weight will be increased and its fertility regulated to convenience the farmer. High levels of oestrogen are now known to aggravate cancers of the breast, ovary and lining of the womb in women. The highly controversial anti-oxidants, butylated hydroxytoluene (BHT) and butylated hydroxyanisaole (BHA), now banned in the United States, are routinely used in animal feed to prevent destruction of vitamins A and D. Binders are also used to produce animal concentrates such as feed pellets and feed nuts and colouring, flavouring and spices are added to the feed of poultry. Hens receive drugs to make the yolks of their eggs yellow. Pesticides and other chemicals are also added to feedstuff imported from the Third World to prevent the growth of pests and lengthen the life of the feed. Appetite suppressants and stimulants are occasionally employed in animal farming and animals are now not often reared in meadows and fed traditionally on grass in the summer and silage or root crops in winter. When raised in bulk they are fed as cheaply as possible using cereals, animal protein such as fish meal and all sorts of waste products including offal, skimmed milk powder, vegetable proteins, poultry fats and oils and synthetic protein, which are by-products of the petrochemical industry.

So all in all, if you are eating factory-reared animals you are ingesting a very nasty cocktail of chemicals. Hospital surveys conducted two years ago showed that 70% of staphylococci in hospital patients were resistant to penicillin because of the drug resistance being transferred through meat.

And that is not the end of the story. Once meat is processed chemicals and preservatives are often added to it. Additives such as nitrites have also come under scrutiny as they may well turn into carcinogenic substances in the digestive tract causing stomach and other intestinal cancers.

Nutritionists now recommend about 50 g of protein a day for the average woman and 75 g for teenagers, so almost no one in the Western world suffers from protein deficiency. Indeed most people far exceed the recommended daily allowance. Nuts, seeds, peas, beans, lentils, sprouted beans and whole grains are all rich sources of proteins. Vegetarians are often warned about the lack of B_{12} in their diets but this fraction of the B complex is easily available and readily assimilable in other food sources such as yeast extracts, soya milk, some seaweed-based foods, fermented foods, brewer's yeast and freshly sprouted seeds. Besides which B_{12} will be manufactured intrinsically in a really healthy digestive tract.

If you must eat meat, eat it in very small quantities and get it from organic sources (for suppliers see Appendix). Cut the fat off meat, skim the fat off stews and avoid gravies. Meat provides about one-third of our current fat intake. Grill rather than fry. Chicken, turkey, game, offal including hearts and kidneys are all lower in fat than beef, lamb, pork, mince, hamburgers, sausages, frankfurters, salami, liver sausage, fatty black pudding, fatty haggis, pies, pastries, and corned beef.

DAIRY PRODUCE

About a third of our fat intake comes from diary products. It is advisable to reduce fat consumption to about 75% of current levels and dairy produce is particularly high in fat.

Cow's milk was designed to feed calves. At birth they weigh 70 lb (30 kg) and once their weight has increased ten-fold they have reached adolescence and live off grass alone. This process takes less than a year. Humans, on the other hand, are designed to increase their weight much more slowly. Besides this many of us do not produce enough lactase to digest cow's milk properly and consequently get wind, indigestion and mucus and sinus problems.

Pasteurized milk is not the answer. It is vastly deficient in vitamins A, B and C, calcium, iodine and the enzymes that make it more digestible. Nor is homogenized milk. The tiny globules of fat in it pass through the intestinal wall unaltered and the xanthine oxidase (an enzyme that leads to deterioration of heart function) in these globules is now believed to be one of the major causes of heart failure. Under ordinary circumstances when fat globules remain their normal size xanthine oxidase merely gets excreted harmlessly. Nor is low fat milk the answer because the more fat is received the less calcium is assimilated. By reducing the fat content the fat soluble vitamins A and D are also proportionately reduced, and these are often added back synthetically – which is about as silly as putting petrol in a car without wheels because the fat in milk facilitates the passage of vitamin D into your bloodstream.

Goat's milk is preferable to cow's milk because it contains fat and protein molecules which are much smaller than those in cow's milk, making it easier to digest. Cow's milk takes 2 hours, goat's only takes 20 minutes to digest. Sheep's milk, admittedly still a rarity, is better still. For one thing it has no taste which tends to be the problem with goat's milk and it has even smaller fat globules. For another it contains more protein and B vitamins than either of the other two and it freezes beautifully. Greek sheep's yoghurt is now widely available commercially.

YOGHURT

A good alternative to any form of milk is yoghurt or kefir, both of which actually lower cholesterol in the bloodstream. Be wary of 'no sugar added' yoghurt – it is a label which may mask the fact that the fruit added could have been previously treated with sugar and remember that sugar kills acidophilus, the benign flora in yoghurt which helps to protect the intestine. All the vegetable gums and gelatines added to commercial yoghurt for thickness actually denature the yoghurt and so invalidate its bacterial content. The thickest, creamiest yoghurts often do not have any live yoghurt culture at all. If in doubt read the label and look for the word 'live' or the name of the bacteria in the yoghurt, usually *Lactobacillus bulgaricus* or *Lactobacillus acidophilus*.

CHEESE

Home-made cottage cheese has less fat in it than any other. Avoid cheese containing artificial colouring and go for goat's milk and sheep's milk cheeses and those from organic farms. Danish feta cheese is made from cow's milk with additives in it. Don't buy it. Greek feta cheese is salty and needs to be soaked overnight in water and then drained.

BUTTER VERSUS MARGARINE

Ever since margarine came on the market there has been noticeable rivalry beween butter and margarine manufacturers and it is not surprising that the average person is somewhat confused as to which is best. Personally I come down very heavily in favour of unsalted and preferably home-made butter. Ghee (clarified Indian butter) has an ability to protect against atherosclerosis and its gentle nutty flavour enhances food as no vegetable oil can. It is possible to make it at home but it is widely available from Indian grocery stores.

Vegetable oils used to make margarine have first to be solidified by a process called hydrogenation. They are then mixed with skimmed milk and re-worked to add salt and remove excess water. The solidification process used frequently turns the unsalted fats into saturated fats, so raising the cholesterol content of the product. Since 1960 many margarine producers claimed to have solved this problem and now produce a low cholesterol margarine made with polyunsaturated fats. But before you get too excited about this process take a closer look at how margarine is made.

Hydrogenation is the next step after refining – hydrogen gases introduce the liquid oil in the presence of a metallic catalyst, usually nickel or cadmium. This succeeds in bonding hydrogen ions onto the oil molecules, saturating them and transforming them from a liquid to a solid. The resulting hydrogenated oil actually has the same molecular structure as plastic when examined under a microscope. No microbes will attack it nor will it grow mould in the normal way. Not good news. This means it is an entirely dead product.

The other problem I have with margarine is with the labelling. Any label that states 'high in polyunsaturates' plays down the fact that hydrogenation is in itself a saturation process. What this really means is that the oil is high in polyunsaturates before it was hydrogenated so that margarine could be made from it.

Butter may be saturated and contains cholesterol but it is at least a real food. So if you must eat fat use unsalted butter, preferably home made with organic milk, and eat it in moderation, no more than three level teaspoons daily.

SALT

We eat about ten times as much salt as we need. Because sodium and chloride are so widely distributed in natural foods, it is almost *never* nutritionally essential to add salt to food. Salt with food is an acquired not an inborn taste. The only circumstances in which it is necessary to add salt to your diet is when you do long strenuous exercise in extremely hot weather to which you have not already had a chance to acclimatize. Remember that nearly 90% of the salt you eat is actually hidden in food. The amount of salt needed daily by an adult in a temperate climate is 4 g, and this can always be obtained from natural foods. Canned and processed foods invariably have added salt, and the additives in them, including monosodium glutamate, sodium bicarbonate, sodium nitrite, sodium benzoate, sodium propionate and sodium citrate also contain salt. Foods containing salt include some surprising examples like hard cheeses, dried, evaporated or condensed milk, baking powder and breakfast cereals. Remember that all salt, whether it be rock or plain table salt, has virtually the same chemical composition and sodium content; so there is no point in just switching to another kind because it sounds healthier.

There are various salt substitutes on the market, some of which contain mostly potassium chloride, and others which are generally a mixture of potassium chloride and ordinary salt. Check with your doctor before using these if you are a diabetic or have heart or kidney disease.

If you are cooking with these substances you can replace salt in exactly the same quantities although some manufacturers recommend that those which contain mostly potassium chloride should be added towards the end of the cooking time as prolonged heating can accentuate a bitter after-taste.

It is worth experimenting with herbs and spices as flavouring instead and of course for children it is better to discourage the taste of the salt and salty foods at a very early age. A good salt substitute is two parts kelp powder mixed with one part parsley, one part marjoram, one part garlic powder, and one part cayenne pepper.

SUGAR

Too much sugar not only causes tooth decay but, far more seriously, diabetes and increases the likelihood and severity of many other diseases. The average Westerner eats over 1½ lb (750 g) of sugar every week where in 1850 we ate 3 lb (1.5 kg) a year. We certainly do not need sugar for energy, and it does not provide any vitamins or minerals. Brown sugar and honey are just as bad for the teeth and also high in calories. Aim to cut your intake by at least 90%.

Sugar inhibits the ability of the white blood cells to destroy bacteria. Tests show that a couple of teaspoons of sugar can undermine the strength of white blood cells by 25%. Sugar can reduce your resistance to everything from colds to cancer.

Use dried fruit to make up for the lack of sweetness as you are weaning yourself off sugar. But if you find this absolutely impossible stick to small amounts of honey or blackstrap molasses or try sweeteners like rice syrup, barley malt or date sugar which do not depend on sucrose for their sweetening power.

ARTIFICIAL SWEETENERS

Many soft drink manufacturers are using aspartame for their diet drinks but the cans in this country do not even carry a warning (as US products are legally obliged to do) that the phenylalanine in aspartame may damage children suffering from phenylketonuria. A recent study of 95 volunteers aged 18 to 22 in Leeds show that people actually felt hunger after eating foods sweetened with aspartame, an effect which is not desirable in view of the fact that most people using artificial sweeteners do so to lose weight or stabilize their weight.

I suggest that you avoid artificial sweeteners in all forms, no matter what their source. Note also that substances like thaumatin, kacesulsamek, mannitol, xylitol, hydrogenated glucose syrup, isomolt and sorbitol are increasingly being added to manufactured foods instead of ordinary sugar so read the labels before you buy.

BRAN

Bran has become a national fetish but be wary of the kind of bran which you ingest. Wheat bran scours the delicate lining of the bowel and if someone is constipated it will often make the condition worse, not better. I have found that 30% of my patients are wheat intolerant. High levels of wheat can inhibit the absorption of iron and iron minerals. I far prefer flax-seed or psyllium mixed with fruit or vegetable juice and taken twice daily between meals, beginning with a teaspoon of seeds taken in plenty of liquid and increasing to a tablespoon. These seeds are soft, mucilaginous and don't scour. Flax-seed has the added advantage of actively deodorizing the bowel because the tiny amounts of linamerase in them block the absorption of poisons. It does not cause bloating or wind even in the elderly. Better sources of bran are soya and oatmeal. Oatmeal has the dual advantage of slowing down the absorption of sugar and reducing the cholesterol content of the bloodstream.

Advice on correcting constipation gently and permanently is given later (see p.127). However if you are just starting on bran introduce it into the diet very slowly beginning with just a couple of teaspoons and gradually increasing to three level tablespoons a day. Unlike laxatives bran will not work suddenly – it may take a few weeks to help establish regularity, during which time it may also cause some quite strong intestinal gas. I do not much like elderly people and pregnant women using bran if they have not tried it before and prefer to direct them to flax-seed or psyllium husks.

ALCOHOL

Keep your alcohol consumption moderate. A maximum of one or two drinks a day is actually healthy but these should always be taken with meals. Wine is closer in composition to our gastric juices than any other drink but it may be loaded with chemicals (none of which needs legally be listed on the label). Many asthmatics react severely to the sulphur dioxide used in wine to halt fermentation and kill bacteria. Another common additive is white sugar (manufacturers are permitted up to 53% water and/or sugar in certain wine). Other additives (there is a choice of nearly 100 in all) may mean you are virtually drinking a chemical factory. Buy organic wine wherever possible. For suppliers see Appendix.

FOOD COMBINING

Proteins are the only food digested in the stomach. The digestion of starchy foods begins in the mouth and ends in the intestine. If starches and proteins are mixed together the starches are trapped in the stomach while the protein is digested and the starches ferment and become sour. If you mix acid fruits and starchy foods together it also encourages fermentation and indigestion. It is advisable to separate protein from starch in any one meal and not to mix fruits, fresh or dried, with starchy foods. There is an excellent book by Doris Grant and Jean Joice which deals with the subject of food combining. It is listed in the references in the Appendix.

SUGGESTIONS FOR A *HEALTHY DIET*

You will notice that I have not given you any hard and fast rules about diet. I have observed an extraordinary fact over the many years of working with my patients and it has repeated itself so often that I know it to be true. Once you have cut out all junk food from the diet and cleared the rubbish away from the system your body will tell you instinctively what it needs. I have worked with people who have vomited up even a cup of herbal tea at the beginning of any dietary reform. This is because the body is so toxic and the digestion so battered that it cannot deal even with the simplest bit of pure nutrition and in this instance I get the patient to start with just a few teaspoons of the tea and graduate from there. Accurate instincts about diet only begin once you have cleaned out the body. At first you will find that instinct appears in fits and starts because the new way of eating is rather like learning to ride a bike. You tend to wobble about a lot and fall off several times but if you are persistent and keep remounting you eventually get the hang of it. Eventually the speed, once you have mastered it, is wonderfully exhilarating!

Don't attempt to change your diet all at once unless you have phenomenal willpower. Vegetarianism, for example, isn't for everyone. I have encountered people who have adapted better than others to having a lot of meat in their diets. These people may feel wonderful when they first switch to a vegetarian diet, but soon find the feeling of super energy dwindling and then notice that they never feel totally well again. These initial good effects are similar to those induced by fasting. A meat-free diet has less toxins and requires less energy to digest. But if your metabolism needs meat, meat it should have. There is no one ideal diet that suits everyone. If you find you need meat, eat it in moderation with enthusiasm and don't feel guilty about it. But for your sake and the sake of the animal you are eating try to track down a source of meat, poultry or fish that treats living creatures with the respect they deserve.

Alter only one aspect of your diet at a time. Set yourself one challenge and having achieved your aims enjoy the satisfaction of that and then go on to something else. If you change your allegiance to a more imaginative balanced wholefood diet you will notice something very intriguing beginning to happen. Your taste buds will get sharper and fussier and you will actually feel nauseated not merely naughty when you eat foods which don't suit you. Or if you get aches and pains, a rash, diarrhoea, headaches and bloodshot eyes or halitosis, you will quickly conclude that it is simply not worth drowning in your own poison.

Try not to become a fanatic but on the other hand don't let other people's opinions bother or sway you. If you are going to be naughty, relax and savour every single mouthful and really enjoy it, because nothing upsets the indigestion more than guilt, self-hatred or worry.

Diet alone will not achieve good health. There are other essential

psychological and physical factors involved. Consider all the other aspects of your life-style. Do you smoke? I hardly need to let you know about its dangers. Are you a passive smoker? If you sit next to somebody who smokes 30 cigarettes a day in a closed office you will be ingesting the equivalent of five cigarettes a day simply by breathing in that inconsiderate smoker's exhaled poisons. Do you take illegal drugs? The dangers far outweigh any possible benefit that might result from their use. Any high you achieve will be temporary and the toxic residues left behind horrendous. Try not to take drugs for any reason at all including medical ones, unless they are absolutely essential. There are more ways to ease a headache than rushing to the medical cabinet for an aspirin. Consider meditation, lying down in a darkened room and having a short nap, a massage with some lavender oil, a couple of teaspoons of cold feverfew tea, ice cubes on the forehead, or a hot-water bottle on the back of the neck.

Regular physical exercise is necessary in order to maintain good health. Aim for three sessions of 40 minutes a week of moderately strenuous exercise which will raise your pulse level to half as much as its resting recording. Enjoy the type of exercise you do. I am very careful to suggest exercise which is appropriate for the person concerned. There is absolutely no point in soldiering on with something which makes you feel miserable because sooner rather than later you'll stop altogether.

Have you ever thought about taking regular mental exercise? The mind undoubtedly governs the body in many ways. Good mental health is a prerequisite to physical health. I have noticed that watching large amounts of television or videos has an almost hypnotic effect on some people, particularly children. Besides which too many people hug the television set by sitting far too close, and so are bathed in the radiation which leaks from every television set. Playing a board game or intricate card game, studying a new subject with concentration, designing a dress from the pattern onwards, even doing a difficult crossword puzzle all help to get the mind working.

People who set themselves achievable goals in life often have much more positive attitudes and something to live for. You've heard it before but I will say it again. All work and no play makes you dull. I make it a rule to work at my clinic only 3 days a week simply because I believe that variety is the spice of life. In the remaining 4 days I pursue my other hobbies and interests, which give me even greater zest to tackle my work with enthusiasm and a clear mind.

I have noticed that people who continually avoid their responsibilities get dragged down with misery and guilt. Stress caused by a sense of failure and self-recrimination is far worse than the stress caused by taking on extra responsibilities.

People who live in dirty, untidy environments tend to encourage the same internally, physically and mentally. While I am not a fanatic about cleanliness it is difficult to feel relaxed and serene in surroundings that are chaotic or dirty.

HEAVY METAL POISONING

Lead, mercury, aluminium and cadmium are all toxic minerals which are becoming increasing threats to our health in today's industrial society. Prolonged exposure to them decreases vitality, shortens life, and generally aggravates disease.

LEAD

Exhaust fumes are the main sources of lead, followed by lead piping and solder used in food cans, cigarette smoke and lead-based pottery and glazes.

There is now irrefutable evidence to suggest that increased body burdens of lead poison the nervous system and so reduce IQ, decrease mental concentration, increase the rate of miscarriage, birth defects and stillbirths, can lead to criminal and delinquent behaviour in children, increase the chances of getting cancer and generally accelerate the ageing process.

MERCURY

Mercury is present on the fungicides used to protect grain, in fish, in mercury-saturated seeds, certain fabric softeners and floor waxes, mercury vapour lamps, some cosmetics, adhesives and dental amalgams. Like lead, mercury is capable of crossing the equal placental barrier during pregnancy, so that pregnant women exposed to it, though showing no signs of mercury poisoning themselves, may produce babies who are grossly mentally and physically deformed.

CADMIUM

Smokers are known to have much higher levels of cadmium in their livers than non-smokers, and cadmium is also present in tap water from galvanised or plastic water taps, tin cans, instant coffee, many processed meats, drinks which include caffeine like cola and refined cereals which have a low zinc to cadmium range. There are scientists who believe that cadmium is an even greater threat to health than lead or mercury. Cadmium poisoning manifests itself in hypertension, possibly emphysema, arteriosclerosis, cerebral haemorrhage, kidney and liver damage and eventually a painful and irreversible softening of the bones.

Unlike lead and mercury it is hard to leach cadmium out of the body quickly. Cadmium antagonists include calcium, iron, vitamin D and zinc.

ALUMINIUM

Aluminium in the form of aluminium cookware, aluminium foil and illuminated salt, baking powder and antacids, certain toothpastes, cigarette filters, buffered aspirin, cosmetics, hot water heaters with aluminium cathodes, processed cheese, cosmetics and pharmaceuticals is ubiquitously

with us. Toxic symptoms include persistent indigestion and gastro-intestinal upset, psoriasis, cystic fibrosis and senility. Aluminium is highly reactive to alkaline saliva, so that by the time food cooked in aluminium saucepans reaches the stomach gas is being produced in just the same way as baking powder acts as a cake rises. To some extent the hydrochloric acid produced in the stomach keeps this under control, but the real problem begins in the duodenum. So it is essential to cook in earthenware, china, glass, stainless steel or enamel-lined saucepans but *never* cook with baking aluminium or aluminium saucepans. The aluminium in food ingested from saucepans goes on reacting producing with the digestive tract painful gas further upsetting the delicate pH of the whole digestive system, flooding the bloodstream and burdening the bodies in the organs. Aluminium is cumulative, so the overall effect gets worse as we get older. Aluminium may be leached from the body by eating foods high in pectin, particularly bananas, apples, lemons, lemon rind and flower seeds. It is also possible in some health-food stores to get pectin in powdered form and to take this in fruit juice.

If you are disturbed that the mineral content in your body may be distorted, it is possible to get a mineral analysis of your hair done by a reputable laboratory.

HEAVY METAL DETOXIFYING PROGRAMME

The following programme should be adhered to for 3 consecutive months.

1. *Two level teaspoons of kelp powder to be taken daily. (The seaweed derivative sodium alquiate is useful for removing lead from the body tissue.)*

2. *Pectin is a natural detoxifier and so will help remove heavy metals from the system. Eat 1 cup of home-made apple sauce a day. Cook the apples with a squeeze of lemon juice and plenty of grated lemon rind. During digestion the apple pectin is transformed into galateuric acid, which combines with toxic metals to form an insoluble metallic salt, which is then excreted. The best utilized source of pectin as far as the body is concerned is home-made apple sauce rather than fresh apples but bananas, carrots, and all citrus fruit contain a reasonable level of pectin and as previously stated it is possible to get pectin powder from a health food shop and to take it on a daily basis. If using this take 2 dessertspoons daily stirred into fruit juice.*

3. *Calcium acts as a buffer against lead in the digestive system slowing down its absorption. Dairy foods actually increase lead absorption so it is best to stick to other natural sources of calcium such as bone meal, alfalfa, sesame seeds, camomile, parsley and wheatgerm.*

4. *Vitamin E is known to be a protective agent of metal toxicity, so begin with 400 IUs daily gradually building up to 1000 IUs. As wheatgerm oil goes rancid so quickly it is best to take vitamin E in powdered form (Nature's Best supply this, see Appendix).*
Vitamin E should not be taken by people who have any history of rheumatic fever or by those with high blood pressure.

5. *Vitamin C is an extremely powerful anti-toxin. Take it to a point just short of diarrhoea. Individual dosage will therefore vary.*

6. *Vitamin A helps to activate the enzymes needed to detoxify poisonous metals, so eat plenty of the golden, orange and red plants.*

7. *Eat two cloves of raw garlic in a salad dressing or if this is too antisocial powdered garlic put into gelatin capsules, 6 of these daily. Like the seaweeds garlic is rich in a sulphur containing amino acids, methionine and cysterine. If you can't stand garlic use onions instead, but you need more, about 2 daily, best taken in onion soup. Alternatively you could use half a cup of cooked pulses or beans daily which will perform the same task.*

8. *Two tablespoons of lecithin granules daily will protect the myobin sheaths of nerves from lead damage.*

Take a cup of the following detoxifying tea with each meal:

3 parts burdock root	½ part ginger root
3 parts gipsy weed	½ part plantain
3 parts yellow dock root	

9. *As far as diet is concerned avoid refined foods and large fish like tuna which may contain mercury although it also contains selenium which is a mercury antagonist. Shellfish, mussels and clams are often high in toxic metals depending on where they come from. So check your sources of fish. Alcohol increases the absorption of lead so reduce consumption to only 2 oz (60 g daily) or the equivalent, that is 2 glasses of wine or 2 pints (1.2 litres) of beer daily. Refined grains lower zinc levels so ensure you only eat whole grains. Water for drinking or for boiling should be filtered. For water filter suppliers see Appendix. Vegetables should be washed or have their outer leaves removed if there is possible contamination. Be careful where you buy them. It seems that those grown within a 10-mile radius of Marble Arch are unfit for human consumption, so are vegetables sold in the heart of busy towns, particularly those left outside on pavements, and should really be avoided. If you must buy them scrub them very well or better still peel them.*

ANTIBIOTICS

Even doctors are becoming increasingly worried about the number of their patients being exposed to such irrefutably useful drugs as antibiotics – not just through prescription but because they are widely used in animal feedstuffs and the end product is eaten by humans. In view of this constant barrage, people are, not surprisingly, becoming immune to antibiotics, so much so that there are some within the medical establishment who are worrying about the day when antibiotics are remembered only as a 'temporary and historical' form of treatment.

Besides destroying the unwanted bacteria in a local area, antibiotics upset the entire ecology of the body, often inducing yeast infections or irritable bowel syndrome as a side effect. Those particularly at risk are people on long-term antibiotics as a preventative for rheumatic heart disease or skin problems.

Their long-term administration can be even more worrying. Sulphonomide antibiotics when administered to those with liver disease can produce malabsorption of fat and water-soluble vitamins and if taken during pregnancy can induce pernicterus in new-born babies. Tetracycline, often used to treat acne, is known to interact with certain minerals especially calcium and iron, so calcium-rich foods need to be eaten well away from tetracycline dosage so that it can be absorbed properly. If taken during pregnancy it will lead to poor growth in the foetus.

It is possible that zinc and copper may also be affected by antibiotics. My feeling is that antibiotics should only be used in a life-threatening situation such as a severe staphylococcal infection which may result in bacteremia and death. If they are used take vitamin C, 3 g daily, and several strong B complex tablets separately from them while on the dosage together with 6 Probion daily to fend off the possibility of yeast infection.

HERBAL ANTIBIOTICS

The best herbal antibiotics are echinacea, eucalyptus, thyme, wild indigo, chaparral, wormwood, nasturtium, garlic, onion, cajaput, goldenseal, horseradish, watercress and mullein. A good herbal antibiotic is:

2 parts echinacea
1 part barberry
½ part cloves
1 part garlic
1 part goldenseal
1 part mullein
1 part thyme

Take two 'O' capsules of the finely powdered herbs hourly as needed.

If antibiotics need to be taken while breastfeeding take the following tincture instead. Equal parts of:

butterbur	nasturtium
garden cress	watercress
horseradish	

Dosage 40 drops in a cup of water, a teaspoon to be taken every 15 minutes while the infection is acute reducing 10 drops 3 times daily as long as it persists. This is Dr Vogal's remedy, commercially available as Petroconale (see Appendix).

To treat cuts externally wash the area in running water and then flush with goldenseal, calendula or echinacea tea and apply Tea tree oil, eucalyptus or thyme oil direct to the skin. Reapply the oil every 2 to 3 hours. Avoid prolonged soaking in water or salt water and expose the cut to as much air and strong sunlight as possible. Tea tree oil is also antifungal while thyme oil is eight times stronger than phenol.

THE PRINCIPLES OF NATURAL LIVING

All good health is concerned with balance. Efficient assimilation must be equally balanced by good elimination. Repairs can only take place in the midst of decay. No one facet of health dominates any other. All are equally important.

ASSIMILATION

The famous maxim 'you are what you eat' could be much more accurately stated as 'you are what you assimilate'. I have seen patients eating the world's most nutritious diet and eliminating with the precision of a sergeant major but if they are not making full and proper use of that food it is all, literally, a waste of time and money. I have encountered those who fill themselves with vitamins and minerals until they rattle and are still creeping around half dead because there is some organ, gland or system which is damaged, malformed, traumatized or underdeveloped and so unable to function efficiently metabolically. There are many things you can do to ensure efficient assimilation.

CHEWING

Correct digestion begins in the mouth. Saliva is permeated with ptyalin which helps to break down starch so if you gulp your food or talk excessively while eating you won't be able to make full use of it. Try and chew your food patiently until it is a liquid pulp before swallowing it.

STAY CALM

The metabolic processes of the body are much more upset by negative feeling such as distress, greed, rage, fear, shock, guilt, anxiety, jealousy, depression and grief than a mouthful of naughty food. You need emotional equilibrium to digest your food properly. If you are upset miss a meal. If you are upset but still feel very hungry sip a small glass of freshly pressed fruit or vegetable juice slowly. Try not to eat to comfort yourself or to relieve tiredness. It is an easy trap to fall into and one to which I have often succumbed. Remember not to force other people to eat. It is a habit which taken from childhood into adulthood can prove very destructive.

It takes 4 hours to empty the stomach completely so the ideal eating pattern is a light breakfast at 8 o'clock, preferably one of fruit only while the body is still on its cycle of eliminating which begins at 4 in the morning and doesn't finish until midday. Take a sustaining lunch observing the rules of food combining between 12 and 1 o'clock and eat a light evening meal between 6 and 7 o'clock. This does not apply if you are hypoglycaemic and need to eat little often. By following this pattern you won't tax your body's enzymic systems or its patterns of assimilation and elimination.

For those who suffer from digestive problems, apart from noting the very sound advice about food combining, I would recommend the following digestive tea to be sipped before a meal.

DIGESTIVE TEA

Mix all the herbs together and store in an airtight jar.

2 parts allspice	*1 part cinnamon bark*
2 parts dandelion root	*1 part meadowsweet*
2 parts fenugreek seed	*flowers*
2 parts ginger root	*2 parts scullcap*
2 parts holy thistle	

Brew as an infusion 30 g/1 oz of herbs to ¾ litre/1 pt of water and save the residue in the fridge. Drink one cup hot while eating. This will soothe and comfort the stomach, intestines, nerves and glands including the pancreas and liver. It will normalize stomach acids helping to remove any excess acid, stop burping and any mucus congestion and, an added bonus, it tastes spicily palatable.

Supplementation

It has been said that if you eat a truly excellent diet there is no need for additional supplementation by way of vitamins and minerals. But such dietary maxims are illusive, surrounded as we are by processed foods. Of all the food we eat, 90% is tampered with in some way chemically and goes through the hands, or more accurately, the machines of food processors. I am a great believer in taking supplementation, on a health maintenance level, from natural sources. While it may be true that a molecule of synthetic crystalline ascorbic acid is chemically identical to the ascorbic acid present in rosehips, the rosehips contain vital accessory factors as well as minute traces of other probably vital nutrients which as yet we know little about. These substances interact with one another to ensure the full absorption and utilization of ascorbic acid and this is true of all herbs. It must be remembered that no vitamin will work without the aid of minerals and herbs are rich in both. Valerian, for example, has the highest yield of magnesium phosphate of any vegetable. Parsley is rich not only in ascorbic acid but vitamin A, essential oils, flavones and various minterals, all combine to assist to increase the flow of saliva, cleansing the mouth and reducing the bacteria there.

The following vitamin/mineral formulation contains the full range of vitamins and minerals as well as amino acids and alkaline protein and it is easily assimilated.

HERBAL VITAMIN/MINERAL SUPPLEMENT

2 parts alfalfa	1 part horsetail
2 parts kelp	1 part Icelandic moss
2 parts rosehip	1 part Irish moss
2 parts spirulena	1 part parsley
1 part cayenne	1 part watercress
1 part comfrey	1 part yellow dock
1 part ginger root	

Take two rounded 5 ml teaspoons of powdered herbs stirred into vegetable juice once a day, with a meal. The dose can be adjusted according to need and should be increased for convalescence, pregnant and lactating women, menopausal women and anyone under stress to two rounded 5 ml teaspoons with every meal.

ELIMINATION

An iridology test is perhaps the most valuable way of finding out exactly how your eliminative organs are functioning. Determining a person's true iris colour will often be an invaluable guide to the state of assimilation and elimination in a body. Over the years I have discovered that nearly 80% of the people who consult me are in some way drowning in their own poisons.

Most people think that what they see in the toilet is what they ate a couple of meals back but in truth normal 20th-century diet ensures that a lot gets left behind in the colon and doesn't come out at all. You may find starches that haven't been digested properly by pancreatic secretions, drugs and barium meal as well as catarrh-forming foods like dairy products, sugar and eggs get stuck and pasted on to the sides of the colon, turning into encrusted mucus the weight of which often forces the wall of the

colon outwards to form diverticular pockets. In some people this encrusted waste can cause the colon to weigh as much as 40 lb (18 kg) and to balloon out from the customary 4 in (10 cm) to as much as 9 in (23 cm). The most immediate and obvious problem that this causes is constipation. You should have a bowel movement for every meal you eat. Therefore if you eat three meals a day you should have three reasonably copious bowel movements a day. Constipation is the hub of the mechanism in the disease process. The heart of the problem lies in the passage of toxins and micro-organisms through the intestinal wall into the body in general causing an endless array of disturbances. When the body absorbs poison from the decaying waste in the colon the end result is self-poisoning. Meat, fish and eggs provide the most harmful metabolites which on entering the bloodstream create a toxic load for the cells throughout the body, in particular the liver. The self-poisoning of auto-intoxication causes fatigue, poor concentration, irritability, insomnia, headaches and muscular aches and can lead to all the degenerative diseases including cancer. It should be remembered that diarrhoea is often the sister face of constipation because its cause is a substance which irritates the colon so badly that peristalsis goes into overdrive in an attempt to expel it. The build-up of faecal matter trapped in the colon becomes so large that these themselves induce the state of continuous peristalsis resulting in chronic diarrhoea.

I have described the ideal bowel movement (see p.134) and given Dr Christopher's excellent herbal combination to aid improper bowel functioning (see p.131). A properly cleansed bowel means better food assimilation, increased vitality and better absorption of nutrition and it often reduces the desire to eat as much food. When a person is chronically constipated generally only about 10% of the food eaten is utilized. Do remember that most laxatives are poisonous and merely serve to irritate the bowel doing nothing to remove the encrusted mucus. If laxatives are used regularly, the colon becomes addicted to them and in time grows weaker from over-stimulation and irritation so that a dose of laxatives has to be increased. Also the three-sided triangle, environmental, emotional and biological or physical stress which are the basis of many illnesses apply particularly to the bowel. People will often be reluctant to let go of faecal matter because they are so 'uptight' by nature. In this case simple relaxants such as lady's slipper, scullcap or valerian are often very helpful, serving to relax the bowel enough to allow it to do its work naturally.

Inefficient excretion particularly if it is caught early on is one of the most easily corrected bodily problems. Anyone with life-long elimination difficulties will always lean towards serious disease sooner rather than later in life.

Dr Christopher offers the following formula to regulate very debilitated bowels.

3 parts comfrey root	3 parts psyllium seeds
3 parts flax seed	1 part lobelia
3 parts liquorice root	
3 parts marshmallow root	

The dosage of this formulation will be according to need, but I would suggest you begin with three size 0 capsules with each meal.

A simpler formulation for children which is very safe and extremely effective is:

1 part carob powder	1 part psyllium seed
1 part flax seed	1 part raisins
1 part liquorice root	

Soak two tablespoons of this mixture overnight in a cup of boiling water. In the morning you will notice it is very spongy, having expanded. Take three tablespoons at a time every hour if necessary adding a fruit juice which is strong-tasting to make it more palatable. I would particularly recommend pineapple juice.

THE LIVER

The main function of the liver is to maintan the body's dynamic balance by preparing fats, carbohydrates and protein for its use, by storing some nutrients, by manufacturing enzymes, bile, antibodies, specific proteins needed for blood clotting and by maintaining the proper blood levels of glycogen, amino acids, hormones and vitamins as well as neutralizing any poisons which enter the bloodstream. In other words the liver is an amazingly sophisticated chemical factory.

Our livers have a particularly hard task today because they are inundated with so many chemicals, either the result of environmental poisoning or the result of totally synthetic food. We eat man-made substances which are so heavily processed that they can no longer be recognized as food. I recently encountered a list of 8 additives in so-called wholesome brown bread rolls and a further 6 additives in the flour used to make bread. So our long-suffering livers certainly have their work cut out for them.

Signs of liver disorder are a feeling of heaviness or discomfort on the right side in the area of the lower margin of the ribs coupled with a feeling of general sluggishness and tiredness for no reason. Indigestion with flatulence may go on for years as well as alternating constipation and diarrhoea. The tongue is often thickly coated, white or yellow, and bad breath may be a problem.

The obvious solution to maximizing liver health is to eat only natural healthy foods and to live in a clean environment wherever possible. Stressed livers particularly hate all processed, fried and fatty foods especially

all dairy products. They need plenty of vitamins A and D and calcium to assist them to maintain healthy internal mucosa. Alcohol should be taken in moderation. Livers particularly benefit from a daily ingestion of lecithin granules (available in health-food stores). Simply add two tablespoons to any cereal, soup or natural yoghurt. Livers also appreciate plenty of garlic and onion soup.

Spring Liver Cleansing

Spring is a particularly appropriate time to do a liver cleanse because the body is just emerging from a winter of heavy fatty foods and not enough exercise.

First ensure that your diet is moving towards a lighter one which is rich in raw foods, whole grains and seeds and very light in protein (not more than 1 oz (30 g) daily. On rising mix 4 tablespoons of olive oil with 8 tablespoons freshly squeezed lemon or orange juice and 3 crushed cloves of garlic. Save the pips from the fruit. Wallop this cocktail back as quickly as you can. You will appreciate it is rather antisocial as far as standing close to strangers is concerned but it is not as horrendous as it sounds. Then sip a small glass of fresh orange juice while you prepare a decoction of fennel, liquorice and aniseed tea, the herbs to be mixed in equal parts. Drink this sweetened with honey if you prefer and chew the lemon or orange pips that you have saved for at least a quarter of an hour before swallowing them. Their bitter essence serves to stimulate the liver. Do not eat any breakfast. If you have to go to work or want to be sociable chew a clove which will help to mask the odour of garlic. At mid-morning eat an abundant serving of any fresh fruit of your choice.

Follow this routine every day for 2 weeks, doing it for 6 days a week and resting and fasting on the seventh day on carrot and beetroot juice. You will notice your faeces may produce a bit of green colouring during the cleanse. If you get constipated as some people do during the cleanse, raise the amount of garlic and liquorice. If you go the other way and get diarrhoea omit the liquorice and take a mid-morning snack of millet porridge well laced with powdered cinnamon and sweetened with honey. If you have high blood pressure omit the liquorice altogether.

The simplest way of decongesting the liver on a daily basis is to drink dandelion coffee made from freshly ground dandelion root and nothing else. Apart from being an exceptional hepatic it also acts on the kidneys and is rich in minerals including calcium, manganese, sodium, sulphur and silicic acid. Do not use the adulterated dandelion coffee available in some health-food shops which is heavily laced with lactose (a refined form of milk sugar). Make sure you buy the real thing which is the pure and simple roasted root.

THE KIDNEYS

While the liver acts internally to neutralize and eliminate poisons the kidney's role in elimination is all too obvious. Any job which ought to be done by the kidneys but which is not will result in impure blood returning to the heart and this is one of the reasons why diuretics are often prescribed for heart problems by allopathic doctors. However all chemical diuretics work by irritating the delicate tubules in the kidneys forcing them to pass water and in doing so leaching potassium from the body, so much so that synthetic potassium has to be given in its place.

Herbal diuretics have the inbuilt advantage of containing potassium and the various complex nutrients needed to maintain an efficient input and output. They raise both potassium and sodium levels so that the cellular pump-action improves both ways. For example celery is high in sodium with a touch of potassium while dandelion is high in potassium with a little sodium.

Healthy kidneys need to be constantly flushed out so drink lots of purified water and potassium-rich broth made from the tough outer green leaves of vegetables and potato skins. Also drink fruit and vegetable juices but avoid tea, coffee, cocoa and salt absolutely (see p.20) focusing on a diet rich in fresh fruit and vegetables, no animal products and keep it free as far as possible of processed foods. Strawberries are especially helpful in dispelling uric acid and the only vegetables and fruit you have to be wary of are spinach and rhubarb, both of which contain large quantities of oxalic acid.

Never ignore a full bladder. I am continually surprised how seldom many of my patients urinate, often only two or three times a day. By holding on, the lining of the bladder gets intensely irritable as its contents are subjected to chemical change if harboured too long. A full bladder will press down on all the pelvic organs, especially the lower bowel and reproductive organs, and aggravate the possibility of prolapse. If we are eliminating efficiently we lose about 1 gallon (4.5 litres) of water every day through the skin, the kidneys and other eliminative organs. If your kidneys are not functioning properly you will notice evidence of water retention including puffy ankles, swollen fingers and feet which spill over the sides of your shoes. Waterlogged kidneys are evidenced by dark circles and bagginess under the eyes. A gentle and palatable diuretic can be made by mixing 1 oz (30 g) of aniseed with 2 oz (60 g) each of dried melon and dried cucumber seeds. Grind them together in a meat mincer and mix to a paste with honey. Use a teaspoon of this mixture with each meal.

Barley water is an ideal drink to soothe and cleanse the kidneys and maintain them in peak condition. It has the added bonus of strengthening the nails and improving the quality and quantity of the milk of lactating mothers as well as helping to relieve asthma because of the hordein it contains.

Pour 1½ pints (900 ml) of water over 1 oz (30 g) whole grain barley (pot barley won't do) and boil until the quantity is reduced by half. Add the zest of the rind of one lemon (i.e. not the white pith) and sweeten with a little honey or apple juice if desired. Drink freely at room temperature. It tastes very pleasant. The safest herbal diuretic is dandelion coffee made as a decoction (see p.34). Stronger ones need to be administered under the supervision of a medical herbalist, some herbal diuretics irritate the kidneys and unless you are certain what you are doing it would be unwise to administer them yourself.

THE SKIN

If you are worried about the texture of your skin or worse still if it is covered in spots or blemishes you can certainly help the problem not just externally but, more fruitfully, internally. If the bowel is chronically congested the bloodstream will also carry the back-up and therefore to cleanse the skin it is essential to purify the bloodstream. A good combination of juices for blood purification is:

4 parts apple juice	*1 part nettle juice*
1 part beetroot juice	*1 part potato juice*
1 part carrot juice	*1 part spinach juice*
1 part celery juice	*1 part watercress juice*
1 part cucumber juice	

Dr Christopher offers an excellent blood-purifying formula which contains not only blood rebuilders but cleansers and astringent herbs which increase the range and power of circulation, particularly to those parts of the body which have been deficient (usually the extremities like hands, head and feet). This formula will remove cholesterol, kill infection and elasticize the veins while strengthening the artery walls so that the herbal nutrients in it will travel efficiently through the blood and lymph fluids and be effectively utilized. The formula consists of equal parts of:

buckthorn bark	*peach bark*
burdock root	*poke root*
chapparal	*prickly ash bark*
liquorice root	*red clover blossom*
Oregon grape root	*stillingia*

All herbs should be finely powdered and put into size 0 gelatin capsules. Take three capsules with each meal. If you get diarrhoea it means that the formulation is working on you too hard and would also indicate the necessity for bowel and liver purification. Attend to these two and then try a reduced dose.

Regular exercise involving profuse sweating will also help the skin. The sweat excreted from such exercise contains more toxic waste than the sweat you flush out during the course of a Turkish bath or sauna.

However, these do help too so don't reject them (although neither treatment should be taken if you have high blood pressure or are pregnant).

Too many people suffocate their skins with synthetic fabrics. Wear only natural fabrics next to the skin. The healthiest fabric is cotton or failing that linen, silk or wool. Remember the palms of the hands and soles of the feet are particularly richly endowed with sweat glands so don't suffocate these areas with non-leather shoes or nylon socks.

I don't approve of the routine use of soap all over the body and feel it should only be used on sweaty or exposed parts. However try to choose an organic not a detergent soap (see Appendix). Several alternatives for cleansing the skin include marshmallow or soap wort but they do not lather like man-made soaps. They are particularly effective for delicate sensitive skin and both are prepared as decoctions and used strained. Indeed soap wort is used to wash the tapestries in the British Museum, some of which are hundreds of years old.

Always remember that the skin is a two-way street, flushing outwards and ingesting inwards. So don't put anything on your skin you wouldn't be prepared to eat. A few drops of a herbal essential oil mixed in a carrier base of almond oil and added to bath water will act therapeutically on the skin as well as moisturising it. Never use mineral oil (sometimes sold as baby oil) or products containing it – as most commercial cleansing creams do.

Don't use deodorants. If you smell particularly obnoxious it is because your body is offloading some poison through your skin and you need to look at the inside not the outside to remedy the problem. Washing twice a day should keep you smelling sweet. Alternatively wash more often until your body purification is complete. Do try to avoid the use of anti-perspirants or deodorants, both of which to a greater or lesser extent block the skin's natural cleansing action. They also destroy the natural bacteria on the skin, upsetting its delicate protective pH balance.

Don't wash your clothes with detergents that contain enzymes. In some people the body's defence mechanism responds to enzymes by launching an assault as if it were attacking an infection and sooner or later you may end up developing a serious form of irritation.

Help the skin to eliminate by dry skin brushing daily. To do this you need a natural bristle brush, not one made of nylon or synthetic fibre. Your body should be dry and you should begin with the soles of your feet working briskly upwards towards the heart missing delicate areas like the nipples and genitals. Use clean sweeping strokes not rotary scrubbing or back and forth motions. Any area above the heart (but exclude the face) should be in a downward motion towards the heart. The benefits of dry skin brushing are enormous and include the removal of dead layers of skin and other impurities so allowing your pores to eliminate without obstruction and stimulating the circulation, thus enabling the body nourishing those organs of the body which lie near the surface to reach them effectively. Dry skin brushing also increases the eliminative capacity of the skin while stimulating the hormone and oil-producing glands as well as the nerve endings of the skin. It is an excellent way of removing cellulite. Five minutes of energetic skin brushing is the equivalent of 25 minutes of jogging or any other physical exercise as far as body tone is concerned, although obviously skin brushing does not have an aerobic effect on the heart. It is also a very effective technique for moving the lymphatic system effectively. In my own experience it certainly contributes to the youthful look of the skin, improving its elasticity and immunity. For suppliers of the natural bristle skin brushes see the Appendix.

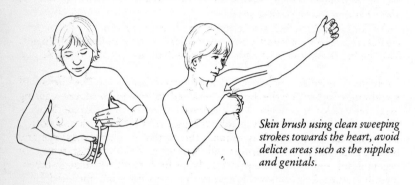

Skin brush using clean sweeping strokes towards the heart, avoid delicte areas such as the nipples and genitals.

THE RESPIRATORY SYSTEM

Most of us are inefficient breathers, using only the top third of our lungs and this type of laziness results in lack of vitality and an acceleration of metabolic disorders and degeneration of the tissues all over the body. Most pathological changes in such tissues can be prevented if they are constantly surrounded by life-giving oxygen. We are, in the deepest and truest sense what we breathe and correct breathing is the best preventive medicine of all. The problem is that most of us forget how to breathe once we get beyond the stage of nappies. Women particularly are prone to moving their shoulders up and down rather than drawing breath into the lungs so deeply that the chest ribs are lifted up and out and stomach muscles well outwards.

Correct Breathing

You need to begin by improving posture. Stand and sit tall and when you lie down make sure you are well stretched out. Keep your head well up and don't tuck your chin in or let it jut out. An easy way to check your posture is to stand barefoot against a wall without a skirting board. Then

try to flatten the whole length of your spine against the wall keeping the back of the head against it too, stretch up and breathe out deeply. Take a step away from the wall holding this position and the way you are at this moment is how you should always stand and walk.

If you can, avoid areas with a high pollen count and polluted air. The poisons in the heart of cities are often dangerously high and passive smoking is becoming a real problem. Cases have been recorded in Poland of nicotine intoxication among new-born babies breastfed by mothers smoking cigarettes. The correlation between lower birth weight and the number of cigarettes smoked daily by mothers-to-be is now widely recognized, but not many people realize that women can affect the foetus almost as much with passive smoking.

An ionizer which helps to control the balance of ions (tiny electrical particles) in the air around you is particularly useful and can be plugged into the bedroom socket at night where it will do its good work while you sleep.

Mucus is normally produced as a protective barrier on the surface of membranes but when the body is irritated it is over-produced causing excessive sticky mucus in which germs are easily harboured. Mucus-forming foods include dairy products, eggs, meat, sugar, tea and coffee, chocolate, anything which is refined, the gluten in wheat, oats, rye and barley, potatoes, swedes, turnips and parsnips and any other starchy root vegetables. Foods which are particularly useful for cutting through mucus include nettles, kelp, onions, horseradish root, garlic, and sprouted fenugreek. Or try making the following jet-propelled mucus-clearing tonic. Put equal parts of fresh horseradish root, ginger root, onions, garlic and cayenne in a jar and cover in cider vinegar. Macerate for 2 weeks, strain and rebottle, stoppering tightly. Take 1 teaspoon before each meal. This is Sensai Cayenne's formulation, a well-known herbalist in the USA and one of my best teachers. I've found it extremely effective.

Oil or syrup of garlic is particularly useful for treating colds, flu and chest infections as well as bronchial congestion and sore throats.

A diet which is high in vitamins A and D to strengthen and desensitize your internal mucosa also helps. A single drop of aniseed oil placed on the back of the tongue will help to clean infected sinuses. Fennel oil used as a herbal steam bath will vapourize mucus and loosen irritants, causing it to degenerate so that the eliminatory process can move it through the bloodstream far more effectively than can be done by coughing, sneezing or blowing the nose. Use 10 drops of fennel oil to 1 pint (600 ml) of freshly boiled water. Put this in a basin and cover your head with a towel holding your face 8 in (20 cm) away from the infusion. Keeping the eyes closed breathe in and out steadily through the nose ensuring that the mouth is closed. Do this for 20 minutes at a time repeating morning and evening.

There is an arsenal of herbs to help strengthen and cleanse the lungs but the following formulation which is a general one will prove particularly useful:

3 parts coltsfoot	*1 part echinacea*
3 parts mullein	*1 part ginger*
1 part aniseed	*1 part liquorice*
1 part chickweed	*1 part sage*
1 part comfrey	

Make an infusion and drink one breakfast cup three times a day.

THE LYMPHATIC SYSTEM

This can best be described as the body's vacuuming system. It is closely allied with the mucous membranes and the bloodstream. But unlike the blood circulation it doesn't have a heart to act as a pump, relying instead on the movement of lymphatic fluids around the body by the action of the muscles and lungs through a one-way valve system. The lymphatic vessels are particularly concentrated in the groin, behind the knees, in the armpits and under the chin but they spread like a gossamer network of tubes about the diameter of a needle throughout the body covering every area except the central nervous system. Lymph vessels have a vast population of white blood cells whose purpose is to attack and ingest invaders, cleaning out waste. Different types have different specialized roles. The B-lymphocytes produce antibodies which immobilize the invader when it comes whether it be from chemical or bacterial sources. The T-cells actively hunt for foreign invading cells, bacteria, fungi, viruses and allergies by producing lymphokins and macrophages. Between them they act as a good policing team ensuring that your auto-immune system is doing what it should. However if they falter the lymphatic system backs up and one or more of the lymphatic nodules swells up with poisonous waste. What you may feel is a lump or you may see bleeding or an enlarged mole and at this stage your lymph system needs very urgent attention.

The lymphatic system has particular difficulty in combatting constant exposure to heavy metals and industrial chemicals whether you breathe them in, put them on your skin or eat them.

There are simple ways in which you can assist your lymphatic system including vigorous exercise which acts as a powerful pump for the lymph glands and the body heat you generate burns up any excessive fat being marshalled in the lymph vessels. One of the finest ways to get the lymph moving is to trampoline on one of those mini trampolines approximately 4 ft (1.2 m) across – but please don't use one of these if you are prone to prolapse. All muscles have got to be in pretty good shape before you start any kind of vigorous exercise so if in doubt begin with long brisk walks really striding out and swinging arms. You can graduate to running if you

are very strong providing you keep to soft surfaces like grass. Cement or tarmac can be very shocking to your internal organs. Swimming long steady laps solves this problem as you are comparatively weightless in water but please try to find a pool which is free of added chlorine.

Herbs which are particularly effective for helping the lymph system are those that are high in iron with good traces of copper and a diet which is high in vitamins A and C as well as zinc coupled with the avoidance of red meat, dairy products, sugar, anything artificial – alcohol or fried food will help to de-congest the lymphatic system.

The following herbal formulation will aid in the stimulation of bile flow and actively assist in the production of white blood cells which help to clear any poisonous chemicals ingested into the system:

1 part bladderwrack	½ part fenugreek
1 part blessed thistle	¼ part cascara
1 part echinacea	¼ part ginger root
1 part nettles	¼ part goldenseal
1 part thuja	

Take three size 0 capsules of the finely powdered herbs three times a day before meals. Fruit pectin powder has been used extensively in Russia to remove environmental toxins and radiation from the body. This is available in some health-food shops. Take one to three tablespoons in freshly squeezed fruit juice once daily.

THE NERVOUS SYSTEM

We are only able to heal ourselves when we are asleep so sleep is vital for rejuvenation. Besides this our dreams can carry out the nightly task of sifting through the day's unsettled problems, emotions and thoughts. The therapeutic effect of dreaming, although it may make no sense to us, is vital for the general health of the body. One of the simplest techniques for inducing sleep is barefoot walking on soil or grass. It sounds crazy but what actually happens is that the excessive electrical charge built up in the body during the course of the day walking on synthetic surfaces is released and literally grounded into a natural substance beneath the feet. My teacher Dr Christopher recounts a story in which he cured a lifetime history of insomnia in an elderly male patient simply by asking him to get up in the middle of the night when he was unable to sleep and having put on his dressing gown go out and walk barefoot in the grass of his back yard. The gentleman concerned was naturally extremely sceptical but desperate enough to try it and within 2 weeks he was sleeping comfortably for a good 6 hours nightly. Barefoot walking should be carried out for a minimum of five minutes on grass, sand or soil, then the feet should be dried vigorously with a rough towel and then warm socks and dry shoes or

slippers put on. If you are popping straight back into bed (and try not to worry unduly about what the neighbours think) you need a pair of warm socks on your feet. Alternatively going to bed in a pair of loose fitting wet cotton socks covered by a larger pair of woollen socks is very helpful for inducing sleep.

Naturally you should sleep, if you use any clothing at all, in natural clothing and in cotton sheets and a bed should be well aired. A healthy body will lose at least 1 pint (¾ litre) of fluid overnight into surrounding material.

Dr Christopher has an excellent nerve herbal food combination for relieving nervous tension and insomnia. It is totally non-addictive, reducing irritability and excitement while being mildly stimulating and acting as a gentle anodine. Equal parts of:

black cohosh	*mistletoe*
cayenne	*scullcap*
hops	*valerian*
lady's slipper	*wood betony*
lobelia	

Put the finely powdered ingredients into size 0 capsules and take two three times a day. This formulation contains herbs that will feed and revitalize the motor nerve at the base of the skull as well as build and feed the spinal cord. It contains herbs which will rebuild capillaries and nerve sheaths as well as the nerves themselves. I have used it to extremely good effect in my own practice for many years now.

There are several very simple teas that can be drunk in isolation to induce more restful sleep including the flowers of lime tree, camomile, lemon balm leaves, hops (although this tastes more palatable if mixed in equal quantities with Earl Grey tea) and elderflower. Sip a cup of any one of these soothing herbal teas just before retiring. I occasionally advise insomniacs with whom I am working to have a thermos flask of one of these teas by their bed at night so they can use it readily without having to go down to the kitchen in the small hours and make some fresh tea.

I do a lot of travelling and consequently my body clock is thoroughly disordered crossing several time zones. If sleeping difficulties are short term for similar reasons I would recommend the following tea:

2 parts kava-kava root	*1 part camomile*
2 parts lemon balm leaves	*1 part liquorice root*
2 parts lime tree flowers	

Make a decoction, sweeten with honey and drink one or two cups before sleeping.

I have also found the addition of camomile or lemon balm oil to a deep warm bath very helpful for soothing the body into a good night's sleep.

Admittedly it is pointless telling someone to relax when they simply don't know how to. Yet it is possible to learn relaxation just as it is possible to learn to read or ride a bike. The choice of methods is wide and not all methods are suitable for every person. Meditation, yoga, self-hypnosis, visualization, autogenics, biofeedback; keep trying until you settle on a method that is right for you. Above all don't be discouraged if you are not instantly brilliant at it. After all surely you could not learn to play a musical instrument in a week could you? The secret is to find a method you like and persist with it.

If you have just been through a nasty operation and are feeling weak and debilitated, or indeed if you are going through a period of convalescence for any reason at all the following herbal formulation will prove useful. Equal parts of:

alfalfa seeds	nettles
cayenne	Oregon grape root
dandelion root	St John's wort
kelp	

Take two size 0 capsules with each meal. It is advisable during such times if at all possible to fast on freshly pressed juices. Slippery elm gruel is a superb nutritive tonic and will help to normalize bowel functions and soothe any internal swelling or irritation.

The following formulation is ideal for debilitated, fatigued and weak bodies but should be used for a short time only. It is designed to support over-worked adrenal glands. Equal parts of finely powdered:

borage	hawthorn berries
cayenne	liquorice
ginger root	mullein
ginseng	

Take ¼ level teaspoon with a little sugarless jam or juice 3 times a day.

Please note ginseng should not be taken if there is an acute illness. Simply omit it from the formula.

GENERAL HEALTH

If you are looking for a tea to take to support your health in general I would recommend the following one. It contains a blend of herbs designed to encourage homeostatis in the body by gently detoxifying while stim-

ulating blood circulation, purifying the blood and acting as a very mild and safe antiseptic:

2 parts agrimony	½ part nettle
2 parts elder berries	½ part parsley
2 parts raspberry	½ part rosemary
½ part cayenne	½ part yellow dock
½ part comfrey root	root

Make a decoction and drink a cup with each meal.

At the beginning of this chapter I touched on our responsibility to get ourselves fit before conceiving children. A tremendous part of our inheritance as far as illness is concerned is the result of genetic programming. When we fall in love with somebody and decide to set up home together generally the last thing on our minds is whether this person had a grandmother who died of tuberculosis or whether they themselves suffer from chronic asthma. Quite naturally we tend to think about the heart rather than the head under such circumstances but disease in previous generations will often surface in future generations. The greatest killers of the previous centuries were leprosy, tuberculosis, syphillis and gonorrhoea. Today it's cancer, heart disease and more recently AIDS. While it is very difficult to uproot such poor genetic inheritance it is possible to strengthen our bodies to such an extent that the chances of having healthy children are very much higher than they would have been in the previous generation. If couples are using oral contraception I always advice them to switch to another method for at least six months before trying to conceive a baby. The Pill can cause many unpleasant side effects in certain women including migraine, oedema, depression, weight gain, extreme mood changes, circulation problems and nausea and recently it has been shown to have a tendency linked to both cancer of the cervix and cancer of the breast. There is also a school of thought that suggests that children born from a woman who has been taking the Pill for many years could develop sexual problems as they grow up. It takes some months for the Pill to be totally removed from the body and for a normal menstrual cycle to re-establish itself. Use the sheath, a diaphragm or the temperature method. The latter is only advisable if you have a full understanding of it. Do not use a copper IUD as it depletes zinc levels in the body. Take the following pre-conception formula:

1 part squaw vine root
1 part true unicorn root

Make a standard infusion and take half a cup three times daily. Dr Christopher has an excellent female reproductive formulation designed to

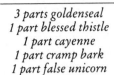

tone, strengthen and regulate the gynaecological organs, rebuilding, harmonizing and healing the reproductive system:

3 parts goldenseal	*1 part ginger root*
1 part blessed thistle	*1 part red raspberry*
1 part cayenne	*leaf*
1 part cramp bark	*1 part squaw vine*
1 part false unicorn	*1 part uva-ursi*

Drink one cup of the tea morning and evening.

The following formula combined with bowel and lymphatic cleansing will strengthen the male prostate gland. Equal parts of:

buchu	*gravel root*
burdock	*hydrangea root*
cayenne	*marshmallow root*
echinacea	*mullein*
ginger	*parsley*
goldenseal	

Take three size 0 capsules of the finely powdered herbs morning and evening for 8 weeks with a cup of decocted pumpkin seed tea. Pumpkin seeds are rich in a male androgen hormone which will also cleanse the prostate gland. They may be eaten separately gently roasted on a baking sheet in the oven and they taste absolutely delicious.

Men should give up smoking and drinking especially in the few months prior to attempting to conceive and while the couple is attempting to conceive in order to improve both the quality and quantity of the sperm. Dr Bayer, a German obstetrician, has stated categorically that he has never known a mentally handicapped child to be born to a father taking vitamin E on a regular basis for many months prior to conception. The dosage of vitamin E should depend on the history of diseases in the family such as rheumatic fever and hypertension. Seek professional help with this.

FASTING

Fasting is undoubtedly the most effective preventive medicine I have ever encountered and I encourage my patients provided they are not hypo-glycaemic, emaciated, extremely weak, elderly, psychotic, pregnant, suffering from exophtalmic goitre or extremely physically active or diabetic to fast on a regular basis.

Fasting is a wonderfully effective tool in emergencies and works well to accelerate the healing of long-term illnesses. Done on a regular basis it can help to rebalance the body mentally, spiritually, physically and emotionally. It does so by periodically unburdening the body of accumulated waste, thereby nipping minor health problems in the bud, decelerating the ageing

process and if done regularly will stabilize body weight and help to prepare the body to utilize nutrition far more effectively after the fast is broken.

How to Fast

Don't fast on water alone, particularly if you have never fasted before. It can be a miserable experience if the body is groaning with toxins – particularly potent ones ingested from insecticides and poisonous metals. They pour into the system so rapidly that you would finish up drowning in your own poison. Far better to choose either one type of fruit (a mixture would decrease the potency of the fruit's digestive enzymes) or vegetable juices. Purists insist that eating fruit is not strictly fasting and certainly the digestive organs are not allowed to rest as much as if only liquids were being processed. But eating fruit certainly ensures the discriminate incineration of old tissue (leaving behind tissues that are ageing but are still useful) which is the strict requirement of fasting. Besides which I find fruit fasting is good for people who have never done it before and are nervous about going the whole way and especially beneficial for anyone suffering from chronic constipation. In such instances the colon actually needs something rich in fibre to bite on to encourage peristalsis (the automatic wave-like movements by which food is propelled along it), and fruit passes rapidly through the system, requiring very little action by the digestive enzymes to make use of it.

The problem is that most people make the mistake of starving themselves and not eating enough fruit on a fruit fast. They then wonder why they get hungry or irritable. The secret of successful fasting is to eat as much of your chosen fruit as you can without being ridiculous about it. You will notice that as the fast lengthens appetite diminishes, but ensure that, even on a long fast, you eat 6 servings of fruit daily. The ideal is to aim for somewhere between 4 and 6 lbs (2–3 kg) of fruit a day depending on body weight. Chew each piece of fruit slowly and carefully until every last drop of juice is extracted before swallowing, and eat all the fruit including the skin and the seeds unless the skin is obviously inedible as it is with pineapples and bananas for example. You are permitted to discard the inedible pips like cherry stones and wooded stalks but you should eat the pips from oranges, grapes, apples and pears.

If you can't manage your 4–6 lbs (2–3 kg) of fruit daily, juice the remainder and 'chew' the juice well before swallowing. Indeed a juicer is one of the first tools I require anybody working with me to purchase as it is an irreplaceable tool in a wholistic healing programme. Juices bought from health-food stores and supermarkets by and large tend to be boiled and so leached of many of their nutrients.

Freshly pressed fruit is particularly beneficial because you can ingest so much more in terms of quantity and therefore absorb more vitamins, trace elements, minerals and enzymes. Fruit juices help to maintain a stable

electrolyte balance thereby ensuring that the circulation remains
stable. Water taken alone has the dangerous capacity to distort
circulation. Besides all this, juices are easily assimilated and do not
put a strain on the digestion. They do not stimulate the secretion of
hydrochloric acid in the stomach (particularly important for those with
ulcers or tender stomach lining). They contain an unidentified factor
which stimulates a micro-electric tension in the body and is responsible for
the cells' capacity to absorb the nutrients from the bloodstream and so
promote the effective excretion of metabolic waste. Some people believe
that juices actually increase the healing effects of fasting and feel the
concentrated sugars in juice strengthen the heart.

You should aim to drink 1 fl oz (30 ml) of juice for every pound
(roughly 500 g) of your body weight every day. This means you may well
be drinking up to a gallon (4.5 litres) of liquid a day.

The most effective juicing machines are those that spin juices out
centrifugally and operate continuously. Juices should be served at room
temperature and pressed freshly as needed to minimize oxidation and they
should be chewed before swallowing. That is, they should be swished well
round the mouth to ensure that they are mixed with plenty of saliva. By
fasting one day regularly every week, choosing the same day, the body will
get into a comfortable natural rhythm allowing it to dump its toxins on a
regular basis. The herbs you will be taking when you are not fasting (all
herbs should always be discontinued on a fasting day) are, in my experience,
utilized more efficiently by the body. While fasting you should skin brush
regularly morning and evening, and do some barefoot walking to help
calm and refresh the body. Follow the natural rhythm of the day by
getting up when the sun rises and consider going to bed shortly after it
sets. You should avoid watching television and be selective about the
things that you read bearing in mind that fasting is also a form of spiritual
cleansing. If you fill yourself with mental rubbish it will leach your
emotional energy and may even give you bad dreams. Don't neglect your
exercise – take long brisk walks making sure you are well wrapped up and
breathing deeply. You may choose to use extra aids as mentioned in this
book including poultices, hydro-therapy, massage and reflexology.

DIAGNOSIS
IRIDOLOGY: A DIAGNOSTIC TOOL

The observation of changes in and around the eyes is very ancient. Runes inscribed for the iris which are thought to be thousands of years old have been found carved on stone tablets in Central Asia. The Chaldeans were recorded as 'reading diseases from eye' 1000 BC. The Japanese and Chinese many thousands of years ago were familiar with the art of recognizing various diseases by looking at the whole eye apparatus, including the sclera (the white of the eye) the correlation of the eyelids as well as that of the pupil and iris. Indian Shamans would often sit and study the eyes of their patients for a long time before prescribing the relevant remedies. There are references to iridology in the work of the Hippocratic school, in the medical school of Salerno and in Philostratus.

There is also a reference to iridology as the observation and diagnosis of disease from the iris by Meyens in his book *Chiromatica medica* published in Dresden in 1670 but the true discoverer of iris diagnosis in its present form was the Hungarian physicist Dr Ignatz von Peczely (1822–1911). As a child he fought with an owl he had tried to capture, and the bird had dug its claws into his arm as it fought for its life. In the confusion that followed the bird's leg was broken. As the boy splinted and bandaged the owl's broken leg their gaze met and Ignatz immediately noticed a small black dot in the bird's eye. The next morning the dot had become a black line running from the pupil to the outer edge of the iris. After its leg healed the owl lingered. It had grown attached to the boy and several months later Ignatz noticed the black line beginning to fade from the owl's eye, until all that remained was a white line. The boy grew up with a burning ambition to study medicine, and especially to examine his patient's irises. This then was the beginning of modern iris diagnosis. Von Peczely began to formulate the first iris chart; each organ having its specific place in the iris.

Over a number of years iris charts were slowly developed by the many pioneers who followed Peczely; Liljequist charted the genital organs; Pastor Felk who gave a clear definition of constitutional types and introduced many others to the study of iris diagnosis including Magdalene Madaes and her daughter Eva Flink; Hense was one of the first to take iris photographs and Schnabel who contributed widely to iris topography. Modern pioneers include Angerer, Deck, Jaroszyk and Kriege. German-born Deck proved many iris–body correlations. In 1952 he showed that: 'among the clinically proven renal patients 92% showed substance marking (organ markings) in the renal sector of the iris'.

HOW DOES IT WORK?

By way of the direct neural connections of the surface layers of the iris with the cervical ganglion of the sympathetic nervous system, impressions from all over the body are relayed to the iris, so establishing the neuro-optic reflex.

WHAT DOES IRIDOLOGY DO?

Iridology is the study of the neuro-optic reflex. To the trained and experienced practitioner the iris reveals inherent characteristics of body tissue, the presence of toxic metals, acids, catarrh and anaemia potential. It is possible to gauge the acute, sub-acute, chronic or destructive stage of any effective organ through its corresponding sectors in the iris. The relationships with various organs to the condition of the autonomic and cerebro-spinal nervous systems can be determined, as well as whether the various endocrine glands are hyper- or hypo-active. Iridology can also act as a preventive tool by revealing a predisposition to certain disorders and disease processes long before, often years before, they have reached the awareness threshold. So iridology is a wonderful tool for assessing a person wholistically. After all, disease is not an actual entity. It is a name given for classification purposes to the primary symptom manifestations. No two individuals are alike in sickness or in health. Though two people may be herded under the same disease classification, the pattern and processes that manifest the influence of so-called disease are demonstrated by the iris to be highly individualistic and for this reason I almost never treat two patients with the same 'disease' in exactly the same way.

Because iridology is such an excellent wholistic diagnostic aid it functions in three ways. Physical structure and function may be determined but environmental and emotional influences may also be seen by the experienced practitioner. It is well known, for example, that a heart can fail as the result of an overwhelming bout of grief or shock as well as from the physical build-up of cholesterol plaque yet the same sign in the iris would be recorded for both and the final result will be the same – heart failure.

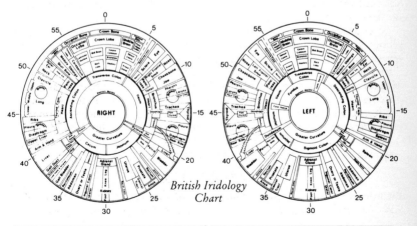

British Iridology Chart

So iridological analysis offers information that is unavailable to a conventional laboratory test and interpretations of a patient's symptoms. These may signal that something is wrong, but they seldom reveal which organ is affected. Iridology does this, effectively and reliably without requiring tissue biopsies, exploratory surgery, injections of dyes or chemical to make some organ appear distinct on X-ray, or other uncomfortable and expensive diagnostic aids.

Above all it is safe, painless and non-invasive.

It is not uncommon for me to be confronted by patients who have been told, in spite of all sorts of conventional medical tests, that there is nothing wrong with them. They come to me insisting that they feel ill. In these instances the other contributing factors to disease, emotional and environmental, may often be the missing ones that have not so far been considered, and it is here that iridology very often will come into its own. I recall a young girl coming to see me who was extremely pale and thin, trembled all over constantly and breathed so badly initially it looked as if she had asthma. The doctors had rejected her as incurable pronouncing her a hypochondriac but iridology soon determined that she was in fact suffering from heavy metal poisoning – in this particular instance cadmium as the result of living in the area where potteries used specialized paints. Patients have come to see me on more than one occasion who have been very disillusioned. They had had ECTs and only a few weeks or months later suffered from a heart attack. In both the instances that I have in mind the cause of the heart attacks was emotional and this could not possibly have been picked up by an ECT test. However the heart would have been recorded as a vulnerable area in the anterior leaf of the iris of the eye and the marking would have been present some years before the event.

The iridology course in which I trained was formulated to the recommended standards approved by the World Health Organization for courses in natural medicines. A proper iridological examination conducted by an experienced practitioner is an interesting experience and not at all frightening. Good iridologists see themselves as health educators whose role is to help others gain awareness of their bodies and an understanding of the fundamental relationships of its parts. Little equipment is actually indeed for the examination. Vital necessities include a flash light, a highly powered magnifying glass, and comfortable chairs for the patient and examiner. A thorough examination may take 30 minutes to an hour using lupe and torch intermittently interrupted by much question and answer from both sides. A trained iridologist is 75% accurate in diagnosis using only the lupe and torch, the remaining 25% of the diagnosis is done by iris photography and stereo-microscope. I find the camera a very useful item in as much as iris photos are reliable records which can then be kept and filed and used on a comparison basis at future iris readings. I like to take fresh pictures of my patients' eyes on a yearly basis. But as far as accurate analysis goes nothing can take the place of direct eye-to-eye examination. Because of the iridologist's ability to move about and to view the iris from all angles conditions may be discovered that can't be seen by a camera alone. The shadows and depth revealed by moving the light around are capable of telling a whole story in themselves. Iris photographs are an excellent means of explaining specific conclusions to the patient and more importantly, educating them about their own possibility and potential as far as their individual health pattern is concerned. It is also a very exciting experience seeing your own iris photograhed blown up to 6 ft by 6 ft (1.8 m × 1.8 m) in such minute detail and most patients really enjoy this aspect of their consultation.

It must be emphasized that the patient needs to cooperate whole-heartedly with the iridologist. Only in this way can an accurate reflection of the patient's health be achieved. As you can see iridology is absolutely nothing to do with a palmistry-like approach.

THE DANGERS OF SELF-DIAGNOSIS

Self-diagnosis is dangerous and irresponsible. While I am perfectly happy to nurture and trust the intuition of those I work with (and it is interesting that this intuition becomes much stronger as the body purifies itself) I am not prepared to acknowledge that people can evaluate their symptoms correctly and diagnose their disorders accurately. Hence my use of my own science, iridology, as a diagnostic tool. Of course there are other reliable diagnostic methods used by allopathic and alternative practitioners.

CLINICAL ECOLOGY

Clinical ecologists are concerned with detecting chemical allergy however it is induced. This is a new and growing science practised by alternative and allopathic practitioners (many of the latter are forced to practise privately as the result of indifference from the National Health Service) (See Appendix.)

ACUPUNCTURE

The Chinese diagnosis by pulses is central to an initial examination by an acupuncturist. In Chinese physiology, blood is not the same as the blood recognized in Western physiology. It is recognized as flowing not only through the blood vessels, but also through channels or meridians. These meridians are sometimes on the surface and sometimes deep within the body as they descend to reach the organs to which they relate and are connected. Additional acupuncture diagnosis is carried out by feeling the pulse with the fingertips and can differentiate between 28 different categories of pulse, organized by depth, speed, width, strength, length and rhythm. Any Chineses acupuncturist will, like his Western counterpart, look at the patient's general demeanour and appearance but the most important inspection is that of the tongue. Its appearance, colour, type and the quality of coating, size, mobility and so on are all noted and interpreted. The pulse point felt is in the radial artery of the wrist and the acupuncturist examines it by using 3 fingers on each wrist giving a total of 6 pulses in all. Each pulse is felt at 3 degrees of pressure, superficial, medium and deep. During the second half of this century an electronic point detector has been developed in an attempt to monitor the electric discharge of acupuncture points and this machine is often used by Western acupuncturists.

APPLIED KINESIOLOGY

This was pioneered by the American chiropractor Dr George Goodhart. It is a way of revealing the balance of the energy in body systems by a series of muscle-testing procedures which are carried out manually.

AURA DIAGNOSIS

The aura is a magnetic energy field which is said to surround the human body. People who claim to be able to see it describe it as an oval light radiating various colours and these change with the mood of the individual and can be analysed for the purposes of diagnosis and prognosis. In the 1920s a Kilner screen made of a special type of glass was developed by the British scientist Walter J. Kilner to enable non-psychics to detect a person's aura. Since then Kirlian photography has been pioneered by Semyon Kirlian, a Soviet engineer, and his wife Valentina. Such photography shows healthy parts of the body as a radiating aura of lights, flares and sparks while unhealthy parts appear dull, dark and lifeless. So a Kirlian photograph can show disease before it appears physically.

BIORHYTHMS

Biorhythms are the three rhythms of life which are associated with variations in physical, emotional and intellectual capacities of any human being. These rhythms were discovered jointly by two scientists working separately at the beginning of this century – Dr Hermann Swovoda in Vienna and Dr Wilhelm Fliess in Berlin. The theory of biorhythms has since been scientifically applied to increase efficiency and prevent accidents and an expert in this field can work out your own biorhythms aided by exact knowledge of the time and date of your birth.

ELECTROENCEPHALOGRAPHY

This is a special electrical machine that records the electrical activities of the brain. In order to do this, electrodes are usually attached to the scalp. The instrument helps to diagnose brain damage and disease. The American Joe Kamiya, using similar complex electrical apparatus, discovered that he could train people to increase a particular type of brain wave called alpha waves. This procedure became known as biofeedback and is currently used to treat an increasing number of illnesses.

RADIONICS

This is a method of diagnosing disease at a distance from the patient by means of instrumented Radiesthesia. Radiesthesia uses dowsing to diagnose disease and prescribe specific remedies. Diagnosis is carried out by the use of a pendulum suspended over a sample of the patient's hair, saliva or blood and the choice of a remedy (usually homeopathic) is arrived at by swinging the same pendulum over a list of likely cures. In radionics the instrument used measures electromagnetic vibration emitted by the disease and by the remedy and the different vibrations can then be analysed and identified appropriately.

REFLEXOLOGY

Formerly called zone therapy reflexology is a very old oriental medical practice in which the feet are deeply massaged in order to heal functional disorders in all parts of the body. Diagnosis is carried out by pressing parts of the soles of the feet with the tips of the thumbs and asking the patient's response. If the area is painful in any way the area in the body to which it relates is judged to be malfunctioning.

CHAPTER 2
HERBAL PHARMACY

HERBAL CHEMISTRY

The chemistry of any herb is both subtle and complex and all herbs are very powerful chemical factories. The principal groups of active chemical constituents of herbs are alkaloids, glycosides, saponins, mucilages and essential, sometimes called volatile, oils. In order to understand what I mean by active principles from a herb it is necessary to emphasize that ultimately any food which enters the mouth orally, or indeed anything which is injected anally or into the bloodstream will influence the body through its chemistry.

ALKALOIDS

These are stable crystalline substances which occur naturally in all plant tissues. They are odourless and colourless distinguishable chemically because they contain nitrogen. In general a plant will contain a group of closely related alkaloids, for example, morphine, codeine, papaderine and thebaine all of which are present in the opium poppy. Strychnine, quinine, nicotine, caffeine and mescaline are all well-known examples of alkaloids.

GLYCOSIDES

Put simply these are the sugar proportion attached by a special bond to a non-sugar proportion of a plant. The most chemically significant glycosides are the cardiac ones which increase the efficiency of the small muscle of the heart, especially in the case of heart failure. The best known of these is digitalis which is very poisonous and needs to be prescribed by an experienced practitioner in small doses.

Anthraquinone glycosides are valued for their laxative action and are present in such plants as cascara sagrada, turkey rhubarb and buckthorn.

SAPONINS

Similar to glycosides in chemical action they produce a soapy lather when shaken vigorously in water and have a markedly irritant effect on the intestine. They are toxic although some have therapeutic properties acting as expectorants for the upper respiratory organs. Yucca contains such saponins as does fumitory and soap wort.

ESSENTIAL OILS

These are also sometimes called volatile oils because they evaporate. They have a pleasing fragrance and are the liquid components of plant cells. Many essential oils are used for food flavouring because their taste and aroma is so distinctive (see p.69).

MUCILAGE

This is a chemical compound of sugars known as polysaccharides. They are partially soluble in water in which they swell up and form a mucilaginous

gel. Examples of herbs which contain such mucilage are slippery elm, marshmallow, comfrey and fenugreek. All mucilage soothes inflamed internal mucosa particularly in the upper respiratory tract and digestive organs and promotes regular rhythmic peristalsis in the latter, so having a mild laxative action.

TYPES OF PREPARATION

It should be remembered that a lot of disease begins with the malfunction of the digestive system. When digestion fails disease will certainly follow sooner rather than later. It is for this reason that herbal medicine is often used to correct the body in a way which does not disrupt the digestive system still further. There are a number of ways of correcting the balance of the body without orally ingesting any herbs.

1. *Smelling herbs: this may be done by inhaling the vapour of essential oils put into boiling water, breathing in the fumes from burning herbs (this was a method often used in ancient times for healing the respiratory tract and coltsfoot and mullein were popular herbs for this purpose), rubbing the oil into pulse points in the skin where it could be easily smelled. The oil of herbs used in this way was usually put in a carrier base of beeswax, lanolin or nut oil. The oils can also be rubbed directly inside the nose although generally it is more comfortable to put them into some sort of salve to dilute their action because nasal membranes are very sensitive.*

2. *Introducing liquid into the anus, vagina, ears or nose or inserting a tampon soaked in herbal preparation or a pessary made of herbs in a carrier base such as coconut oil.*

3. *Applying the herbs onto the skin by administering poultices, fomentations, rubbing in creams or oils often accompanied by special massage movements, or even using the herb infused or decocted in water (although other carrier bases are employed from time to time such as milk), using herbs to bathe only certain parts of the body as with using an eye bath or soaking of the feet only. Warming the body by steaming in the evaporation from herbs put in boiling water.*

4. *Gargling with herbs and then spitting them out.*

5. *Massaging herbs into the gums, usually in a powdered form, and leaving them there.*

It is often sensible to try to apply a remedy to the affected face area: that is the mouth, eyes, ears or nose.

So you can see there are many available paths of treatment before any medicine need be taken orally. In the western world we generally think we must eat something medicinal or otherwise to make us well, but fasting is often the finest medicine of all.

EXTERNAL BODY TREATMENTS

These can be administered in water, oil, or alcohol, although occasionally other substances are used such as milk.

WATER-BASED PREPARATIONS

If taken internally such preparations are generally called teas but externally are called baths (and there are a fair variety of these) or poultices or fomentations. This is certainly the simplest way to prepare herbs but the liquid will only contain the water-soluble principles of the plant. If used methodically over a long period of time the water-based preparation can be extremely effective and certainly in small children I have noticed it will have a discernable effect within a few minutes. Fresh herbs should be gently crushed to break down the cellulose of the plant, thereby releasing the active principles. To do this use a stainless steel knife, your fingers or a pestle and mortar. Dried herbs should be chopped or pounded and a pestle and mortar is the best tool here. You should remember that water-based herbal preparations decompose rapidly so they need to be made freshly each day.

Delicate parts of the herb like flowers, leaves and stamens need to be steeped in water for 20 minutes. Use 1 oz (30 g) of ther herb – remembering that fresh herbs will take up a lot more room than dried ones – and pour over them 1 pint (600 ml) freshly boiled filtered water, which has first been allowed to stand for 30 seconds. Water that is actually boiling is too harsh and destroys the potency of the herb. Stir the preparation with anything that is not aluminium. Cover the container tightly and leave to steep for 15 minutes, then strain through muslin, nylon, a stainless steel or silver tea strainer or, if using a large quantity of herbs, a sieve.

Seeds, roots, bark or very tough leaves like bay leaves all need rigorous processing to make them surrender their medicinal property. Their cell walls are very strong so more heat is needed here than would be for flowers, leaves and stamens to ensure that the active constituents are transferred into the water.

Put 1 oz (30 g) of the herbs in the bottom of a glass, enamel or stainless steel saucepan, cover with 1 pint (600 ml) filtered water with a tight-fitting lid. Bring to the boil and simmer very gently until the water is reduced by half. You will find this generally takes about 15 minutes. Strain and use as required.

If you need to use both the wood of a herb and the flowers of a herb in one mixture it is better to make infusion and decoction separately and then combine them. An infusion is the term used for preparing easily damaged herbs like leaves, flowers and stamens and a decoction is the term used for the more rigorous process of boiling up roots, berries, seeds, bark and tough leaves such as bay leaves.

Please note that all seeds, roots and barks need to be well crushed using a pestle and mortar or coffee grinder. Burdock root and cinnamon only need steeping in freshly boiled, not boiling water: valerian should be steeped in cold water for 24 hours to ensure that the valerianic acid and essential oils are not lost. Decoctions will stay fresh for 3 days, infusions tend to stay fresh only for 36 hours.

Store what you do not need immediately in the refrigerator in a glass jar covered with muslin or linen to allow the water-based preparation to breathe. If you see fine bubbles popping up to the surface the preparation has begun to ferment so throw it away; your garden would be grateful for it! However, if you make only a pint (600 ml) at a time you will generally find it will be finished within a day so this should not be a problem.

ALCOHOL-BASED PREPARATIONS

The advantage of these is first that alcohol is a better solvent than water on certain types of plant constituents and secondly that they can be kept indefinitely if properly stored. An alcohol-based preparation is called a tincture.

Use good quality brandy, gin or vodka, never use alcohol in the form of surgical spirit or methanol as these are poisonous. You will generally find the final amount of alcohol is only one-third of the original amount as the herbs, which are strained out, absorb much of it.

Combine 4 oz (125 g) powdered or very finely chopped herbs with 1 pint (600 ml) alcohol. Keep the container somewhere warm, an airing cupboard is ideal. Shake vigorously daily or twice daily if you have the time and strain after 14 days.

Tinctures should be started with a new moon and strained with a full moon 14 days later. The power of the waxing moon helps extract the medicinal properties. Evidence to support this theory is available in *Moon and Plant* by Agnes Fyfe (published by the Society for Cancer Research, Arlesheim, 1975). In this book the author discusses the moon's nodal cycle in relation to both the earth and plants on it. Over a period of many years she conducted 70 000 consecutive single tests on plant sap which proved that the moon has a chartable influence on the way sap rises and falls in plants.

She was aware that medicinal plants were gathered in the past at particular times according to some faculty and knowledge now lost to people today. Her experiments have provided us with scientific proof that such practices were not arcane but vital if herbs were to be used at their most effective. (There are diaries which chart the course of the moon which may be obtained from local stationers' shops.) Once the tincture has been made strain it through coffee filter paper into a labelled bottle and cap it tightly. For external use tinctures can be rubbed on to the skin directly or applied on poultices previously dampened with water. When I travel I always take a small bottle of tincture of plantain with me to apply to insect stings or bites, and it is most effective.

Having established three ways of preparing herbs for external use let us consider their application.

POULTICES

These seem to have gone out of fashion but they are a very useful form of treatment for external wounds or grazes, for ulcers and for drawing out boils. In addition they will supply nutriment to skin by way of the lymphatic and blood circulation to the tissues and organs beneath. Poultices are also a good way of softening and dispersing material that has become hardened such as breast lumps. You will need:

1. *Herbs – fresh herbs need to be liquidized in a little water, while dried ones should be macerated in a little hot water. Powdered ones can stay as they are.*

2. *Slippery elm powder, cornflour or arrowroot, as a carrier base.*

3. *Cider vinegar.*

4. *Fine white cotton. A man's handkerchief usually does beautifully depending on the size of the area to be treated but gauze is also suitable.*

5. *Two large plates and a large saucepan of boiling water.*

6. *Plastic sheeting such as a piece of bin bag or any large clean piece of plastic or cling film. You will also need a supply of stretchy cotton bandages and safety pins.*
The amount depends very much on the area that needs to be treated. For example, if you are applying a poultice to the abdomen it is going to take a lot more bandage than a poultice applied to your wrist.

You will therefore need to estimate how much of the herb will be necessary to be treated to a depth of ¼ in (6 mm). Now mix the herbs with an equal quantity of the carrier base, whether it be slippery elm, cornflour or arrowroot and add enough cider vinegar to form a thick paste, using a china or glass basin and a stainless steel or wooden spoon to mix. Spread the piece of cotton on a plate and put this over the saucepan of boiling water. Scrape the mixture on to one half of the cotton only, keeping it from the edge to stop it squelching out when you use it. Fold the other half of the cotton over the top and press the edges together. Cover the whole poultice with the other plate and allow it to become really hot. Remove it and apply as hot as is bearable to the affected area, but obviously do not burn yourself. Cover the poultice with plastic; secure with bandages and then safety pins, or, if the area is very large, a thin towel. Leave it on all night. If the poultice is to be applied somewhere on the trunk wear a tight cotton T-shirt to hold it firmly in place.

The next morning peel your poultice off and warm it up again using the plate method. While waiting for it to warm cleanse the area by bathing in a warm decoction made of echinacea root. Strain the decoction before use. Reapply the poultice but this time use the other side against the skin. Repeat again in the evening using a completely fresh poultice and reusing the other side again in the morning until the area is healed. In other words the poultice will need to be refreshed every 24 hours.

Poultices are useful for emergency outside treatment such as bites and stings (see pp. 234 and 239). They may be made by chewing the relevant herb and wrapping it into a pulp, mixing it with plenty of saliva in the process and not swallowing it while doing so. Spread the herb directly onto the swelling and if you have it to hand, cap it with a piece of plastic or cotton to hold it in place until you can get indoors and do a proper job. I have found equal parts of cayenne and plantain work wonderfully well to draw out splinters.

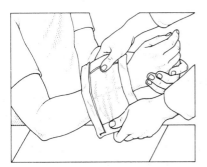

Poultices should be applied as hot as is bearable and secured firmly.

COMPRESSES

These are thin liquid poultices which are particularly useful if large areas are to be treated. They assist the circulation of lymph or blood to a specific area, so relieving swellings like varicosity and goitre, muscular aches and cold. Cold compresses ease head congestion, insomnia, fever, indigestion, sprains, bruises, and sore throats. I tend to use a lot of hot and cold compresses in my practice and although my patients grumble about going to bed accompanied by the rustle of plastic bags which is not too romantic (the plastic is necessary to hold in moisture from the compress) they nevertheless agree that they are extremely effective especially used on a

regular cyclical basis. Compresses have the special advantage of often giving almost instant pain relief. As well as being made from fresh, dried or powdered herbs they can be made from warmed oils, plant juices or tinctures diluted in water. Plant juices can be extracted from mucilaginous plants such as comfrey by putting them through a juicer.

HOT COMPRESSES

Make a double strength herbal decoction by using 2 oz (60 g) herbs to 1 pint (600 ml) water and strain, remembering to mash the herbs well down in the sieve to extract every last bit of goodness from them. Powdered herbs are particularly effective for this. Reheat the liquid and dip into it white, pure cotton cloths (bits of old sheet will do nicely) wringing them out lightly but firmly. Wrap around the part to be treated and secure with bandages and cling film or a piece of some other plastic. This will keep the moist heat of the compress intact and protect the bed sheets from seeping dampness. It may also be necessary to protect the bed sheet with a towel to prevent it from staining especially if you are leaving the compress on all night.

If the compress needs to be re-used the simplest way to do this is to turn a slow cooker or saucepan on high and drop in the damp compress, leaving the lid off. The compress will heat up very quickly and if compresses are needed one can be kept hot and within reach while the other is being used. If applying a compress for more than an hour it may be necessary to refresh it with enough herbal decoction or infusion to re-dampen it.

If you are treating a whole arm or a leg with a compress it is best done by soaking either cotton tights or a long cotton glove in the herbal mixture. This saves using bandages which, if they have to be wrapped all the way up the arm puttee style, are often awkward to remove. Silk stockings although difficult to find are a good alternative to cotton tights although any natural material will do. Poultices are very effective on limbs being treated for varicosity and thread veins as well as eczema, psoriasis and ulcerous conditions. You will need to sustain the heat over the area concerned for as long as you can with a hot water bottle.

COLD COMPRESSES

These are made in exactly the same way as hot ones but allow the liquid to go cold before dipping the cloths in. The cold compress applied for 5 to 15 minutes will encourage the blood to move quickly to the surface in cases of high temperature, sprains and bruises. For fever it is necessary to change the compress every 5 to 10 minutes as it heats up. A cold compress left on for 20 to 30 minutes will relieve indigestion and insomnia and may be repeated if necessary once every two hours. A cold compress left on all night will relieve a sore throat and bring down the swelling. It is especially effective for swollen joints. Cold compresses can be used in conjunction with applications of hot water to achieve certain interesting effects. For example, a cold compress applied to the back of the neck at the same time as a hot foot bath relieves headaches and congestion. Hot and cold compresses, 3 minutes for the hot and 2 minutes for the cold, are often used alternately for the first 48 hours of an injury until healing is complete and are particularly effective for sprained ankles.

BATHS

We are all familiar with taking baths at home but if they are to be therapeutic they should last only for 2 to 10 minutes. Very hot immersion baths if taken daily encourage debility, mental lethargy, physical weakness, poor circulation and even depression. The best way to take a bath is to enjoy a deep, hot one for only 2 to 10 minutes interspersing it with ice cold showers of water. If you do not have a shower as part of your bath use one of those rubber ones you can purchase from a chemist and attach it directly to the taps. If this is inconvenient because you have a mixer tap and such an apparatus won't fit, have a couple of large jugs of cold water on standby.

However, prolonged hot baths may be beneficial if taken when menstruation is late or for dysmenorrhea (painful menstruation) as an antispasmodic.

HERBAL BATHS

Add a gallon (4.5 litres) of strained decoction or infusion to a half-filled bath. Immerse as much as possible of the body under the water for 15 to 20 minutes protecting the head on a folded towel or bath pillow which makes a comfortable resting place.

Clean the skin *before* you take the bath by vigorously skin brushing (see p. 37) and washing any really dirty bits with a non-detergent soap or flannel. Don't use any kind of soap *after* any sweating therapy as it stops the cholesterol coming out through the pores.

EPSOM SALT BATHS

This treatment is *not* to be used by those with high blood pressure or heart conditions. It is an excellent way of dispersing acidity from the system, soaking up aches and pains, getting the skin to work properly, inducing a short sweat for therapeutic purposes and cleansing the system of fungus. It is also a wonderfully effective bath to be taken at the onset of a cold and is particularly beneficial for any kind of deep purification and healing. It needs to be taken on alternate days for 6 days, resting on the seventh day, if possible detoxifying the body with a fast on fruit or fruit juices on the seventh day.

Buy 1 lb (500 g) of Epsom salts and mix it with enough almond oil to give it the texture of wet sea sand. Carry this into the bathroom in a large basin and rest it on the side of the bath. Now put the plug in the empty

bath and stand in the bath massaging yourself all over with this mixture, using small circular movements working upwards towards the heart. This exfoliates dead skin. Let the salts and oil pour into the empty bath and step out carefully filling it as deeply as possible with hot water adding an additional cup of Epsom salts and one of apple cider vinegar. (Don't worry about the dead skin cells, they will be invisible to the naked eye and will anyway disappear down the plug hole when you drain the bath away.) Stir with the hands to dissolve. Soak yourself in the bath for 30 minutes adding more hot water as it cools. Drink as many cups of any diuretic tea (ginger, peppermint and elderflower are all particularly pleasant tasting) as you can manage. Elimination through the skin is vital. Normally the skin does only one-twentieth of the work of the kidneys but by speeding it up with herbs and hydrotherapy it can take on one tenth of their work so relieving the kidneys of any added burden.

It is advisable to have some ice cubes on standby and a bowl with a couple of flannels so you can use these on the face, neck and forehead if you feel dizzy, faint or sick. As the water drains out of the bath run a cold shower over your face and body allowing it to cool down thoroughly. Alternatively fill up plastic jugs with cold water drizzling it slowly over your body. Go to bed warmly dressed and pack yourself round with hot water bottles to encourage free perspiration. I have known some of my patients to sweat so prolifically that they needed to get up in the middle of the night to change into fresh nightwear which is all to the good. Don't wear any kind of body lotion after this treatment. It will stop the skin breathing freely. Having sweated profusely during the night take a hot shower followed by a cold one the next morning.

SALT GLOW

This is an excellent way of dislodging superficial catarrh in the tissues and I strongly recommend it to be carried out 3 to 4 times a week on those patients of mine who suffer from chronic catarrh which nothing seems to move. I have found it extremely successful.

Standing naked in an empty bath shower the skin all over with warm water. Mix 1 lb (500 g) of fine salt with enough water to turn it into a soft slurry and picking up palmfuls of this at a time massage vigorously into the skin using a brisk circular movement. Begin with the soles of the feet moving upwards towards the heart. Areas above the heart should be massaged downwards. Do not massage the salt into the scalp or the face and avoid the genital area and nipples. Rinse off the salt with a forceful warm shower followed by a brisk very cold shower. Stand under this for as long as you can manage. Get out of the bath or shower and dry vigorously.

TURKISH BATHS AND SAUNAS

Turkish baths and saunas increase circulation, skin function, respiration and general vitality as well as stimulating the nervous and hormonal systems and encouraging mental relaxation and sleep. While in a Turkish bath throw basins of cold water over yourself and in a sauna you will need to come out and take cold showers every 2 to 3 minutes after perspiration becomes noticeable. Skin brushing either before or after such baths is particularly helpful for stimulating the nervous and hormonal systems and increasing the circulation.

For those with bronchial congestion or sinus problems a few drops of eucalyptus, peppermint or camphor oil mixed with water which can be dashed over the coals in a sauna is helpful. In a Turkish bath take a small cotton cloth soaked in a few drops of one of these oils and hold it on your face. In both cases breathe in deeply through the nose and out through the mouth.

HAND AND FOOT BATHS

These baths are a particularly useful way of getting children to ingest herbal medicine. I have also used them on some of my adult patients with extremely good effects.

Mix double strength unstrained decoctions or infusions of herbs with an equal quantity of freshly boiled water and pour it into a large heat-proof enamel, china or glass container. Immerse the feet in the water, which should be bearably hot, for 8 minutes exactly. Do this on rising before breakfast. Hand baths should be taken before supper for the same length of time. Continue this topping and tailing cycle for 3 days, reheating the mixture as you go then throwing it out so that you can begin again. Take the bath for 6 days weekly resting on the seventh day and preferably detoxifying the body with a fast on this day.

Mustard hand and foot baths work wonders for aching and burning feet, leg cramps and are a preventive measure against chilblains. Add 1 tablespoon of mustard powder to a bucket of hot water and soak up to the knee or elbow in it for 10 minutes. Massage the hands or feet afterwards with equal parts of a simple tincture of benzoin and camphor.

SITZ-BATHS

These are probably the most awkward baths to take but often prove to be the most rewarding. A sitz-bath increases the circulation of blood and lymph to the pelvic region, removing internal congestion and improving tissue vitality and nutrition.

In institutions which use hydrotherapy there are often specifically designed sitz-baths which tend to look like two water filled armchairs facing one another. One is filled with very hot water, the other with ice cold. You can sit with your bottom in hot water and feet in cold for three minutes and then reverse, leaving your feet in hot water for only 1 to 2 minutes. You alternate back and forth from hot to cold for 3 immersions in each temperature finishing with the bottom in the cold bath. After drying vigorously with a rough towel you then exercise until sweating is produced. Alternate hot and cold sitz-baths are useful for any disorders of the uterus, ovaries or the fallopian tubes, for prostatis, constipation and digestive disorders.

These baths can be imitated at home. Use two large plastic tubs or galvanized wash tubs. (Baby baths do very nicely.) They need to be big enough to accommodate the bottom easily and hold enough water to cover you from navel to mid-thigh. The hot water temperature should be as warm as the body can comfortably bear and the cold should be very cold. If necessary melt ice cubes in the cold water to facilitate this.

For maximum benefit carry out these baths at least once and sometimes three and four times daily as instructed.

COLD SITZ-BATHS

An easy way to do this is to fill your bath tub with 6 in (15 cm) of cold water so that when you sit in it the water comes up to your navel. Now climb in, sit down and raise your feet to above the level of the water resting them on the edge of the bath. If this is tiring you can put in an upended plastic bucket as a foot rest. Let your knees fall apart and sweep up handfuls of water, vigorously splashing it over the abdomen while you count slowly to 60. A cold sitz-bath is particularly useful for bedwetting, impotence, difficulty in conception and malposition of the womb. When you get out, wrap yourself in a towel without drying and lie down for at least 10 minutes. If you feel a nice warm glow after this, gradually increase to a slow count of 180 over 12 sessions or more so that you are sitting in the bath for up to 3 minutes at any one time.

HOT SITZ-BATHS

Do this in the same way as cold sitz-baths but the duration can be longer, anything from 3 to 10 minutes. Take the water as hot as you can manage. It is useful in the remedy of colic and spasm or pain due to menstrual cramps, lower back pain, haemorrhoids and intestinal disturbances.

Anyone with rectal pain which is so bad that sitting in a hot bath is unbearable should fold 2 bath towels into quarters and place them one under each buttock. This will help to turn a hot sitz-bath into a positively enjoyable experience.

A SITZ-BATH SUBSTITUTE

Stand with your back to the shower so that the warm water is aimed at your lower back only. Now bend over back into the shower parting the legs so that the water runs down between the buttocks and gradually increase the temperature to the hottest you can manage. Now turn the shower to cold and have it running forcefully while you count up to 40. Once you have mastered this increase the count to 80. When you have finished dry vigorously with a rough towel then exercise until sweating is produced.

GARGLES

For maximum effectiveness use these as hot as possible. They can be made from infusions, decoctions and tinctures and even salt (provided you do not swallow it) to relieve sore mouths and throats, and for those unfortunate enough to be stung in the throat. A few drops of tincture of myrrh in half a cup of hot water is good for mouth ulcers and a double strength infusion of sage leaves with a teaspoon of cider vinegar added to each cup is excellent for sore throats including laryngitis. A decoction of ginger root tea with one teaspoon of cider vinegar, two teaspoons of honey, a teaspoon of garlic oil and a generous pinch of cayenne is a delicious mixture to gargle with and then drink, and will soothe bacterial throat infections. Tonsillitis can be helped by gargling with a teaspoon of Tea tree oil diluted in warm water.

EYE BATHS

These should be made with very gentle herbs like marigold, raspberry leaves, eyebright and cornflower. Brew them freshly, straining them meticulously several times through a coffee filter paper. Always wash out both eyes, even if only one is affected; use a sterilized eye bath and change the wash for each eye. Alternatively apply lukewarm compresses and keep changing them as they cool.

VAGINAL DOUCHES

Douches reduce the instance of non-specific vaginitis, relieve painful periods and are essential after the use of vaginal boluses (see p.70). They are a very active form of treatment so use only mild herbs well strained at body temperature unless otherwise directed, and never take more than 2 douches daily, and even this is only permissible when trying to contain infection. Stop douching as soon as the infection clears otherwise the delicate balance of natural bacteria in the vagina will be altered. The addition of a tablespoon of cider vinegar or a teaspoon of fresh strained lemon juice to every 2 pints (1.2 litres) of herbal infusion or decoction helps to maintain the pH balance.

Your douche kit needs to be kept scrupulously clean for obvious reasons and never share it with anyone else. Make an infusion or decoction (depending on the herb used) and strain through coffee filter papers. Allow it to cool to body temperature. Hang the douche bag (the ones I sell have a strong hook attachment) on the wall over the bath 2 ft (60 cm) above the hips. Climb into the bath and lie down. It helps to warm the bath up first by running hot water around it and then letting it drain out. Insert the nozzle slowly and gently into the vagina so that it touches the cervix and lie back. Now release the closed tap slowly allowing the herb tea to flow into the vagina. Then using both hands seal the vaginal opening around the nozzle so that the vagina literally becomes flooded. If you do this correctly you will detect a slight sensation of pressure as the vagina expands to accommodate the fluids. When it feels full shut the tap with one hand releasing your hold with the other and allowing the vagina to drain. If you do it correctly the liquid will be rapidly expelled with a swoosh. Now repeat the whole procedure until all the tea is used up. Douching while sitting on the toilet or bidet is tantamount to useless; don't bother with it.

N.B. *Pregnant women should never douche and should avoid douching for at least 4 weeks following delivery.*

ENEMAS

These are used to treat nervous complaints, pains and fevers; to cleanse the bowel and stimulate the detoxification of the liver, spleen, kidneys and lymph; and to carry nourishment into the body. If women have experienced an enema at all it is usually just before childbirth and it has usually been administered amidst fear and discomfort. Often soapy water is used which induces violent and painful peristalsis as well as wiping out all the benign bacteria from the colon. I am not therefore at all surprised that when I mention enemas, particularly to women, most of them get very apprehensive.

Please let me reassure you. An enema is really easy and comfortable to administer if done correctly. Give yourself plenty of time and privacy and lay everything out in advance because the more relaxed you are the easier the whole process is.

Enemas do not make a mess. Your anal sphincter muscles will hold the liquid in the colon until you decide to release it. Initially the stimulus the enema fluid gives the bowel may make you want to rush straight to the toilet and release it but you will acquire more self-control with practice.

Taking an enema is really quite logical. No sensible person would attempt to unblock a drain from the top end of the waste pipe. Using the same analogy a blocked colon needs to be relieved from the bottom end. In the event of a fever an enema is the quickest way to relieve the bowel of toxic waste. If you are so weak that you cannot eat then an enema of spirulena or slippery elm will supply some nourishment.

You will need:

1. *Herbal decoction or infusion – 3½ pints (2 litres). Cool or cold enemas are used for cleansing and warm ones for treating nervousness and spasms. Always use plain spring water bottled in glass. Never use tap water. It certainly contains chlorine which upsets the bacterial balance in the colon and may also contain fluoride.*

2. *An enema kit (see Appendix).*

3. *Oil, vaseline or KY jelly.*

4. *A large bath towel or a piece of plastic sheeting.*

TAKING AN ENEMA

1. *Fill up the enema bag with a strained tea (warm or cool as appropriate) and hang it from a hook at shoulder height.*

2. *Lubricate the tip well with vaseline, oil or KY jelly.*

3. *Lie down on your right side with your knees tucked up to your chest and gently press the lubricated tip of the enema tube into the rectum.*

4. *Release the tap and allow the liquid to flow slowly into the rectum. If it encounters a block of impacted faeces (you will know because you will feel marked internal pressure) turn off the tap, roll over on to your back with your knees bent and the soles of your feet flat on the towel and massage the area in an anti-clockwise direction. Once you feel comfortable roll over on to your right side and reopen the tap.*

5. *When the enema bag is emptied of its contents turn off the tap and remove the nozzle tip.*

6. *Wrap yourself up warmly in a bath towel and go and lie down with your bottom raised on some pillows.*

7. *Retain the enema for 20 minutes if you can. Get up carefully and release while sitting on the toilet.*

N.B. *Enemas should not be taken while fasting except in emergencies when they are being used to treat fevers. They should never be relied upon in place of a proper bowel movement nor should they be abused by over-use.*

OTHER EXTERNAL AIDS

HERBAL OILS

Pure essential oils are extracted from aromatic herbs by a complex process of distillation and it is not possible to make these at home without sterilized equipment. It is far easier to buy the oils from specialist suppliers and the ones I like are listed in the Appendix.

Simpler oils are possible to make at home. Pound 2 oz (60 g) of the freshly picked herb with a pestle and mortar. In this instance dried ones are less effective. Scrape the herbs into a wide-necked glass container and cover with 1 pint (600 ml) vegetable oil preferably olive or almond oil. Add a tablespoon of cider vinegar to assist the breaking up of the cellulose of the herbs. The container should be large enough for there to be a gap at the top

so that the contents can be shaken vigorously. Ideally the jar should be placed outside in strong sunlight. It should be embedded in fine sand which attracts and holds the heat for hours after the sun has disappeared. Bring the jar in at night. Shake again and store it in the airing cupboard until the morning. Keep up this routine for 2 to 3 weeks then strain the oil through muslin initially then coffee filter papers. Bottle in dark glass and label. If this routine is impractical the jar should be left in the airing cupboard all the time instead of putting it out in the sun during the day.

This process can be speeded up by using artificial heat but I never find the results quite as good. Place the jar in a pan of boiling water and keep the water just below boiling point for 2 hours. Top up the water as needed. This will need more or less constant attention. Strain and bottle when cool.

St John's wort, using the yellow flowers which exude caporic acid, is a very good example of an effective home-made oil. It comes out a glorious rich ruby red and is excellent for sunburn and to heal wounds.

Taken internally oils are best mixed with a little hot water and in this case take 3 drops of the oil 3 times daily. Essential oils bought from the supplier will need to be diluted. A number of essential oils have an antiseptic effect, the best known being garlic. Put 2 drops into a teaspoon of vegetable oil before applying to the skin. Do not get such essential oils near mucus membranes unless gargling with them.

OINTMENTS

These are useful for their protective and emollient effects and are usually made with herbal oil and beeswax or cocoa butter. Use a pint of herbal oil to 2 oz (60 g) melted beeswax or cocoa butter, beating vigorously while the mixture cools and thickens. Add essential oils when the mixture has cooled considerably, but before it begins to set. Beeswax gives a stiff pasty consistency while cocoa butter gives a rich oily one. Ointments are particularly effective for drying and cracking skin and need to be applied generously and rubbed in thoroughly.

CREAMS

Being lighter versions of ointments, creams are easily absorbed and excellent for treating sore and chapped skin and protecting and moisturizing healthy skin. This moisturizing effect is enhanced if you spray first with a flower water or diluted apple cider vinegar. Many such creams are readily available from health-food shops and the ones I find particularly useful are listed in the Appendix.

PESSARIES AND BOLUSES

These are simply internal poultices. They are made by adding enough finely powdered herbs to gently warmed cocoa butter to form a doughy paste. A vaginal bolus is shaped into a sausage the size of a regular size tampon. A pessary should resemble your little finger in size, and if it is being used to treat the colon not just the rectum it should be at least 2 in (5 cm) long and two should be inserted, one behind the other.

The best way to roll out the paste is on an oiled marble slab or inside a plastic bag. The pessaries or boluses can then be left overnight on a flat surface in the refrigerator to harden and then stored in sealed plastic bags, each pessary or bolus wrapped in greaseproof paper.

Once unwrapped the pessary or bolus should be inserted as deep into the rectum or as high into the vagina as possible just before bed. The body heat will then gently melt the cocoa butter and release the herb. The bed linen should be protected with an old towel and you should wear cotton knickers and a press-on sanitary towel. Rinse the anus or the vagina well the next morning preferably in a warm followed by a cold sitz-bath. A new pessary should be inserted after every bowel movement, a new bolus on the evening of every second day. You should douche on alternate evenings (not the evenings on which you insert a bolus) resting from both douching and the boluses or pessaries on the seventh day.

Pessaries and boluses are useful for astringing (i.e. tightening) internal tissues, soothing, cleansing, drawing out toxins and carrying herbs to the requisite area internally to treat infections, irritation, cysts, tumours and, in the case of pessaries, haemorrhoids. Boluses and pessaries need to be used properly over a period of 6 to 7 weeks to work well. Expect all sorts of discharges and odours as they do their work.

INTERNAL HERBAL TREATMENTS

There are almost always as many ways to administer herbs internally as there are externally and these include those based on water, alcohol, sugar, honey, glycerine, milk, or preparations where the herb is taken chewed fresh or in its dried, finely powdered form.

HERBAL TEA

To prepare a herbal tea follow the instructions on page 58 for water-based preparations but avoid powdered herbs which quickly turn into a muddy and unappetizing soup. Keep a teapot especially for your medicinal tea. Your ordinary teapot tends to get stained with tannin and if you brew an iron-rich tea like yellow dock in such a pot, the iron from the herb in the tannic acid from the staining will bond to form tannate of iron, a very strong styptic (that is, an agent that is extremely astringent and contracts tissues, specifically a hemostatic agent which stops bleeding by contracting the blood) which induces acute constipation and digestive problems.

Always use boiled, filtered water. Water filters are readily available from health food shops and chemists. Those that also take the nitrogen out of water are a relatively new introduction to the market and even more

effective than those that only take out heavy metals. Do not take water straight from the tap. It is laden with chemicals.

The quantities of a medicinal tea are always the same unless otherwise specified. They are 1 oz (30 g) to 1 pint (600 ml) of boiled filtered water. Drink 1 cup of the strained herbal tea with every meal. Many medicinal herbal teas drunk at this strength taste very strong and somewhat unpalatable so can be sweetened with honey, maple syrup, date sugar, liquorice or a dash of apple or grape juice or even grape sugar, but there are certain instances when a tea should not be sweetened and this will be mentioned as it occurs. Decoctions are particularly strong tasting and so need this additional help. If a tea is specifically designed to act on the digestive system, in particular the stomach, liver or pancreas, it may be necessary to drink it without any masking with sweet additions. Teas can be drunk hot as well as cold. Some people find cold decoctions more palatable than hot ones. However hot teas are more stimulating and will act more quickly on the body than their cold cousins.

ALCOHOL-BASED PREPARATIONS

These are made in exactly the same way as tinctures for external use (see p.59).

If you are a teetotaller and cannot face the thought of alcohol even for medicinal purposes or fear your children may be in need of frequent medication with tinctures use cider vinegar instead of alcohol but add a teaspoon of glycerine before bottling.

The dosage for tinctures is generally 1 teaspoon or 10 drops in a cup of water 3 times a day with meals.

GLYCERINE-BASED PREPARATIONS

It is possible to base a tincture on glycerine which treats the digestive tract more gently than its alcoholic counterpart, but such tinctures have the disadvantage of not dissolving oily or resinous materials as effectively.

To make a glycerine tincture mix 1 part of glycerine with 4 parts of filtered water so that you make up 1 pint (½ litre) of the mixture in all. Add 4 oz (125 g) of the dried, ground herb and leave it in a well stoppered container for two weeks, shaking it vigorously daily or twice daily if you have the time. After 2 weeks strain and press or wring the mixture out of the cloth catching it in a large basin. Coffee filter paper in this instance is not helpful as the glycerine will not pass through it. Put the glycerine tincture into a labelled bottle and cap it tightly.

SUGAR-BASED PREPARATIONS: SYRUPS

This is a good way of preparing medication for children as the syrup masks the strong taste of the herbs. To a strained decoction add a quarter of its weight in liquid honey and trickle in slowly over heat, stirring with a wooden spoon until the mixture turns syrupy. You will need to skim off the rising scum from time to time. Alternatively mix one part of tincture with the equivalent weight of honey, stirred over a low heat if necessary to amalgamate the two. Decant into a labelled glass bottle. Take one tablespoon as needed. Syrups are an excellent basis for cough mixture. Syrups are also very pleasant to gargle with if diluted in their equivalent weight of hot water. Whether the gargle is spat out or swallowed the child should be encouraged to clean the teeth afterwards.

DRY PREPARATIONS

These are probably the most potent and effective form of herbal medicine because the whole herb is used, not an extract. I tend to favour the powdered herbs (generally encapsulated in gelatin capsules) at my own clinic. However, in some instances it is essential to taste the herb, as when using bitter herbs, as their effectiveness depends on the neurological sensation of fitness in order to stimulate the digestive process. In this instance powdered herbs are best not put into capsules but mixed with a little honey and thoroughly chewed. A dried herb also takes longer to be absorbed by the system because it is unprocessed by water or alcohol but this may be just as well because the action ultimately is far more powerful. You can buy herbs already finely powdered from the suppliers listed in the Appendix. Alternatively you can powder your own by putting them through a coffee grinder with a very powerful motor but even this will not touch some of the very hard roots and barks. In this instance you will need to prepare them in an alternative form with tinctures, or by decocting them.

GELATIN CAPSULES

These are small cylindrical capsules made up of animal gelatin in which the herbs are compressed. Unfortunately over the many years in which I have been in practice I have not yet been able to track down a source of vegetable gelatin capsules. For those who are ardent and committed vegetarians the alternative way to orally ingest powdered herbs is to mix them in some alternative carrier base such as honey, unsalted butter, sugar-free jam, yoghurt, or fruit juice. Animal gelatin capsules are available in sizes ranging from '00' to '4'. The stock size is '0', which is the correct size for an adult. To fill the capsule, separate it and press both halves firmly into the powdered herbs until each is as full as possible. Then close the capsules carefully so that one side slots into the other.

If you have a choice and don't mind the strong and bitter taste of most medicinal herbs I would recommend that you use a carrier base rather than capsules simply because the bitter principles facilitate digestion and therefore any medication taken will work far more quickly.

However, if using gelatin capsules take two or three size '0' capsules as prescribed right at the beginning of each meal with lots of liquid, preferably herbal tea or fruit or vegetable juice.

(Should you have difficulty in swallowing capsules but can manage tablets, or vice versa, it may be because you are using the same swallowing technique for both. For a tablet or pill place it in the mouth with a small amount of water, and tilt the head backwards and you will find that you can swallow readily. Follow with more water, herbal tea or fruit juice. This method does not work for a capsule which, because it is lighter than water, will float forward and so be difficult to swallow. Instead tilt the head or upper part of the body *forward* then the capsules will float backwards and be swallowed easily.)

PILLS

These are helpful when herbs cannot be finely powdered but can be roughly chopped and for those who do not have the dexterity or patience to fill capsules. Mix 1 oz (30 g) of the herb with enough firm set honey or melted unsalted butter to make a malleable paste. I find a food mixer handy here. Divide the paste into 100 equal size portions by rolling it into thin sausages, then cut it into pellets and shape it into balls. Roll each ball in a little slippery elm and spread them on a stainless steel baking sheet, drying them out overnight in an airing cupboard.

> N.B. Hyopglycaemics, diabetics and anyone with pancreatic imbalance should *not* use honey and people trying to lose weight should avoid both butter and honey.

Take 2 or 3 pills at the beginning of each meal with plenty of liquid.

DOSAGES

As a general rule the dose of any herb should follow the body weight. Doses in this book are as for an adult weighing 150 lbs (75 kg). Bear this in mind and adjust the dose accordingly. From my own experience I have found that people who are underweight or highly strung, or possibly both, are best advised to spread the dose of the herb out on a more continual basis throughout the day. That is that you take the recommended dose appropriately adjusted to body weight but they would divide the dose up into 6 portions over the course of the day rather than 3.

HERBAL TEAS

One breakfast cup with meals 3 times a day.

POWDERED HERBS

Two size '0' capsules before meals 3 times a day.

SYRUPS

One tablespoon between meals 3 times a day or as needed.

TINCTURES

One teaspoon or 10 drops in a full cup of water 3 times a day.

ACCURATE DOSAGE FOR CHILDREN

There is a simple way of determining the correct dosage for a child according to age. Take the age of the child *on their next birthday* and divide it by 24 which will give you the fraction of the adult dose recommended. That is the dose for a 7 year old would be 8 divided by 24 equals one third of the adult dose.

So if the formulation calls for 1 breakfast cup full of herbal 3 times a day for an adult it will be approximately one-third of a cup of herbal tea for a 7 year old 3 times daily. If an adult dose calls for 2 size '0' capsules 3 times a day before meals then a 7 year old will take one-third of this which amounts to two-thirds of one size '0' capsule before each meal. Always remember in treating very young children only the very mild herbs should be used such as camomile, lemon balm and catnip. Camomile taken in a standard dose of 1 oz (30 g) to 1 pint (600 ml) often causes nausea, so I always recommend for an adult dose to use ½ oz (15 g) to 1 pint (600 ml). If in doubt administer herbs to children through the skin by using hand or foot baths or full bodied baths. This is certainly safer than any other method. Safer, however, does not mean weaker, it is extremely effective.

STORING FORMULATIONS

Anything made with alcohol or vinegar will keep well over a year if stored in firmly stoppered opaque glass bottles, but please remember that any herbal mixture, no matter how effectively dried or preserved, will grow less effective with age. So throw out any dried herbs once they have passed their first birthday. Syrups will keep indefinitely as honey is such an excellent preservative, but should be stored in a refrigerator tightly covered, preferably with a vacuum seal. Essential oils will keep indefinitely in small, sterilized opaque glass bottles but air gaps should be eliminated by transferring them into smaller and smaller bottles as they get used up. Poultices and compresses should always be freshly made and cotton or gauze bandages should be well boiled after use, dried and stored in sealed plastic bags. If they become sticky with ointment throw them out.

Herbal preparations which have rotted and gone off begin to smell odd, fizz or turn ominous colours, in which case your compost heap will still be grateful for them. Always sterilize containers before use with a thorough boiling, and screw on sterilized lids or plug uncapped bottles with generous swabs of cotton wool. Corks need first to be boiled and then sterilized in diluted vinegar.

WHEN NOT TO ADMINISTER HERBS

The strict rule when using herbs at home is that no herb should *ever* be taken even in small quantities unless you are personally totally familiar

with its properties and any contra-indications. If in doubt ask for professional help. For those who have experience in using harmless herbs for bodily correction there is no need to justify their use.

One of the enormous advantages of herbal medicine as a therapy is that it is completely safe – *when correctly administered*. But I have known amateur herbalists run away with the erroneous belief that all herbs are benign and beneficial and consequently to administer them in a spirit of cavalier abandon. This is irresponsible and dangerous. It should be remembered that herbs are very potent healing tools and there are many which are poisonous and should not be used at all. In general they are certainly far safer than orthodox medicines and many still provide the raw materials for today's allopathic remedies.

Every year, amateur herbalists poison themselves or worse still, someone else, by ingesting poisonous plants. (When I was at university there was an epidemic of hemlock poisoning, the result of enthusiastic students on a 'food for free' kick eating what they thought was wild carrot.) You must remember that many plants have not yet had their biochemical qualities, both toxic and therapeutic, fully documented. There are, for example, 300 species of lupin, two species of laburnum and many others which are intensely poisonous even when taken in minute quantities. What constitutes a toxic dose of the normally therapeutic herb depends largely upon the herb. Often the toxic dose may be 300 times the medicinal dose and herbs in this quantity would be extremely difficult to ingest. There are other herbs that have a toxic dose so close to the therapeutic one that any attempt by the amateur at self-medication may end in disaster. Such herbs are listed on pages 77–85. Please read this section. I have also included warnings specifically about treating pregnant women and children. In general it is best to treat an acute condition without any herbs at all. Instead fast on fruit or vegetable juices. I have said it once but I will reiterate it – fasting is the best medicine of all. However if you are confident about managing fever there are herbs which are useful for accelerating the patient through this stage (see p.237).

Qualified herbalists know that when two or more herbs are married in one prescription their individual properties react together in such a way that other effects are produced that are not normally found when either of the herbs is prescribed separately. This marvellous internal cooperation between herbs results in the extraordinary situation of two plus two equalling five. So if a formulation is given in this book which includes more than one herb please do not change it unless I give you an alternative. Never alter the dose of any herb and if at all doubtful about treating children, don't. Seek the advice of a professional.

CONTRAINDICATIONS

Biological activity is a two-edged sword. This should never be forgotten. Herbs can heal and herbs can kill. Healing herbs used in more than the recommended dose or administered in the wrong way or used for too long a period of time can aggravate a condition. Poisonous herbs are occasionally used by very experienced practitioners in minute amounts to accelerate healing. As far as the amateur use of herbs is concerned some herbs should not be used at all, or should not be used in certain circumstances.

Here is a check-list of herbs which are contraindicated, read through it carefully before embarking on taking any herbal medicines.

ACONITE

The aconites belong to the Ranunculaceae family, of which there are some 30 species, all containing the deadly poisonous alkaloids aconitine and pseudoaconitine. If these are ingested in anything but the most microscopic quantities the results are fatal.

ALOE JUICE

Not to be confused with the whole herb, aloe vera, or with aloe gel, both of which are more potent in their action and should *never* be used internally. Externally a cut leaf of aloe rubbed over burns, rashes, psoriasis, insect bites and itching is extremely helpful but if you ingest the whole plant it will cause internal ulceration and piles. The juice taken internally actually heals internal ulceration but it tends to cause griping so is best mixed with a little strong ginger root tea (see Appendix).

BELLADONNA

This should only be used by qualified medical herbalists being part of the Solanaceae family and one of the most notorious plant poisons.

BROOM

It should not be used if there is high blood pressure or during pregnancy.

BUTTERCUP

The sap is extremely poisonous taken orally.

CAMOMILE

Often regarded as the gentlest of herbs, overstrong infusions can cause nausea, so I generally specify that it is to be taken at half the normal infusion, that is ½ oz (15 g) to 1 pint (600 ml) of water and infused for only 10 minutes before drinking. I always feel camomile has rather an uninteresting straw-like taste and advise my patients to cheer it up with a pinch of cinnamon or to stir honey into it with a cinnamon stick.

CAYENNE PEPPER

Cayenne should be taken uncooked. It can cause burning on defecation and should always be mixed in some sort of carrier base such as soya milk or vegetable juice, particularly if you have a sensitive stomach. I have noticed that if I have administered it for 5 or 6 months at a time without remit it has caused a great deal of mucus to appear in the stools and I feel this may be the result of irritation of internal mucosa rather than healing. However it is a superb remedy for stomach ulcers and will heal them extremely effectively, contrary to public opinion.

CELERY

Ascertain the soure of the seeds, which are usually dressed with fungicide, and only use it if you can be confident that this is not the case. As it is a uterine stimulant, it is not to be taken in pregnancy.

CLOVER

Some varieties of white or Dutch clover contain hydrocyanic acid, which can break down into prussic acid in the digestive system and prove extremely poisonous. Admittedly New Zealand is the only country to record a death from clover poisoning but incidents of toxicity occur regularly. If using clover externally on the skin it is always advisable to mix it into a carrier base such as slippery elm as prolonged contact with the skin can cause burning and soreness.

COOKED SPICES

Most cooked spices aggravate. They are much more therapeutic if taken raw. This particularly applies to cayenne pepper, see above.

FALSE UNICORN

This contains oxytoxic agents, rather like goldenseal, and promotes delivery so it should not be used during the course of pregnancy except to resolve potential miscarriage problems and during the last 6 weeks of pregnancy (see p.178). However it is a superb herb for inducing fertility in women being one of the most positive stimulative tonics to the uterus and ovaries.

FOXGLOVE

If taken in excess it is deadly so should not be used by amateurs.

GARLIC

The whole clove eaten is very beneficial for high blood pressure but processed garlic in the form of pearls or tablets can sometimes aggravate the condition, so approach with caution. I have never found parsley particularly useful to sweeten the breath after eating garlic but chewing a clove is extremely effective and gives the breath a lovely spicy fragrance.

GINSENG

This is best used in chronic diseases where the patient is weak, cold and debilitated. It should never be given to those with hot acute diseases (as with a fever) nor to those suffering from high blood pressure, nervous tension or anxiety, or to women with menstrual irregularities. I get quite distressed listening to people in health-food shops who know very little about the herb recommending it to women who are experiencing menopausal or menstrual problems.

It should never be taken with anything containing caffeine. For the elderly or for prolonged treatment of debilitation the maximum dose is 800 mg of the dried root daily. The young and active should not take it for more than 3 weeks without stopping for at least a fortnight between doses. For short term use the maximum dose is 2 g daily in this instance.

All this advice applies to Asiatic ginseng (*Panax ginseng*) and Siberian ginseng (*Eleutherococcus senticosus*), which if anything is even stronger, and to a lesser extent the American ginseng (*Panax quinquefolium*). The best way to take ginseng is to use all 3 mixed together in equal parts (see Appendix for suppliers of a mixed formulation).

GOLDENSEAL

This should not be used by diabetics because it lowers blood sugar levels. Taken for more than 3 continuous months at a time a patient may begin to exhibit hypoglycaemic symptoms. If this occurs, drink liquorice tea (provided there is no high blood pressure) or fenugreek tea. Taken over the long term it will stop the assimilation of B vitamins. However it is useful in the short term especially as an infection fighter. Large doses contract the uterus so women who have a tendency to miscarry should not take it. If you need to use a herbal formulation containing goldenseal for more than 3 months replace the goldenseal with equal parts of wild thyme and garlic.

GREATER CELANDINE

It has been called the best and the most wicked of herbs and in large doses it is extremely poisonous. I use it only externally and its sale is restricted to medical herbalists only.

GROUNDSEL

Excessive use over short periods may cause cirrhosis of the liver.

HAWTHORN BERRIES

Do not use these if you have low blood pressure.

HEART'S EASE

Excessive doses may cause a cardiac reaction. The maximum dose is 4 g of the dried whole herb taken 3 times a day.

HEMLOCK

The hemlock that Socrates drank was adminstered with opium because otherwise death would have come by an excruciatingly slow progressive failure of the respiratory system; the opium made this horrible end a little more bearable. Also avoid *Cicuta*, water hemlock, which is equally fatal.

HOLLY

The leaves are sometimes used to treat rheumatism but the berries are poisonous. Watch children particularly over Christmas if holly is used to decorate the house.

HORSETAIL

This is a strong diuretic and therefore its long-term use is dangerous as it can scour the kidneys. Always use it with a demulcent herb to soften its effect. (Slippery elm, comfrey root or marshmallow root are all excellent demulcents.) Horsetail contains silicic acid, saponins, alkaloids and a poisonous substance called thiaminase which causes symptoms of toxicity in both humans and animals. Thiaminase poisoning causes a deficiency in vitamin B, and may lead to permanent liver damage.

Please remember all diuretics need to be approached cautiously. The only really safe diuretic is dandelion root, which contains plentiful amounts of potassium but is not as potent in its action as horsetail, uva ursi, buchu, or juniper berries.

JUNIPER BERRIES

Juniper berries are wonderful for clearing up a brief attack of cystitis but should only be used for this kind of emergency, never for prolonged treatment.

LIME TREE FLOWERS

Ensure your supplies are fresh. Old fermenting leaves and flowers can cause hallucinations and I know of at least one case in which a herbalist did not check supplies and got a severe shock when the patient phoned up complaining of hallucinating.

LIQUORICE

This decreases the contraction of the uterus and should not be taken during labour or in the last 6 weeks of any pregnancy. Indeed, unless specifically prescribed by a qualified medical herbalist, it is best avoided altogether during pregnancy.

You will notice throughout this book my frequent cautions about its use. Large and frequent doses exacerbate high blood pressure because liquorice is a cardiac stimulant with a high sodium ratio. (Most other herbs are low in sodium and high in potassium.)

LOBELIA

This is not available to the general public as it is considered a poisonous herb in Britain. However herbal practitioners are able to prescribe it and I find it one of the most useful herbs in my own pharmacy because it has a wonderful way of catalysing other herbs and getting them to work in the parts of the body where they are most needed. Administered in small doses it acts as a superb antispasmodic, relieving asthma and helping to bring up mucus. In large doses it is an emetic and so useful for certain types of poisoning (see p.241). A reasonable substitute for lobelia is ginger root if used in a multiple formulation but ginger is not an emetic.

MISTLETOE

Government authorities are sensitive about this herb particularly because of its anti-carcinogenic reputation but also because it contains large amounts of viscotoxins. The berries of mistletoe are therefore not permitted to be prescribed by anyone other than a registered medical herbalist. The rest of the plant is now coming under scrutiny on the basis of assumed dangers although none of these has been proved clinically as yet. So mistletoe should be taken only under qualified medical supervision.

NETTLES

Do not use the foliage in its fresh state after mid-summer as it becomes a laxative. If you feel you need nettles for treatment during the winter the young leaves are best and after picking should be finely chopped and frozen in plastic bags or containers in your deep freeze. These can then be made into soups or stirred into stews.

NUTMEG

This contains a poisonous alkaloid, strychnine, and should not be used at all except by qualified medical herbalists. It can cause abortion. Of course it is perfectly acceptable to use it in small quantities in cooking.

PILEWORT

This should never be ingested fresh or rubbed on the skin fresh – it may cause irritation. Once dried toxins in the plant break down into reasonably innocuous anemonine and it is safe to use.

POKE ROOT

The leaves are extremely poisonous. It contains mitogenic substances (that is substances that distort cell structure) and should not be taken in doses of more than 1 g every 24 hours, and then should only be used for 6 days, after which it should be given a wide berth for 3 months. Properly administered it is a wonderful cleanser for the lymph and blood and is excellent for chronic catarrh and benign cysts.

RED RASPBERRY LEAF

This contains fragine, which strengthens the uterus but cannot promote uterine contraction unless a woman has a genetic background of strong pelvic muscles. Its high iron content makes it useful in pregnancy but it is best administered, even then, with at least the same quantity of another herb.

RUE

If inhaled in large amounts it is hallucinogenic.

SAGE

Because it is rich in tannin it should not be used on a daily basis. Tannin builds up proteins and eventually reduces the assimilation of the B vitamins and stops the effective absorption of iron. Very prolonged use of astringent herbs that contain tannin have occasionally been associated with throat and stomach cells becoming cancerous, so herbs rich in tannin are all best used only in the short term. If they have to be used for some time, mix them with milk to neutralize the tannin. Herbs high in tannin include the bark of bayberry, cascara and blackberry, the roots of comfrey, sarsaparilla and yellow dock, and some leaves like peppermint, cleavers and uva ursi.

Sage also contains a toxic ketone as part of its essential oil complex, and if the essential oil is consumed regularly over several months, this may produce an emmenagogic effect in women, causing womb spasms and the possibility of abortion in pregnant women. As sage oil is often administered for menopausal hot flushes please take this into account and do not use it for more than 3 consecutive weeks at a time without resting between doses for at least a further week.

SASSAFRAS

The oil is carcinogenic, so always use the whole herb. Do *not* use at all during pregnancy or for longer than 3 or 4 consecutive weeks.

SQUILL

This can cause drastic diarrhoea and uncontrollable retching. It needs to be prescribed in minute, carefully controlled doses by a qualified medical herbalist.

TOBACCO

Chewed raw or taken as a tea it causes vomiting, convulsions and respiratory failure even in minute doses. Nor is the Italian gypsy habit of applying it as a poultice to a wound to be recommended as it is possible that enough of the toxin could be absorbed into the bloodstream to cause septicimia.

VALERIAN

Once a stressful period is over substitute an alternative nervine. In the short term its action is quick and potent but in the long term it can cause degeneration of the nervous system so its long term use is not desirable. This applies to both its internal and external use.

VIOLETS

Always use the fresh not the dried flowers.

WHITE BRYONY

In large doses it is toxic.

PHYSICAL SENSATIONS

Some herbs like kava kava and cloves will numb the tongue. Lobelia in tincture or tea form can cause a feeling of scratchiness at the back of the throat. Bayberry bark and myrrh cause a tightening sensation in the mouth in tea or tincture form. Prickly ash may make the stomach very hot and will produce heavy sweating. Blue cohosh applied externally is extremely irritating to the mucous membranes as is the fresh juice of poke root, as previously mentioned. Cayenne may cause anal burning on defecation as previously mentioned.

ESSENTIAL OILS

It takes some 7 000 flowers to make a single drop of undiluted essential oil so these oils need to be treated with a great deal of respect and caution. Pennyroyal oil, for example, can cause a painful and dangerous abortion, and coma, bleeding, uncontrollable trembling can all occur with excessive doses of essential oils so they should be taken strictly according to instruction both internally and externally. Externally you will notice I have always asked you to apply them to the skin diluted in a mild carrier oil. Internally they should be dissolved in hot water with a little honey. The only instance in which I have recommended a single drop applied to the back of the tongue to help move mucus out of the body is essential oil of anise and this should not be used for longer than a week.

HERBS FOR SHORT-TERM USE ONLY

Goldenseal

After 2 or at most 3 months of its use take it out of the formulation and replace it with an alternative mixture. Although there is no exact substitute as previously mentioned I like equal parts of wild thyme and garlic.

Poke root

Use for 6 days only and then not for another 3 months. Do not use externally at all without the supervision of a qualified medical herbalist.

Black and blue cohosh

Both are potent herbs and useful in the short term. You will anyway be warned off excessive doses by nausea.

Senna and cascara bark

Used over prolonged period they will actually discourage peristalsis and by prolonged I mean upwards of a year.

POISONING BY PLANTS

Induce vomiting as quickly as possible (unless the herb was taken several hours beforehand in which case vomiting is a waste of time) and then phone the doctor.

Above all keep the patient calm. Panic only increases the speed with which a poison will invade the system. Ipecac syrup (1½ fl oz/45 ml for an adult) will quickly induce vomiting. Lobelia (5–10 ml in peppermint tea) will also do so. Never clear up the vomit until the doctor has inspected it. Undigested plant material in the vomit can give important clues about the nature of the toxic material swallowed and this is particularly important as far as children are concerned.

Vomiting may leave the patient feeling better, albeit rather weak. Do not assume however that the worst is over. Do *not* try to induce vomiting more than once. Please remember *all* poison victims need immediate professional help. This advice is only offered for short term use. You should always contact a doctor or a hospital immediately.

QUALIFIED MEDICAL HERBALISTS

Choosing a competent medical herbalist is tantamount to walking through a therapeutic minefield. There are still some excellent herbalists in practice who have no formal qualification whatsoever except for many years of experience, but these are dwindling in numbers. There is a distressing number who have little or no experience and hide behind a list of weekend certificates that mean absolutely nothing. (For a list of qualifications to look for see Appendix.) As in every profession the skill of a medical herbalist will vary. Choose someone who will fit into your life-style but whoever you choose look for, and expect, absolute professionalism. I always think the best way to make a choice is to talk to other patients working with a practitioner you have in mind. If a patient has been going to see a practitioner for the last 2 years and is not improving there is something wrong. It obviously means that the disease is not being helped. Even those with entrenched illnesses like multiple sclerosis who may need to see a medical herbalist for a long period of time should be experiencing some relief.

Many medical herbalists like to see patients for a yearly check-up on a purely preventative basis. I much prefer to work with people who are basically healthy and want to stay that way rather than those who are on their last legs and have tried every other form of medical help before coming to see me. Choose someone who specializes in one field only. A jack of all trades and master of none will be no good to you. Be prepared to work with someone who will open-mindedly refer you on to another branch of naturopathy if necessary. Herbalism isn't the panacea of all ills. Neither is acupuncture, homeopathy or osteopathy, though some practitioners evidently believe so judging by the jealous way they cling to their patients.

CHAPTER 3
HEAD, EYES, MOUTH, THROAT AND EARS

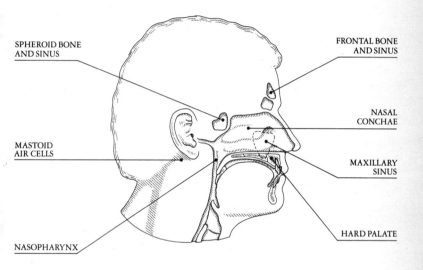

SPHEROID BONE
AND SINUS

FRONTAL BONE
AND SINUS

NASAL
CONCHAE

MASTOID
AIR CELLS

MAXILLARY
SINUS

HARD PALATE

NASOPHARYNX

ADENOIDS

Chronically swollen adenoids block the eustachian tubes, causing congestion and fluid to run into the middle ear and so creating an ideal breeding ground for bacteria. Follow the advice for tonsillitis (see p.97) and treat the cause systemically with the following formulation.

Equal part of:

cleavers	*calendula*
echinacea	*pokeroot*

Take 1 size '0' capsule with each meal. Adjust the dose according to age (see p.74).

CATARACTS AND GLAUCOMA

In my own practice I have found that internal problems of the eye like cataracts and glaucoma are not readily approached by herbal treatment although there is a lot to be said for a systemic rather than a local approach. If cataracts are seen to be developing relatively early in adult life the patient needs careful investigation because disturbances in sugar metabolism or calcium are now known to be a cause of the premature formation of cataracts and people with these conditions can be treated by a specially tailored personal nutritional programme.

The only herbal medication I know which has been used with some success for cataracts is *Cineraria maritima succus*. These are administered as eye drops, one drop two to three times a day.

Vitamin E and selenium may also influence the rate of normal degeneration in the lens of the eye. Alternating hot and cold forceful head showers may be helpful and the Bates' eye exercises are certainly worth a try (see Appendix).

Far too few people visit an optician regularly for a check-up. You should go throughout your life as naturally as you go to the dentist, only not as often; once every 2 or 3 years is fine unless you wear glasses or contact lenses, in which case it should be once every 18 months. After the age of 40 you should go every year, regardless of whether or not you wear glasses or contact lenses, because this is the age at which glaucoma is most likely to develop. An optician can spot not just cataracts or glaucomas but certain types of circulatory problems too. Approximately 4% of the over-40s develop glaucoma and large numbers suffer severe sight restriction or blindness as a result. Yet glaucoma caught early can be treated very successfully by lowering the intra-ocular pressure and keeping it within normal range. Your optician will prescribe drops to do this locally in cases of chronic simple glaucoma and the following formulation is a gentle systemic way to help back up this treatment.

angelica	Oregon grape root
dandelion root	plantain
figwort	scullcap
gentian	turkey rhubarb
gipsy weed	

Take two size '0' capsules of the finely powdered herbs three times a day. In addition to eye drops prescribed by your doctor, decoctions of angelica and eyebright may be used in cooled form as an eyewash.

Also take 200 mg of potassium gluconate and 300 mg of nicotinamide (the non-flushing form of B₃) nightly with one B complex. Cut out all salt absolutely.

COLD SORES (*Herpes Simplex*)

Rubbing or chafing the skin, injury, physical or mental stress, sunburn, fever, a poor diet, excessive anger, anxiety, depression and menstruation can all spark off the viral infection that typically produces cold sores around the mouth – a small blister that when ruptured leaves a thin yellowish crust often exacerbated by broken skin which bleeds or weeps.

Raising the level of the immune system is a prerequisite, as is a dietary strategy which involves the reduction of the amino acid arginine and the simultaneous boosting of lysine, which help to control the duplication of the viral particles. Foods which are rich in lysine include chicken, lamb, beans, brewer's yeast and beansprouts, as well as most fruits and vegetables except peas. Foods high in arginine are gelatine, chocolate, carob, coconut, oats, wholewheat or white flour, wheatgerm, peanuts and soya beans.

While symptom-free take ½–1½ g lysine daily. This is one of the amino acids available in capsule form – for suppliers see Appendix. When the virus is showing signs of activity increase the dose to 3 g daily. Also take vitamin C and bioflavonoids to saturation point, stopping just short of diarrhoea; and B₅, B₆, folic acid, calcium and magnesium according to individual need.

Pat on the following tincture externally. Equal parts of:

garlic
goldenseal
scullcap

To raise the level of the immune system, dry skin brush daily and take the kind of vigorous exercise which will act as a powerful pump for the lymph gland (this includes swimming, trampolining, running, and skipping). Herbs which are particularly effective for the lymph system include echinacea, nettle, goldenseal, cleavers, marigold, red clover, plantain, myrrh and bayberry bark. Echinacea is probably the most helpful of these

as it assists the production of white blood cells and is a supreme lymph cleanser. Take two size '0' capsules three times a day.

Food which clogs the lymph system includes red meat, dairy products, sugar, anything artificial, alcohol or fried food.

COMMON COLD

A cold that is properly managed should last for only 2 days and flow purposefully and freely. It should occur only once or twice a year. A cold that is discouraged and suppressed may drag on in one form or another for 2 to 3 months.

Recently the use of zinc lozenges has been shown to shorten the duration of symptoms of the common cold (for suppliers see Appendix). A herbal alternative which I have found works excellently, provided it is used as soon as symptoms of a cold or flu are felt, is boneset tea. Make an infusion and go to bed propped up on plenty of pillows. Try to drink the whole pint (600 ml) as quickly as is reasonably possible. Cover yourself with plenty of warm bedclothes and settle down to have a good sweat.

A famous herbal remedy for colds is equal parts of an infusion of elderflowers, peppermint and yarrow. Take as for boneset tea above.

To assist the eliminative function of a cold, drink plenty of ginger tea with honey, lemon, a pinch of cayenne pepper and a crushed clove of garlic in each mug. Use hot mustard foot baths to decongest the head and a saltwater douche into the nose using a nasal spray to open up and decongest the sinuses. Hot ginger chest compresses are also helpful as are facial steam inhalations using essential oils of eucalyptus, thyme, cloves, and the combination Olbas oil. If a sore throat is the problem gargle with the ginger tea mixture. (Alternatively see the section on sore throats on p.97).

Fasting on fruit juice for 2 to 3 days also helps (together with the magical ginger tea mixture!). Do not extend the fasting beyond this time as it tends to prolong the cold. Instead go on to a diet which .ncludes plenty of onions, garlic and citrus fruits.

CONJUNCTIVITIS

This is an inflammation of the eye which becomes red, watery, gritty and painful. Its vernal form, meaning the type that frequently occurs in the spring, is often due to calcium deficiency. Contrary to public belief, dairy products are *not* the best or even the most effective source of calcium – plants are by far the best assimilated form of calcium. Take the calcium formulation on page 171. Fast for three to four days using carrot juice and assist the kidneys during the fast with a goldenrod or dandelion tea. Make a decoction of one of any of the following herbs (infusions may not sterilize the herb adequately). Bathe the eyes often with it, remembering to make it freshly and ensuring that it is well strained and use it tepid.

Cornflower, mullein, plantain, marigold, eyebright, fennel, liquorice, camomile, and raspberry leaves are all useful. Also take ten drops of rue tincture before each meal as long as the condition lasts and then discontinue.

N.B. If the redness of the eye is confined to the ring around the front of the eye it is a feature of vitamin B$_2$ deficiency. Bear in mind that food allergy can also cause repeated conjunctivitis.

COUGH

I have found both tincture of plantain (10 drops in water as needed) and syrup of garlic (1 teaspoon as often as needed) both extremely effective for treating coughs. Both coughs and sore throats are often helped by a short fast on apple juice or a diet using warm vegetable broth and soupy grains.

If the cough is prolonged and merely irritating try a cough syrup (see p.72) made of equal parts of wild cherry bark, aniseed, and wild lettuce. Take 1 teaspoon up to 6 times a day. If the cough is very bad and racks the body take equal parts of the following mixture.

bayberry bark	*mullein*
comfrey root	*slippery elm*
Icelandic moss	

Take 2 capsules every 2 hours together with 1 teaspoon of garlic oil and 10 drops of tincture of echinacea in a little water. Place a ginger root compress on the chest (see p.61).

*E*ARACHE

Ears are very delicate, sensitive complex organs and can easily be permanently damaged by neglect or inappropriate treatment. So if you are in any doubt about the cause of an earache, consult your doctor. This is particularly important in the case of babies who can't tell you what is wrong but can only scratch at their ears or pull them or, more likely, yell. If the earache is the result of a chill apply a raw grated onion poultice over the back and sides of the neck securing it with a cotton bandage. Put a few drops of mullein oil into both ears, even if the earache is only in one ear, and plug with cotton wool. Keep the head, neck and ears warm at all times.

Tincture of lobelia dropped directly into the ears is good if the pain comes in spasms. Garlic oil and garlic foot compresses are very useful for ear infections. Hot compresses of camomile applied directly to the ears and neck are useful for acute pain. Alternate hot and cold compresses of camomile are better for chronic pain.

Judging by the number of grommets inserted into the ears of my young patients chronic ear infection is on the increase. In this instance a strict

mucus-free diet is extremely helpful with the addition of mucus-cleansing foods like garlic and onions and plenty of carrot juice.

GINGIVITIS

This is an extremely common infection of the outmost tissue of the gums caused by lack of oral hygiene and poor diet. Seek advice from your dentist as a matter of urgency. The following remedies are also helpful.

1. *Switch to a herbal toothpaste containing echinacea or myrrh.*

2. *Use a mouth rinse of equal parts of echinacea and myrrh several times a day and massage oil of eucalyptus into the gums before bed. It tastes terrible but it is very effective. Rinse it out the next morning with mouthwash.*

3. *Ensure the diet has an adequate quantity of vitamins A, D and C and avoid refined carbohydrates and processed foods.*

CORRECT TOOTH BRUSHING

Dislodge plaque between the teeth with waxed dental floss (a dental hygienist will show how to use this correctly) and then use a soft toothbrush with rounded bristles, spreading it with a little echinacea or myrrh herbal toothpaste. The brush should be held at an angle of 45° to the teeth which should be *gently* scrubbed following this angle. Having rinsed the mouth give the gums a good massage using the fingertip in a small rotary movement.

HALITOSIS

To most people halitosis is a fate worse than leprosy. It is partly an indication of the blocked-up colon inside you and partly oral bacteria so tackle the problem from both angles. Firstly ensure your bowel is clean (see p.131) and that your diet includes lots of natural chlorophyll in the form of green tips of freshly sprouted seeds, the juice from wheatgrass, and dark green leafy vegetables, and be meticulous about oral hygiene – flossing as well as brushing. Mouth washes with lavender or lemon verbena infusions or chewing a clove will sweeten the breath, but only temporarily.

Of those people over 30 who will have their own teeth (and one-third do not) 3 out of 4 have periodontal disease, that is, diseased gums around the teeth. It is the most widespread disease in the world and is often relatively painless until it is well advanced. The first sign is bleeding gums, which most people tend to ignore, imagining it to be the result of overzealous tooth brushing. Don't be deceived. Get to your dentist immediately, and ask to be shown how to both brush and floss your teeth correctly. If left unchecked you will inevitably lose your teeth.

HEARING PROBLEMS INCLUDING DEAFNESS AND TINNITUS

First look to cleansing the bloodstream and the bowl and then improve the circulation, because a lot of ringing in the ears is often due to poor circulation. Catarrh is another causative factor so a mucus-free diet is recommended (see p.255). Make up the following tincture.

Equal parts of:

black cohosh
garlic
goldenseal

Take 15 drops 3 times a day. Regular foot and hand baths of the same ingredients are also helpful.

DOCTOR CHRISTOPHER'S OIL AND TINCTURE COMBINATION

This formula is designed to improve poor equilibrium and sharpen hearing. Every night with an eye dropper put 4 drops of garlic oil into each ear then add 4 drops of the following tincture. Equal parts of:

black cohosh	*lobelia*
blue cohosh	*scullcap*
blue vervain	

Plug each ear with cotton wool. Massage the outside of the ear on the bony section around the back and the dent beneath the skull at the back of the neck with a few drops of the tincture. Continue with this routine for 6 nights and on the seventh gently syringe out the ears with a half and half distilled water and cider vinegar mixture. Professional medical help to do this may be necessary and is advisable. It is possible to puncture your eardrum even with the smallest ear bulb.

Some deafness is due to a cararrhal blockage of the middle ear and a build-up of wax in the outer ear canal can also contribute to deafness. Heavy ear wax seems at least partly related to diet and it is the proportion of saturated versus unsaturated fats that is implicated. So restrict saturated fats and take daily doses of essential fatty acids in capsule form.

INFLUENZA

The initial symptoms of influenza which are weakness, fatigue, drowsiness, nausea, fever and headache are startlingly similar to those of jaundice so do be sure the diagnosis is correct Treat as for fever (see p.237) and use a herbal tea of ginger, pleusrisy root, boneset, and garlic in equal quantities. Drink 8 fl oz (250 ml) every waking hour if possible. Also give tincture of echinacea, 10 drops every hour.

MASTOIDITIS

This is an infection of the bone behind the ear. Before the introduction of antibiotics children sometimes suffered severe complications stemming from untreated bacterial ear infections including hearing loss and infection of the mastoid bone behind the ear. Herbal antibiotics if correctly administered (see p.28) will virtually elminate both of these and properly treated an ear infection will heal in one or two weeks with no long-term effects, though there is often fractional hearing loss for up to three or four weeks after the infection.

In every instance ear infections must be monitored by your doctor to ensure they are healing properly because an untreated or improperly treated viral or bacterial ear infection can lead to serious complications.

MENINGITIS

This is an inflammation of the three protective layers that enclose the brain and spinal cord and can be caused by a bacterial, fungal or viral infection, spreading TB or chemical irritation. Treatment depends on the cause and although this was once treated herbally, allopathic treatment is absolutely essential as this illness is very serious. Contact the emergency services immediately.

Symptoms include headache, stiff neck, fever, nausea or vomiting and intolerance to light and sound often followed by convulsions and delirium.

MOUTH ULCERS

Rub the sore with the following lotion:

6 drops essential oil of coltsfoot
3 drops tincture of myrrh
½ teaspoon of runny honey

Rinse with 1 teaspoon of tincture of white oak bark and 1 teaspoon of cider vinegar diluted in a cup of water. Gargle nightly with warm sage tea sloshing it well around the mouth before spitting it out. Recurrent mouth ulcers can be caused by iron, folic acid and vitamin B_{12} deficiency.

NASAL POLYPS

Follow the advice for sinusitis and, in addition, if the polyps are bleeding use a tiny pinch of tormentilla as a snuff, finely powdered, remembering to sniff it up both nostrils. Otherwise it is possible to paint the polyps with a half and half mixture of tincture of goldenseal and black walnut. You'll need a very fine, thin, camel hair brush with a slender handle to do this and it is quite likely you will sneeze a lot after this delicate operation. Don't worry and do persist. I have treated patients in this way with a good bowel and blood cleanser and they have got rid of polyps altogether.

For sores inside the nose or a chapped nose as the result of too much blowing with a cold apply the following ointment:

1 tablespoon of petroleum jelly
1 teaspoon powdered comfrey
1 drop each of spearmint, wintergreen and wormwood oil

It is thick, somewhat messy but very effective.

PYORRHOEA *(gum disease)*

This is a chronic degenerative disease of the gums where the teeth become loose and the gums spongy. Follow the advice for gingivitis (see p.92) and clean the teeth with the following toothpowder. Equal parts of:

bayberry	*orris root*
bistort	*sage*

Rinse afterwards with a double strength decoction (that is 2 oz to 1 pint 60 g to 600 ml) of bistort. Then surround the gums around the loose teeth with powdered white oak bark and try, if you can, to leave it in all night. If you swallow a bit it doesn't matter. Continue this treatment nightly until the gums have firmed up.

Also treat systematically with high doses of vitamin C, stopping just short of diarrhoea and the following formulation:

2 parts echninacea	*1 part chapparal*
1 part blue flag	*1 part pokeroot*

Drink 1 cup of the tea 3 times a day with meals until the condition has healed. Also urgently seek the advice of your dentist.

QUINSY

This is usually a complication from tonsillitis and results in pus-filled inflammation of the tonsils. Seek expert advice about treatment. Cudweed and red sage are useful used as gargles.

SINUSITIS

Chronic sinusitis is often the result of suppressing or improperly treating colds. One of the simplest ways to treat it is by fasting on grapefruit and its

juice for 3 days, taking a hydrochloric acid supplement with each piece of fresh grapefruit. (For the correct dosage see instructions on the individual container.) This should then be followed up with a mucus-free diet of fruits, vegetables, nuts, grains and seeds, and a little fatty fish and white meat is also permissible. Dairy products and refined carbohydrates will certainly exacerbate this problem.

Check the teeth and gums are in good order. Breathe in the vaporized oil from sage and hot water twice daily, keeping the eyes closed so that the steam doesn't sting. Rub fresh lemon juice externally over the sinuses or spray lemon juice and water as a douche with a nasal spray inside the nose. Nasal sprays are available from chemists.

Take the following formulation made as a tincture, 1 teaspoon 3 times daily. Equal parts of:

burdock	hyssop
garlic	plantain
ginger root	sage

I often prescribe freshly grated horseradish macerated in vinegar, a teaspoon to be chewed before each meal and the tonic for sinus congestion on p.39. My patients don't love me for it but it is extremely effective. This should not be used if there are any digestive problems. Personally I find breathing the fumes in while grating it almost as effective!

A poultice of grated onion on the back of the neck worn all night in bed and secured with a scarf is extremely helpful as is a hot compress of plain water to the back of the neck and ice cubes on the forehead.

Really stubborn cases of sinusitis will respond well to a month's course of a megadose of vitamin A and D as well as vitamin C and zinc but this must be taken under professional supervision.

SNORING

Nasal breathing, an ideal body weight, and a mucus-free diet are the prerequisites in order to correct this problem. The old-fashioned solution of a glass marble in a bit of cloth sewn between the shoulder blades of a snorer's pyjama top is also helpful. This prevents sleeping on the back and generally stops snoring. Its added advantage is that it can go through the wash without damage and is not likely to be left behind if pyjamas have been worn away from home.

A new and relatively simple surgical procedure can cure snoring if it has got way beyond a joke. It involves removing some of the soft palate in the back of the mouth and any extra tissue on the sides and back of the throat. Apparently it is effective in about 95% of cases. I have also seen an electronic device designed to stop snoring which is strapped on the arm and triggered by the distinctive sound waves of snoring to produce a small

stinging sensation in the skin: not enough to wake the sleeper, but enough apparently to stop the snoring. I don't know whether it works, but it sounds worth a try for the desperate.

SORE THROAT

Follow the advice for tonsillitis (below) and gargle with an infusion of red sage. Add a teaspoon of cider vinegar to each cup of the tonsillitis infusion, drink it warm. If the throat is very painful spray with goldenseal tincture.

STYES

Always ensure that the bowels are working properly. Bathe the eyes with a freshly made and meticulously strained decoction of equal parts of eyebright, burdock and sarsaparilla. Take one cup of the same mixture internally 3 times a day with meals.

If the stye is unbearably itchy rub it with a piece of raw potato or, if you can get it, a clean-cut edge of fresh marshmallow root.

TONSILLITIS

If tonsillitis is chronic its cause is certain to be far more deeply rooted than the throat, so seek expert advice on the possibility of quinsy or diphtheria. Consider too that there may be a problem of allergy or nutritional deficiency particularly of the B complex, vitamin C, zinc and iron. A diet with too many dairy products, sugar, starches, and a deficiency of green vegetables will lead to acidity, toxicity, and catarrh throughout the body. Spinal lesions in the neck may reduce blood and lymph flow to the tonsils and adenoids so osteopathic manipulation may be necessary. Certainly it makes no sense at all to whip out the tonsils as was so fashionable a few years ago. Removing them will not make the problem go away. Swollen lymph glands are an early warning system and should not be ignored.

As long as the patient can swallow administer the following herbal tea proportionate to age, three times a day:

2 parts echinacea	1 part goldenseal
2 parts poke root	1 part calendula
2 parts red sage	

Gargle with a teaspoon of goldenseal tincture and one teaspoon of myrrh in a cup of water as often as needed. Spraying neat tincture of goldenseal directly on to the glands using a hand spray obtainable from chemists is very effective. An external compress of 3 parts of mullein to 1 part of lobelia will help swollen glands. If the attack is acute fast on fruit juice only (which shouldn't be difficult as swallowing will be extremely

painful). I remember being given ice-cream as a child for tonsillitis, and this is positively the worst thing in view of its mucus-forming potential. Thereafter follow a mucus-free diet of fruits, vegetables, nuts, grains and seeds and if the throat is too sore to cope with food, drink only freshly pressed juices served at room temperature.

CHAPTER 4
RESPIRATORY SYSTEM

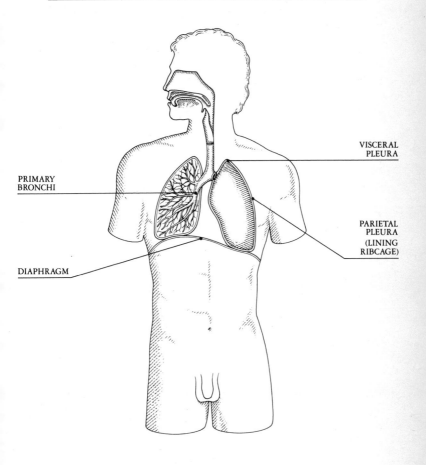

VISCERAL
PLEURA

PRIMARY
BRONCHI

PARIETAL
PLEURA
(LINING
RIBCAGE)

DIAPHRAGM

ASTHMA

Asthma needs professional treatment and careful supervision. There is a disturbingly high chance of death if it is mismanaged. Herbs such as ephedra, lobelia, grindelia, skunk cabbage, blood root, sundew, euphorbia and thyme are helpful. Some of these herbs if improperly used can cause renal malfunction, vomiting, constricted breathing and other problems so you are not advised to try them without supervision.

However the advice outlined under hay fever is useful for asthma. Also check that there is no mould sensitivity and that all damp patches and mildew in the house are eradicated. Animal fur and feathers can sometimes make asthma worse so if there is a pet in the house it is important that the asthmatic avoids physical contact with it and that it should not enter the asthmatic's bedroom at any cost. Mattresses need to be vacuumed thoroughly once or twice a week as does the rest of the house, particularly carpets. A mega-multi vitamin mineral supplement is recommended as is B_6 and possibly digestive supplements. A nutritional programme needs to be individually tailored – so seek professional help.

BRONCHITIS

Stimulate the lymphatic system to assist elimination (see p.40) by administering hand and foot baths of equal parts of eucalyptus and thyme morning and evening. Take the following formulation. Equal parts of:

aniseed	hyssop
coltsfoot	thyme
garlic	

Two size '0' capsules to be given every hour with a hot drink until the infection clears.

Apply hot ginger and mustard compresses to the chest, but be sure to avoid blistering, because mustard if left in prolonged contact with the skin may cause blistering in particularly sensitive individuals.

Follow a mucus-free diet, consisting of fruit, fresh or dried, vegetables including pulses, nuts and nut butters, wholegrains and seeds. Animal produce, anything white or refined, tea, coffee, chocolate and alcohol are to be completely avoided.

If you have the strength, take hot and cold alternative showers daily.

Learn how to breathe properly. Good breathing begins with good posture. Stand and sit tall and when you lie down make sure you are well stretched out. Keep your head well up and don't tuck your chin in or let it stick out. You can check your posture by standing barefoot against a wall without a skirting board. Now try and flatten the whole spine against the wall. Keep the back of your head against it too. Stretch up and breathe out deeply. Take a step away from the wall holding this position – this is how you should stand and walk. Having mastered the art of good posture refer to page 38 for proper breathing technique.

Brisk sustained walking punctuated with plenty of short rests is the best type of exercise. If you want to go further blow up several balloons daily. You can consciously work to improve your lung capacity: breathing while you walk for 4 paces, hold your breath for a further 4 paces (if it feels uncomfortable let it go – don't explode!), then breathe out slowly with control for 6 paces. As you improve, gradually increase the count. Swimming gently and consistently is also good but do remember to shower carefully afterwards as chlorine is intensely poisonous.

CATARRH

Although catarrh generally manifests itself in the nose it is important to remember that it can be present in any area of the body lined by mucus membranes. This includes the whole of the digestive tract, fallopian tubes, vagina, as well as the more obvious areas like ears, nose and throat and upper lungs. Catarrhal forming foods are undoubtedly dairy products, eggs, meat, sugar, tea and coffee, chocolate, anything refined especially refined carbohydrates, the gluten in wheat, oats, rye and barley, potatoes, swedes, turnips and parsnips and any other starchy root vegetables. However, if after cutting these out of your diet for 2 to 3 months no relief is experienced the problem may be the result of food intolerance and therefore a supervised restrictive diet needs to be followed.

I have found a quick way to remove catarrh from the system is to fast a patient for 3 to 4 days on grapefruit and grapefruit juice together with supplements of hydrochloric acid. Then follow a diet which eliminates all potentially catarrhal-forming food and includes plenty of sprouted fenugreek as well as nettles, kelp, onions and garlic. Oil of garlic is especially helpful.

TO MAKE OIL OF GARLIC

Press 8 oz (250 g) of peeled minced garlic into a wide-mouthed jar and barely cover it with olive oil. Close the jar tightly and leave it to stand in a warm place for 3 days. Shake it several times daily. After 3 days press and strain it through a piece of muslin or fine cloth and store the resulting oil of garlic in a cool place in well-stoppered bottles.

Take one level teaspoon (5 ml) mixed into enough honey to form into a paste and chew slowly. Do this 3 times a day.

Fennel oil used as a herbal bath will vapourize mucus, loosening it and causing it to degenerate so that the eliminatory process can remove it through the bloodstream far more easily than can be done by coughing, sneezing or blowing the nose. This process is helped by fennel's high

mineral content. Add 10 drops of fennel oil to 1 pint (600 ml) of freshly boiled water and use this as a facial steam.

EMPHYSEMA

Living as I do in Stoke-on-Trent I am confronted by a lot of emphysema, which is on the increase as a result of irritant inhalants from industrial pollution. Radioactive fallout has also been implicated in its rapid rise and certainly cigarette smoking is central to most cases of emphysema. Improvement with herbal treatment is certainly possible, although some parts of the lungs may be permanently scarred for life. However, this disease needs very careful supervision and management and therefore you are advised to seek the help of a medical herbalist.

Diet is the same as for asthma and bronchitis.

Exercise should be gentle and progressive and preferably carried out in an atmosphere where the mucus membranes of the lungs will not dry out, so swimming is ideal. Spinal manipulation may be necessary. Mucus solvents like garlic, onions, fenugreek and fennel are very useful. Activities such as singing, whistling or playing a musical instrument which involves forceful breathing out help to develop lung efficiency.

HAY FEVER

The treatment of hay fever is often very complex because it is a many-faceted condition. It can be inherited as an allergic predisposition and initially manifest itself as allergic eczema or asthma as well as food intolerance. It can be triggered by the inhalation of grass pollens or an early intolerance of dairy products, wheat or other foods.

It is interesting that hay fever only seems to have become common over the last 150 years. Prior to this it seems to have been a disease of the educated classes. This raises interesting questions as to the causes of it. Sugar only began to be taken in large amounts 150 years ago and at that time only the affluent upper classes could afford it. I often wonder if there is a link here. An intolerance to wheat which is in the same botanical family as grass may also be implicated.

THE AIR YOU BREATHE

Try to avoid areas with high pollen count and polluted air – for example, parts of cities where the poisons are often dangerously high. Use an ionizer to control the balance of ions (tiny electrical particles) in the air around you. An ionizer is particularly useful in the bedroom, where you can spend at least 8 of every 24 hours. You can leave the windows open or closed while they are in use; either way they will cope (for suppliers see Appendix).

Stop smoking completely and avoid smoke-filled rooms.

Avoid inhaled allergens such as pollen and use a synthetic duvet and pillows. Feather duvets and pillows tend to attract dust.

Because the pollen counts are highest on warm, dry days, it is advisable to stay indoors on such days or ideally go to the seaside and away from fields.

Avoid food additives, common food allergies like cow's milk, sucrose and refined carbohydrates, especially wheat. Take the following formula. It was used by Dr Christopher, its originator and the leading herbalist in the USA until his death in 1982, with a great deal of success. Of course he also insisted on body purification and correct nutrition too (see Chapter 1).

DR CHRISTOPHER'S ALLERGY FORMULA

Equal parts of:

burdock root	*juniper berries*
cayenne	*lobelia – half a part*
chapparal	*marshmallow root*
ephedra	*parsley root*
goldenseal	

Take two size '0' capsules three times a day.

The catarrh accumulated during hay fever may be cut by making an infusion of equal parts of ginger and cayenne, adding one crushed clove of garlic and plenty of honey to every cup. Gargle with this and swallow the mixture. Fiery but effective! Take as much of this as often as needed.

N.B. This is a difficult condition to treat and as it can result in serious complications if neglected, you are advised to seek the professional help of a medical herbalist if you are not confident about treating it.

PNEUMONIA

Much depends on whether it is bacterial, viral or bronchopneumonia. Bacterial pneumonia, which often starts very quickly and is severe, needs urgent treatment with antibiotics. Viral pneumonia is generally less serious and can be treated with expert herbal management as for a fever incorporating such expectorants as ipecacuana, garlic, thyme and lobelia. See pages 237–8 and seek the guidance of a qualified medical herbalist. A well-managed convalescence is often essential to avoid secondary complications (see Convalescence, p.235).

CHAPTER 5
CIRCULATORY SYSTEM

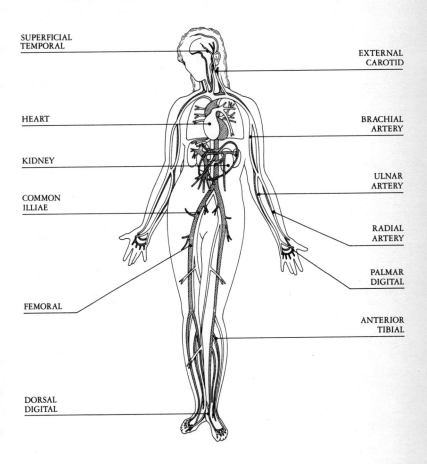

SUPERFICIAL
TEMPORAL

EXTERNAL
CAROTID

HEART

BRACHIAL
ARTERY

KIDNEY

ULNAR
ARTERY

COMMON
ILLIAE

RADIAL
ARTERY

PALMAR
DIGITAL

FEMORAL

ANTERIOR
TIBIAL

DORSAL
DIGITAL

ANAEMIA

It has been suggested that iron deficiency is the most common worldwide nutritional disease and most of the time it goes totally unrecognized. Symptoms of anaemia resulting from iron deficiency include listlessness, fatigue, very obvious heartbeat on exertion, a sore tongue, cracks at the corner of the mouth, difficulty with swallowing, concave nails or pale nails with vertical ridges on them, brittle, wiry, thin lacklustre hair and in children poor appetite, retarded growth and an ability to catch every infection going.

Iron deficiency is the precursor of anaemia and doctors often rule it out if they can find no clear evidence of anaemia. But iron deficiency can exist without any blood changes and without the person being anaemic and this is far more common than realized. One study in Canada showed that 19% of the population had evidence of iron deficiency although only 2% were actually anaemic. Thus poor diagnosis means various other conditions in diseases tend to be missed and remain untreated, often for years. Certainly I find iron deficiency worryingly common in my own practice. Vegetarians are particularly at risk because iron absorption is impaired by whole grains, soya and other legumes although vitamin C improves the absorption of iron and most of my vegetarian patients eat a diet rich in this vitamin. Tea and coffee taken with food radically reduce iron absorption. The stronger the brew the greater the reduction in iron absorption. People who have malabsorption problems, those living on limited exclusion diets for food allergy and those producing very little gastric acid following the removal of part of the stomach are also at risk.

The problem with synthetic iron is that it causes stomach upsets, constipation and black stools. It is far better to get your iron from natural sources. The richest herbal sources of iron are undoubtedly parsley and yellow dock. (Pregnant women should avoid very large intakes of parsley as it may stimulate uterine muscle and lead to miscarriage. During pregnancy the odd sprinkle on food is fine.) All dark green leafy vegetables especially green turnip tops are recommended, as is dried fruit, bananas, grapes, beets, black cherry juice. Liver from organically raised animals, fish, egg yolks, and blackstrap molasses are other rich sources.

Over-supplementation of inorganic iron can lead to serious liver, pancreas and heart problems and cause a form of arthritis. Natural sources of iron are assimilated much more easily in the body and in turn help with the assimilation of vitamins C and E. Natural iron has the added advantage of burning up accumulated poisonous waste, flushing it out of the body, and unlike synthetic iron it does *not* cause constipation.

Iron and folic acid supplementation inhibit the absorption of zinc. Until recently pregnant women in Britain were routinely given iron supplementation and this seems to me both crazy and foolhrdy. Zinc deficiency is commonly associated with a poor pregnancy outcome including possible congenital malformations, so any multi-mineral supplements should contain iron and zinc in the ratio of 1 or 2 parts of iron to 1 of zinc. More iron than this inhibits zinc absorption.

Women lose 15–30 mg of iron with each period and as much as 50 mg during childbirth and pregnant women need as much as 120 mg daily. If you are in any doubt about your iron intake from natural sources use the following formula:

3 parts yellow dock	*1 part comfrey*
1 part burdock	*1 part gentian*

Take two size '0' capsules of the finely powdered herbs morning and evening on an empty stomach. Do not drink tea, coffee or chocolate during the time you are taking this formula. Replace them with herbal teas and coffee substitutes – ideally dandelion root coffee.

If the stomach is not producing enough hydrochloric acid (and the level of hydrochloric acid may be determined by an iridology test) sipping a teaspoon of cider vinegar in a little water half an hour before a meal will help its production and also drinking a cup of rosemary tea. Under-production of hydrochloric acid is nearly always present in people over 45, in my experience. It may be suspected (but will need professional confirm-ation) by the emergence of foods in the stools in almost unchanged condition, belching, vomiting or nausea.

ARTERIOSCLEROSIS *(hardening of the arteries)*

This is a degenerative disease where the arterial walls lose their elasticity and begin to calcify. It has been clearly demonstrated that excessive consumption of white sugar and refined foods is one of the prime causes of hardening of the arteries so follow the diet for angina (see p113). Definitely no smoking and detoxify yourself from lead, copper and aluminium (see p.26 heavy metal detoxification).

It is also vital to reduce fat in the bloodstream (see p.111 for information on cholesterol). To do this take the following steps:

1. *Stop smoking.*

2. *Take moderate physical exercise (see under angina, p.113).*

3. *Increase those foods known to help lower cholesterol and triglycerides in the blood including soya beans, tofu, legumes of all sorts, oily fish, brewer's yeast, wheat, bran and oats, onions, garlic, wheatgerm, sunflower seeds, sprouted seeds of all sorts and lecithin.*

4. *Cut down on animal fats.*

5. *Consider coming off the pill and hormone replacement therapy if you are on either.*

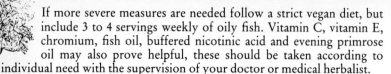

If more severe measures are needed follow a strict vegan diet, but include 3 to 4 servings weekly of oily fish. Vitamin C, vitamin E, chromium, fish oil, buffered nicotinic acid and evening primrose oil may also prove helpful, these should be taken according to individual need with the supervision of your doctor or medical herbalist.

Use daily hand and foot baths of garlic and hawthorn berries equally mixed (see p.65). Mix together the following finely powdered herbs:

angelica	dandelion root
borage	safflower
cayenne	sanicle

Take two size '0' capsules three times daily.

HIGH BLOOD PRESSURE *(Hypertension)*

High blood pressure is not a disease, although many doctors seem to treat it as such. It is simply the body's defensive and corrective measure, an attempt to cope with pathological conditions such as toxaemia, glandular disturbances, defective calcium metabolism, poor kidney function, degenerative changes in the arteries, obesity, and emotionally caused dysfunction of the vaso-motor mechanism. It distresses me to see so many people on a course of allopathic drugs to 'control' high blood pressure which they have been told they must take for the rest of their lives. Mildly raised blood pressure is very common and is by no means serious. Often high blood pressure has no obvious medical cause – although its association with kidney and hormonal disease is well known. The relatives of patients with high blood pressure often have a higher than normal blood pressure so there is a genetic element, however I feel our western society is both socially and nutritionally predisposed to hypertension. It is a waste of time lowering the blood pressure unless the cause of the condition can be removed, and an iridology test will often get to the heart of the problem.

Average blood pressure reads 120/80. It is the lower figure, the diastolic reading, which is the most important figure; this records the rebounding of the blood back through the arteries and the pressure they are under, even at rest. The problem I find with most allopathic remedies for blood pressure, which usually includes a two-pronged approach of mild diuretics with hypotensive drugs, is that the drugs rapidly become addictive and lose their efficacy. The vast majority of hypertensives can be helped by a simple natural approach, and this is particularly successful if the condition is caught early. It does however require dedication and persistence from the participant.

A supervised juice fast for 3 or 4 weeks is an excellent way of bringing the blood pressure down to normal, and certainly produces a sharp reduction in the systolic pressure (which records how the blood bounds outwards from the heart through the arteries) in a very short period of time. Use citrus fruit, blackcurrant, grape, carrot, spinach and comfrey juices – the vegetables ones to be taken with a dash of onion or garlic (a level teaspoon in 8 fl oz – 250 ml). A brown rice fast works equally well. However, I must emphasize that such fasts must be done under the close supervision of a medical herbalist, as they may not be suitable for everyone and you will need an individual examination to determine this. If you prefer something to chew on try a watermelon fast for one week but again seek the guidance of a professional.

A simple way to regulate either high or low blood pressure is a teaspoon of cayenne in a glass of warm water three times daily. You will need to build this up gradually – it tastes pretty fiery. Do not stay on this remedy for longer than 3 consecutive months. Include lots of garlic, buckwheat (for its rutin content), sprouted alfalfa and raw foods in the diet and avoid absolutely salt, tea, coffee, chocolate, cocoa, alcohol, and all strong spices and flavourings except cayenne and garlic. Meals should be small and your weight controlled.

Exercise is of paramount importance. This needs to be done under supervision particularly if obesity is a problem. Aim for a minimum of 12 minutes a day of any sort of exercise that leaves you breathless. Hot showers or baths should be avoided and replaced with warm alternating with cold showers of 2 minutes each, repeating several times and finishing with a cold shower.

Lecithin will help emulsify fat in the bloodstream and vitamin B_3 will help to dilate the arteries loosening adhering fatty molecules. Buffered nicotinic acid is the best way to take this and causes tingling, flushing and skin reddening for about half an hour shortly after taking a large dose, especially on an empty stomach. The buffered form of nicotinic acid helps prevent gastrointestinal upset. Dosage needs to be individually determined by your medical herbalist.

The following formulation will gradually regulate high blood pressure, strengthen the heart, protect the arteries and improve the circulation:

6 parts hawthorn berries	1 part angelica
3 parts motherwort	1 part hyssop
2 parts rosemary	1 part nettles

Mix the powdered herbs and make a tincture using 4 oz (125 g) to 1 pint (600 ml) of vodka. Take 60 drops 3 times daily. Sometimes I will add diuretics to this formulation (dandelion is a very safe one) if the kidneys are implicated.

Always bear in mind that high blood pressure can be purely emotional and so stress, fear, repetitive pressure, and prolonged nervous tension need to be examined. (See advice in this respect for depression, p.186).

DRUGS

If you are taking allopathic medicine from your doctor for this condition it must be reduced very, very gently. I will not alter allopathic prescriptions for the first 3 to 4 months of treatment until I am sure that the programme I have individually tailored for the patient is working well. If it is I may reduce the medication by a third and put the patient on a supervised fast. Once the lower blood pressure reading is maintained over a period of 2 to 3 months I may again consider reducing the dose of allopathic medication. Remember it takes time to reverse the *cause* of this condition, so be patient.

N.B. Liquorice is known to cause sodium and water retention and can therefore raise blood pressure, so anyone with high blood pressure should avoid the use of liquorice in any formulation. (See also p.77 for further explanation of contraindications.)

LOW BLOOD PRESSURE

Many of my vegetarian patients have a normal blood pressure reading of 100/60. It is now known that the risk of heart problems is reduced by 95% by a vegan diet. Low blood pressure which reads well below the average measurement of 120/80 will manifest itself as a general feeling of lassitude and fatigue, and anaemia may be present. Low blood pressure is generally the result of nutritional deficiencies and a backlog of poisons in the body (see Chapter 1). Attend to these and take the following formula:

6 parts alfalfa	1 part cayenne
3 parts hawthorn berries	1 part hyssop
3 parts lime blossom	1 part Korean ginseng

Make a decoction and take 1 cup 3 times daily with meals.

CHILBLAINS

Chilblains are always the result of poor circulation and this may be the result of an impaired blood supply because of the narrowing of the arteries. Provided the chilblains are not broken hot mustard footbaths followed by cold dips are very helpful. Put your feet into the hot mustard bath for 3 minutes and then dip them quickly for 3 seconds into cold water. Repeat this from 6 to 8 times. If necessary replenish with hot water from time to time. Use one tablespoon of mustard powder to a bucket of hot water, the soak should reach to the knee. Dry the feet briskly afterwards with a rough towel and massage with equal parts of tincture of benzoin and camphor. Persistent and regular hot and cold foot baths will restore the circulation to normal again.

If you have the opportunity, a simpler method is snow walking. Walk barefoot on an even stretch of snow for 10 seconds, gradually increasing to 2 to 3 minutes or longer. It is important that you go outside without having warmed yourself up first, and go out well covered except for the feet. Dry your feet by rubbing them well with your hands, not with a towel, and return to bed. This is best done on rising, if you can pluck up the courage!

The Romans used to stimulate their frozen limbs while manning Hadrian's Wall by flogging themselves with nettles – a somewhat radical solution for chilblains! A less painful solution would be to assist the circulation with the formulation on page 109. A supplementation of buffered nicotonic acid, vitamin C, vitamin E, evening primrose oil, magnesium, and rutin are also useful but these need to be individually determined by your practitioner.

TO SOOTHE CHILBLAINS

Cut a leaf of houseleek lengthways and rub the exposed juicy flesh over the chilblains twice daily. Excellent creams are available for chilblains (see Appendix).

BROKEN CHILBLAINS

Soak them, using a light touch, in a warm infusion of dried marigold flowers, then cover with a poultice of the strained out petals, keeping these in place with a bandage. A pair of thick socks helps here if the chilblains are on your feet. Such a poultice will relieve the agony of broken chilblains very quickly and accelerate their healing. Once the skin is healed apply marigold ointment until the redness has completely disappeared.

CHOLESTEROL AND ITS SIGNIFICANCE

I include this entry because cholesterol has been linked to many of the problems discussed in this section and there is a great deal of ignorance or muddled thinking about the issue. In the prevention of coronary heart disease abnormalities in blood fat levels also appear to be important. While many of the public are well aware of cholesterol and its supposedly harmful effects in heart disease, it has now been proved that only _rancid_ cholesterol actually causes coronary heart disease. Pure cholesterol does not. The inevitable conclusion is that it is the harmful effects of any rancid oil which are the primary factor here, not simply cholesterol. It is the combination of sugar or refined carbohydrates mixed with saturated fats which cause the highest increases of cholesterol and triglycerides in the blood. Our saturated fat consumption has only increased by 10% over the last 100 years whereas our consumption of refined sugar and carbohydrates has increased by 700% over the same period of time. Rancid cholesterol is likely to be present in food which has not been stored properly, particularly pre-prepared cake, pastry and biscuit mixes.

It is not generally appreciated that cholesterol is made in every part of the body except the brain. While a dietary intake of cholesterol may range from 200 to 800 mg daily the body will produce 2 g. Cholesterol is vital for the cell membrane structure, bile formation, vitamin D synthesis, and steroid hormone production.

Fats that are ingested have to move from the intestine to the liver where they can be metabolized. It takes several hours before they are cleared from the blood and if the level of cholesterol remains high, any excess is deposited on the linings of the arteries, so narrowing them. Fats are transported in the bloodstream in a protein fat molecule, lipoprotein. The low density lipoproteins are around cholesterol-laden molecules and when they are found at elevated levels in the bloodsteam there is a higher risk of coronary heart disease. High density lipoproteins are smaller molecules with more protein and less cholesterol; when high levels of these are found in the bloodstream they actually reduce the risk of coronary heart disease. So it is the cholesterol to high density lipoprotein ratio which is vital in the fight against heart disease.

Not only does vitamin C have a beneficial effect upon blood fats, particularly cholesterol, but it reduces platelet stickiness. For people with coronary heart disease the dose needs to be upwards of 500 mg a day. Vitamin B complex helps keep cholesterol from collecting as plaque. Vitamin E is known to correct various platelet abnormalities and works especially well mixed with selenium; dosage needs to be individually determined. The oils from oily fish reduce platelets sticking to blood vessel walls and increase high density lipoproteins.

Evening primrose oil has far-reaching effects on prostaglandin metabolism. Lecithin significantly lowers blood cholestrol levels. It is available in capsule form or as granules (for suppliers see Appendix). The minimum dose is 3 rounded teaspoons a day.

Oat bran fibre and oats increase high density lipoproteins and reduce blood cholesterol; finely powdered alfalfa seeds work in much the same way as bran. Garlic oil, garlic and onions have beneficial effects on blood fats as well as on platelet stickiness. The bromelain found in pineapple and pawpaw has beneficial effects on platelet stickiness. Ginger (the fresh or powdered root) reduces platelet stickiness. Yoghurt and buttermilk can reduce blood cholesterol by as much as 5%. A supplementation of acidophilus, the benign bacteria found in the digestive tract, will also lower cholesterol levels. This is available in supplementation form. The best are a combination of Superdolphilus and Probion (see Appendix).

Sweating therapy will help exude cholesterol through the skin.

The following formulation is a blood purifier which will rebuild the blood, cleanse it and increase the range and power of circulation, particularly to those parts of the body which have been deficient (usually the extremities in the capillary circulation). It helps to remove the cholesterol, kill infection and elasticize the veins while strengthening the artery walls. By

this means any other herbal nutrients taken in will travel efficiently through the blood and lymph fluids and be properly utilized:

Equal parts of:

buckthorn	peach bark
burdock root	prickly ash bark
chapparal	red clover blossom
liquorice root	stillingia
Oregon grape root	

All the herbs should be finely powdered. Take three size '0' capsules with each meal.

HEART DISEASE

ANGINA PECTORIS

Coronary heart disease usually expresses itself as angina (that is chest pain on exertion) or a heart attack. Coronary heart disease is a major cause of death in the West.

You may be surprised to learn that it is smoking, not diet, that is the major factor associated with any kind of heart disease. Certainly an elevated level of cholesterol in the blood is associated with an increased risk of heart disease but most people simply need to moderate their intake of dietary fats and not go on a fanatical low cholesterol diet. A diet high in fat and sugar certainly greatly accelerates the risk of heart problems. *Don't* go on to polyunsaturated margarine. It's hydrogenated and contains as much as 40% trans-fatty acids which raise cholesterol and inhibit the production of prostaglandins which help lower blood pressure and reduce platelet dumping. Refined cooking oils (that is, those that are not virgin and cold pressed) are unprotected from oxidation and therefore form free radicals which tend to damage artery walls, encouraging arteriosclerosis. The definition of free radicals is complex. Sufficient to say they are the result of failure of an oxidizing atom to add the requisite amount of electrons to complete the set. The result is an activated molecule which has a nasty tendency to extract another electron from another electron donor which consequently becomes altered and may become pathological. They are directly responsible for the arterial eruptions of arteriosclerosis. With this in mind, you're better on a *little* unsalted butter if you must (no more than 2 level teaspoons daily). When using virgin cold pressed oils, add the content of a capsule of vitamin E to the bottle and keep it in the fridge when not in use.

However for those with very severe angina, or for people who are at high risk of heart attack, a very strict diet of entirely vegetarian foods without dairy products (that is, a vegan diet) coupled with plenty of oily fish is very helpful. This approach, together with monitored graded exercise, some counselling and learning relaxation techniques can reduce angina by 91% in less than a month. The essential fatty acids found in salmon, cod, mackerel, herring, sardines and other cold water fish are known to reduce cholesterol and increase high-density lipoproteins. Whenever lipoproteins are found at high levels in the blood there is a considerably reduced risk of heart disease. If you cannot eat fish, fish oils (maxEPA) taken in substantial quantities will help to reduce platelets sticking to blood vessel walls. Vitamin C reduces platelet stickiness in people with coronary artery disease and upwards of 500 mg needs to be taken. Evening primrose oil affects prostaglandin metabolism, so this also helps to combat platelet stickiness. Garlic oil and ginger root act in similar ways. A combination of hawthorn and mother wort in equal quantities make a superb heart tonic and antispasmodic.

In the event of an attack of angina place warm poultices of cider vinegar around the top of the arms and keep changing them as necessary or put the following compress over the heart:

---

1 part celandine
1 part hawthorn berries
1 part sage

Have the mixture ready brewed and closely covered in the fridge and warm it up as necessary. Leave the compress on for 10 minutes until cool and then replace with a warm one. Also take the same formula as for high blood pressure (see p.109).

Regular exercising 3 or 4 times a week is certainly helpful but it is essential that you consult your medical herbalist or doctor about this before starting. Try simply walking, start with a few minutes with frequent rests on the flat and gently build up until you are walking at a sustained pace for an hour daily. The cumulative effect on the heart's action will soon be noticeable. It was George Macauley Trevelyan, a famous 19th-century doctor, who said, 'I have two doctors, my left leg and my right.' Don't be frightened to use them.

HEART ATTACK

There are three main areas in which nutrition is relevant to heart attacks specifically and coronary artery disease generally.

1. High cholesterol and triglycerides levels can be controlled by diet and nutritional supplements (see p.30).

2. High blood pressure can be controlled by dietary means and herbal supplementation see p.109).

3. Platelet stickiness and clotting can be reduced by diet (see p.112).

For an acutely ill person with a heart attack the use of medications to correct the heart beat disturbances, heart failure and shock and general intensive care are currently the mainstays of treatment. In an emergency situation while waiting for the ambulance/doctor, administer 3 teaspoons of cayenne in warm water initially (this to be drunk all at once) and then half a teaspoon every 15 minutes in warm water. If possible, give foot and hand baths of black mustard powder, 2 handfuls to a litre (1¾ pints) of water. 'Rescue Remedy' (one of the Bach flower remedies, see Appendix) massaged into the wrists, put on the tongue or on the lips is also very helpful for allaying shock and fear. I have heard of it being successfully administered in a hospital by an enlightened doctor through an intravenous drip.

A recent study shows that magnesium given intravenously to patients admitted to hospital with a heart attack radically reduces their risk of dying.

In a semi-acute situation nutrition certainly has a substantial part to play not only in minimizing and hopefully preventing further heart damage but in actively rebuilding the arteries.

PHLEBITIS *(Inflammation of a vein)*

This is clotting of the veins in the leg which may result in painful localized inflammation. This is common in pregnant women as the changes in sex hormones during pregnancy cause the blood to clot more rapidly.

Apply externally compresses of ice-cold witch hazel, arnica, comfrey, marigold or hawthorn berries. Raw onion rubbed over the area externally also helps, as does eating garlic. Also take a mixture of the following herbs:

3 parts dried lime flowers	*1 part horse chestnut*
	1 part yarrow
1 part buckwheat	

Take two size '0' capsules of the finely powdered herbs with a wine glass full of decocted ginger tea with each meal.

STROKE

Since the Second World War the instance of strokes in Britain has been falling, and it is thought that improved vitamin C intake in the British diet has something to do with this in addition to better blood pressure monitoring. Certainly lack of vitamin C results in easy bruising and bleeding and this, coupled with high blood pressure, increases stroke risk. So ensure a good supply of fresh fruit and vegetables every day and take a 1 g supplement of vitamin C. Vitamin B_6 and E may also help certain risk factors in individual patients but these need to be individually prescribed by a knowledgeable practitioner.

Aspirin has been shown to reduce blood stickiness and stroke risk, particularly in those having repeated small strokes. Natural salicylate (which is artificially present in aspirin) are richly present in apples, apricots, avocados, all berries, cherries, currants, grapes and raisins, dates, figs, guavas, grapefruit, lemons, lychees, melons, mandarins, nectarines and peaches, plums, prunes, oranges, passion fruit, pears with their skins, persimmons, pineapple and rhubarb. The following herbs are extremely high in salicylate:

aniseed	oregano
cayenne	paprika
celery seed	rosemary
cinnamon	sage
cumin	tarragon
fenugreek	thyme
liquorice	white willow bark
mace	yucca
mustard	

THROMBOSIS

This is the formation of clots in the bloodstream which block up the vessel or travel, as emboli, around the circulation to lodge somewhere else. The most common forms are cerebral thrombosis usually known as a stroke, coronary thrombosis, pulmonary thrombosis and thrombophlebitis (where the clot occurs in the vein, usually in the leg).

Conditions which increase the risk of blood platelets becoming unusually sticky and clumping together include:

1. Taking oestrogen (notably the contraceptive pill) and hormone replacement therapy

2. High blood pressure

3. Strokes

4. Migraine

5. High blood fat

6. Asthma

7. Rheumatoid arthritis

8. Diabetes

For treatment follow the regime outlined under the heading arteriosclerosis (see p.107). For specific therapeutic agents which have a beneficial effect on the blood stickiness see cholesterol (p.111).

VARICOSITY

Varicose problems are more prevalent where there is a family history of low arterial blood pressure. Nearly a tenth of women get phlebitis or varicose veins shortly after or during pregnancy and this is aggravated by a calcium deficiency, standing for long periods which impedes the circulation, and wearing constricting clothes or shoes.

Vitamin E is essential to keep arterial oxygen at its optimum; so are foods containing bioflavonoids which are known to be anti-thrombotic and essential for the maintenance of healthy capillaries. The best known bioflavonoid is rutin (found in buckwheat but available as a supplement). Take 500 mg daily. Also take lecithin and plenty of naturally occuring vitamin C.

Weight loss is essential if you are obese. Anyone suffering a thrombosis in the veins is particularly prone to varicosity, so refer to p.000 for help with this problem.

Exercise helps, especially treading up and down in a bath filled with cold water, reaching knee-height. Do this for five minutes daily. Also helpful are warm hand and foot baths containing 10 drops in all of lavender, garlic or rosemary oils. Use these twice daily. Massaging the legs with 1 fl oz (30 ml) almond oil with 4 drops each of cypress and lavender oils and 2 drops of lemon oil is soothing. Use long, gentle, upwards sweeping strokes. A simple preventative remedy is equal parts of:

cayenne	*stoneroot*
lime flowers	*yarrow*
prickly ash bark	

Take two size '0' capsules of the finely powdered herbs with each meal.

VARICOSE ULCERS

These are erosions on the lower part of the leg which are the result of poor circulation from that area and are often associated with varicose veins. So the same dietary factors that apply to constipation and haemorrhoids apply here.

Slant board abdominal exercises are recommended, as is vigorous leg and calf exercise, keeping the feet up as much as possible in between bouts of exercise, alternate hot and cold forceful leg sprays where a shower is directed over the relevant area, slippery elm, cabbage leaf, comfrey or clay poultices applied directly to the ulcers and the following herbal tincture with which I have had a great deal of success.

Equal parts of:

arnica	*St John's wort*
horse chestnut	*yarrow*

Take 20 drops 3 times daily in water after meals.

Also see to vitamin and mineral deficiencies. There is often a chronic lack of vitamin C and vitamin E and this may have to be corrected according to individual need.

CHAPTER 6
DIGESTIVE SYSTEM

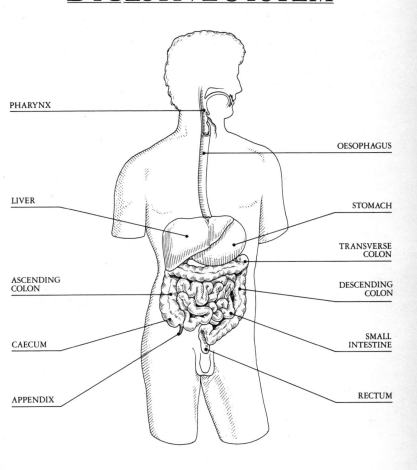

PHARYNX

OESOPHAGUS

LIVER

STOMACH

TRANSVERSE
COLON

ASCENDING
COLON

DESCENDING
COLON

CAECUM

SMALL
INTESTINE

APPENDIX

RECTUM

ANOREXIA NERVOSA

The mortality rate of anorexia is as high as 20% and death, apart from obvious starvation, often occurs as a result of infections and heart disorders. So anorexia is extremely serious and needs urgent medical intervention as well as skilled psychological counselling.

Getting an anorexic patient to accept herbs is a battle in itself but liquid zinc, which is easily swallowed in drinks, is quick to ingest and has been found to help.

Simon Mills, president of the National Institute of Medical Herbalists in the UK, recommends condurango (eagle vine), in a dose of 0.5–3 g of dried bark equivalent to be taken three times daily. Gentian or barberry may also be helpful taken as a tincture or a tea as well as scullcap and lady's slipper. Do not attempt to treat this disease at home. It needs urgent professional medical attention.

APPENDICITIS

It used to be the fashion to remove even a healthy appendix if the opportunity, in the form of an operation on the right-hand side of the abdomen, presented itself.

The appendix is about the size of a small pencil and when it gets blocked by impacted faeces it quickly becomes inflamed and infected. Initial symptoms include colicky central abdominal pains, nausea and vomiting and as the inflammation spreads so the whole of the surrounding area begins to hurt badly. An acute attack will come on very suddenly and may result in peritonitis which is very dangerous and needs urgent medical attention.

However grumbling appendix, a mild irritation, often goes on spasmodically for months or even years and it is possible to treat this by natural means with diet as for constipation (see p.127) and no laxatives although a lower bowel cleanse is an excellent idea (see p.131). Also take:

2 parts echinacea	1 part camomile
2 parts wild yam	½ part liquorice
1 part agrimony	

Drink 3 cups of this decoction 3 times daily for several months.

Dr Kloss recommends using a herbal enema of equal parts of spearmint, catnip, whiteoak bark, bayberry or wild alum root made as a standard decoction and administered 2°F below body temperature. This is to be followed by hot and cold compresses to the appendix and the full length of the spine. At night he recommends a poultice of granulated or powdered lobelia with a large handful of crushed mullein leaves and a sprinkle of ginger. Proportions to be 3 parts of mullein to 1 part lobelia and a generous pinch of ginger. The herbs are mixed into a paste with powdered slippery elm or cornmeal and a poultice is applied as warm as possible over the appendix until cooled. When suffering an attack of grumbling appendicitis go on a liquid diet drinking potassium broths (see p.135), fruit juices and several cups of slippery elm gruel daily.

N.B. When using this combination of compresses and enema and the decoction please be absolutely certain it is grumbling appendix you are suffering from and not acute appendicitis. Grumbling appendix takes the form of recurring attacks of abdominal pain on the lower right side, but the pain tends to be dull not acute, often accompanied by a rise in temperature, nausea and sometimes vomiting.

BELCHING *(Burping)*

This can be caused by swallowing air while eating too fast and talking at the same time. The obvious solution is to eat meals in silence, slowly, perhaps listening to background music. Another cause can be too little hydrochloric acid and pepsin resulting in bacteria going wild in the stomach causing food to ferment and producing gas which tastes terrible and smells foul. For treatment refer to point 15 in the hypo-acidity section of indigestion (see Indigestion, p.146).

BLOATING *(Wind, Flatulence)*

I have seen patients so agonized by this condition that they have confessed it has impeded their careers or inhibited their sex life. What bloating and flatulence signify is that food, for many possible reasons, is not being digested properly.

Certainly the type of food we eat accounts for the amount of wind we produce. Pulses are notorious for this. They are embarrassingly sulphuric and antisocial without and can be uncomfortable within. Such flatulence is the result of two incompatible starches (stachyose and raffinose) which do not pass through the walls of the small intestine, and instead of being converted into blood sugar, intestinal bacteria go to work on them splitting them into carbon dioxide and hydrogen – an intestinal gas bomb.

Soaking pulses goes part way towards solving this problem but it is in the cooking that the job can really be done properly. Use plenty of water to ensure the soaking beans absorb all they can and throw away any beans that still float on the surface. Soya beans are the only group that need to be refrigerated to stop fermentation while they are soaking. A quicker method than simply soaking them is to bring the beans gently to the boil, remove them from the heat and leave them to soak for an hour.

To cook beans generally requires 3 measures of water to 1 of soaked beans, with the exception of soya beans and chick-peas which need 5 to 1. Cider vinegar added to the cooking water will tame the gas-producing activities of beans, but add it only at the very end, otherwise it will toughen the beans and lengthen the cooking time. At the beginning of the last half hour of cooking remove the saucepan from the heat, scoop out a quarter of a cup of liquid and replace it with the same quantity of cider vinegar. Stir the vinegar in with a wooden spoon and add whatever flavouring you want (herbs, spices, celery, carrots, onion, garlic etc.) at this stage. Return the saucepan to the heat and simmer gently. If a bean squashes easily between thumb and forefinger it is well cooked.

Interestingly, the more often you eat beans, the less intestinal gas you create. Apparently the multiplication of the intestinal bacteria responsible for breaking down stachyose and raffinos is promoted by bean eating. Sprouted beans do not cause flatulence because the starch is partially converted to sugar.

Many other foods will cause flatulence in particular people and those concerned can usually be identified and avoided. But sometimes the problem goes deeper than this. Follow all the dictates under indigestion (see p.146). Also consider gall-bladder disease which is often associated with indigestion and with flatulence (see gall bladder, p.138). Investigate the possibility of a parasitic intestinal infection by seeking professional help. An iridology test will help to ascertain this.

Also take one 5 ml teaspoon of tincture of wild yam in hot water every half hour for 2 hours then every 4 hours.

Sipping peppermint, dill, ginger, fennel, caraway or aniseed tea is also helpful as is reflexology (massage of the reflex points in the soles of the feet) and hot sitz-baths during an acute attack or alternatively a hot fennel compress applied over the abdomen.

Do *not* use bran of any sort. Use flax-seed, marketed commercially as Linusit Gold, instead. Bran worsens the condition and may scour the delicate lining of an already distressed bowel. High levels of it can inhibit iron absorption and in any case many people are wheat intolerant.

N.B. If bloating and flatulence persist in spite of stringent adherence to these measures please seek professional help and ask about the possibility of Candida.

BULIMIA NERVOSA

This is related to anorexia where any food that is eaten publicly or even privately is vomited up deliberately immediately afterwards. Acid from the vomit is known to wear away the enamel on the teeth.

Treatment is the same as for anorexia (see p.120).

CANDIDIASIS *(Thrush)*

Since I have been practising as a medical herbalist it seems to me that candidiasis has become an epidemic. For many years the yeast *Candida albicans* has been recognized as an important disease-producing micro-organism. It is most commonly encountered as oral and vaginal thrush and the problem with candida infection is diagnosis. When it is deeply entrenched it can be diagnosed with an iridology test but the initial symptoms will remain invisible in the iris. I list them simply because there are so many of them.

Alcohol intolerance
Anal itching, recurrent cystitis
Constipation or diarrhoea
Craving for refined carbohydrate and/or alcohol
Depression
Fatigue
Fungal nail or skin infections including athlete's foot
Hyperactivity
Hypoglycaemia
Inability to concentrate
Inflamed prostate gland
Iron or zinc deficiency
Irritable bowel syndrome
Joint pains with or without swelling and muscle pains
Menstrual problems
Nettlerash and hives
Recurrent vaginal infections or oral thrush
Sensitivity to chemicals
Upper abdominal discomfort or burning, bloating and flatulence

The symptoms are worse in low or damp places, near new-mown lawns or raked-up leaves or on days when the atmosphere is damp – all symptoms of mould allergy.

The symptoms are precipitated by antibiotics.

There may be an onset of problems during or shortly after pregnancy.

Treatment includes a diet based on the principle that refined carbohydrates act as food for candida in the gut, and yeasted foods particularly increase bloating, flatulence, soreness, itching, disturbed bowel function and lead to an all-round worsening of symptoms. So a meticulous diet which avoids all refined carbohydrates is essential as is the avoidance of yeasted food especially Marmite, Vegemite and other yeast-based spreads, frozen or concentrated fruit juices which are a rich breeding ground for yeast spores, all cheeses, any bread made with yeast (although it is possible to make Irish soda bread with wholemeal flour), alcoholic drinks, grapes and their juice, unpeeled fruits, all dried fruits, peanuts and pistachios,

mushrooms, vinegar, soya sauce and any fermented product, and B vitamins which contain yeast. Read the label, some do not. Carbohydrate intake should be restricted to whole grains only and reduced to 2 oz (60 g) daily. The diet should lean towards one which is high in fish, antibiotic-free meat and eggs and plenty of vegetables particularly dark green leafy ones (the latter with e.g. garlic and onions because they contain naturally anti-fungal agents).

Drugs that promote the growth of candida and other yeast fungi include antibiotics, the pill, cortisones and prednisone and immuno-suppressive drugs such as Imuran.

For candidiasis to be treated correctly on a permanent basis and eradicated altogether the efficiency of the immune system must be raised. There are various normal physiological changes which, if present, predispose candida infection. These begin in infancy, when the immune system is immature. It is possible for a baby to become infected with candida as it passes through the mother's vagina should the vagina be infected. Pregnancy, as well as the use of oral contraceptives, predisposes to candidiasis. In old age when the immune system functions less efficiently it is possible for old people to become run down, particularly as a result of insufficient nutrients in their diet or simply because they can no longer efficiently absorb the nutrients they eat. A lack of immunoglobin A (which is an important antibody), a debilitated stomach wall producing too little hydrochloric acid, and other conditions can predispose a person to chronic candidiasis.

In order to raise the level of the immune system and encourage it to function correctly individual nutritional deficiencies must be corrected and these may include deficiencies of vitamin A, certain of the B vitamins, vitamin C, zinc, iron, and magnesium.

TREATMENT

Swallow 1 medium-sized garlic clove whole 2 to 3 times a day with meals. Garlic capsules may be taken as a substitute but they are not as effective and many of them are made by fermenting garlic in oil. This type of garlic capsule is not advisable. Dried garlic put into gelatine capsules or in pill form is useful but not as effective as fresh raw garlic which is a superb fungicide.

Take one teaspoon of Superdophilus or chew 2 capsules of Probion 3 to 4 times daily. (For suppliers of both these see Appendix.) Superdophilus should be stored at all times in the refrigerator when not in use and needs to be mixed with 8 fl oz (250 ml) of lukewarm purified water for each dose.

While taking Superdophilus do not eat yoghurt of any sort. Probion may cause constipation and if this is the case take 2 teaspoons of psyllium husks in vegetable juice 3 times a day.

Ensure that the bowel is kept working well at all times. If taking Superdophilus it may also be necessary to take the bowel tonic (see p.33).

If there is an external manifestation of candidiasis such as athlete's foot or nail fungus add 10 drops of Tea tree oil to one cup of hot water and soak the nails for 30 minutes twice daily in this. Alternatively add 2 teaspoons of Tea tree oil to a foot bath and soak the feet in this. Also apply Tea tree cream externally (for suppliers see Appendix).

The inner bark of the Taheebo tree which grows in South America is known to be an excellent anti-fungal agent. Otherwise known as Pau d'Arco it is available in tea form (for suppliers see Appendix). Drink 1 cup decocted for 15 minutes 4 times a day.

Caprilic acid is also known to be helpful. (When ordering from suppliers – see Appendix – ask for the individual dose recommended for your body weight. I generally insist patients take a minimal 3 week course, 4 capsules after each meal.)

If there is any vaginal discharge use Tea tree oil pessaries nightly and douche the following morning with 10 drops of goldenseal in 1 pint (600 ml) of lukewarm water. (For suppliers of Tea tree oil pessaries see Appendix).

It is essential to keep transit time of faecal matter through the colon optimal so I always couple all anti-candida measures with a thorough bowel cleanse (see p.131). This also repairs the inner wall of the colon which in the case of chronic candidiasis is often damaged.

Oils which are particularly useful antifungal agents include olive, safflower and linseed. Take 3 tablespoons of one or a mixture of these uncooked daily.

Note that die-off reactions can occur at the start of any treatment. This is simply the result of massive candida death, where the body suddenly gets swamped with the burden of the breakdown of its yeast products. Symptoms may include chronic fatigue, nausea, stomach bloating and flatulence as well as alterations in bowel movements. Hang on in the realization that the anti-candida treatment is working. Such a reaction can be minimized by starting the anti-candida diet 2 weeks before taking any other natural medications to combat it. All treatment will need to last for at least 3 months before any improvement is noticed, and this will include fewer headaches, improved bowel function, a lifting of depression and an uplift in energy.

CIRRHOSIS OF THE LIVER

The functions of the liver are absolutely vital for the body as a whole. Indeed many natural therapists believe that the recovery from cancer depends directly on the degree of damage to liver functions. The liver has an extraordinary capacity to regenerate itself, so partial destruction may be restored provided the deterioration is not extensive and rapid. Conversely the liver can remain damaged for a long time before the deterioration is detected and its great functional reserves will have been consumed. It is here once again that iridology comes into its own because it is so useful in evaluating the exact degree of liver degeneration.

Liver cirrhosis is generally the result of excessive consumption of alcohol. It is known that low levels of nickel occur in people with cirrhosis. A long-term herbal approach is necessary to treat cirrhosis and hepatic herbs that act directly on the liver, herbs which increase the flow of bile, and bitter herbs which promote digestion need to be used selectively according to individual need.

COELIAC DISEASE *(Gluten Sensitivity)*

This is an intolerance of gluten in wheat, oats, rye and barley which can begin at any age and shows itself as diarrhoea, bloating, colic, irritable bowel syndrome, depression, infertility or a variety of gut upsets. Coeliac disease needs to be confirmed by a specialist as gluten intolerance is also possible even if the small intestinal lining is shown to be healthy. It is even possible to be allergic to wheat *without* being intolerant of gluten.

For details of gluten-free cookery books see Appendix.

TREATMENT

Avoid all gluten. Brown rice and carrot juice gruel will help children with coeliac disease.

Apply abdominal compresses of camomile or horsetail and take warm sitz-baths of camomile daily. Herbal remedies which will soothe, heal and renew the lining of the intestine include comfrey root, slippery elm, marshmallow root which can be mixed in equal quantities and taken as a gruel. A good general formula would be equal parts of finely powdered:

agrimony	*meadowsweet*
camomile	*slippery elm*
comfrey root	*wild yam*

Adult dose 3 size '0' capsules with each meal. Adjust dose for children appropriately.

COLIC

Much of what applies to bloating and flatulence applies to colic. I have found colic very rare among babies who are breast-fed unless they are very greedy and suck in lots of air with breast milk or they are being upset by something the mother is eating. Onions, garlic, wheat, yeast and the sulphurous green vegetables are the most usual culprits. Bottle-fed babies are often intolerant of milk, soya milk or sugar in formula feeds. The alternative is diluted goat's milk. Once the child starts to eat look to wheat intolerance and introduce any grains late on, as children can only digest them really well after the first year.

An excellent formula for infantile colic is an infusion of equal parts of catnip and fennel. Give 2 teaspoons every 15 minutes or as needed. Apply a hot compress of peppermint to the stomach. For an older child or adult make a decoction of equal parts of:

aniseed	*pleurisy root*
cinnamon	*wild yam*

Sweeten with honey. Dosage according to age (see p.74).

CONSTIPATION

Chronic constipation is the result of a variety of physiologial and psychological factors including:

1. Liver malfunction (especially gall-bladder disease).
2. Underactive thyroid function.
3. Appendectomy.
4. Anaemia.
5. Addiction to laxatives.
6. Specific food intolerance.
7. Constant worry/depression.
8. Refusing to go to the toilet to defecate when you have a natural urge to do so.
9. A low-fibre diet with too much animal protein in it and resultant putrefaction in the colon.
10. Vitamin and mineral deficiencies particularly vitamin C and magnesium.
11. Diverticular disease.
12. Not drinking enough liquids regularly. Ideally an adult should drink a minimum of 4 litres daily.
13. Irritable bowel syndrome.
14. Drugs and substances that affect bowel motility (opiates, iron tablets, certain anti-depressants, antacids).
15. Long periods of immobility; this particularly applies to the elderly.
16. Painful anal conditions that inhibit the opening the bowels.
17. Spinal lesions.
18. Prolapsed colon.
19. Partial intestinal obstructions like adhesions and cancer.
20. Absence of normal nerve plexus and ganglia on the wall of the colon – a condition which is extremely rare.

Overall poor diet certainly plays the largest part in constipation. The bowel should literally dump pounds of waste every day. Most people get rid of 8–10 oz (250–300 g) and think they are doing well, even if they do

have up to three bowel movements daily, but in truth everyone should eliminate four-fifths of the food they ingest over a 10–18 hour period. It is possible to conduct a rather novel experiment to find out if this is so by liquidizing the entire intake of food for a day, taking a long hard look at it and seeing if most of this emerges at the other end.

Check to see how long food takes to pass through the body. It is not uncommon for people to retain faeces for days. Do this with the sunflower seed test. Eat a heaped handful of sunflower seeds, chewing as little as possible (the only instance in which I let you get away with poor chewing!) and time their passage through the colon. They will show up very clearly, white and grey, in the faeces. (Sunflower seeds are high in vitamin F which helps to rebuild the mucus lining of the colon, so eating them plentifully and chewing them well under normal circumstances helps.) A sluggish colon is just as dangerous as an impacted one. The prolonged retention of faeces can be one of the sources of heart disease because a poisonous bloodstream raises cholestrol in the blood serum alarmingly, predisposing the body to coronary disease. The chemical changes to the bile produced by retention may also be responsible for tumours and cancer. A prolapsed colon and rectal problems can be dealt with by learning to defecate properly and by using the slant board exercises (see pp.141–3). Squatting is the best position to adopt when defecating. In so called 'less civilized' countries this position with thighs flexed against the abdomen ensures the stomach muscles are provided with the support they need.

Our ridiculous western WC units do not suit the physiology of the body. They are too high to allow for a squatting position and the sitting-on-a-chair posture they encourage is essentially passive and unable to assist the body's mechanism. Besides which western clothing actively impedes a squatting position.

Our WC units can be adapted to encourage a healthier alternative which won't involve scrambled clothes and wet hems or trouser bottoms. Sit on the toilet crossing the arms across the chest and drawing the feet back. Or put a small stool, a box or a pile of magazines about 12 in (30 cm) high in front of the toilet to raise the feet and if you are suffering from any internal prolapses defecate while placing your hands on your head. This will relieve the bearing down on rectal muscles, prevent haemorrhoids and relieve the strain on upper abdominal muscles.

There are WC seats designed to encourage a more healthy and comfort-able position even when used on a unit of conventional height. The shape is elongated to provide comfort and room for men and curved to give the thighs the support that the conventional WC lacks, but as far as I can ascertain such seats are only currently available in Italy.

THE MICRO-LIFE IN THE INTESTINES

A healthy colon holds 3–4 lbs (1.5–2 kg) of resident bacteria as indigenous flora. Such flora is composed of 300–400 different species of bacteria whose activities affect our metabolism, physiology and biochemistry in ways both beneficial and harmful. So vital is this intestinal metabolic activity that it even exceeds the liver in the wide range of its metabolic processes. A constipated colon has a much higher proportion of abnormal bacteria in it with a consequently greater potential for cancer.

The bacterioids together with coliforms bacilli and *E. coli* are the putrefactive bacteria responsible for the decaying matter in the colon. They prefer a diet full of protein and fat which accelerates the output of undesirable metabolites like bile salts, urea, phenols, ammonia and other dietary degradation products which are all potentially harmful substances, doubly so if there is constipation or impaired detoxification by the liver. A high population of poor bacteria is one of the main contributory factors in the development of all sorts of degenerative diseases like ulcerative colitis, diverticulosis, haemorrhoids and colonic cancer and most people have a ratio of 85% of these potentially harmful bacteria to only 15% beneficial bacteria.

The 15% beneficial bacteria produce acetic, lactic and formic acid which lowers the pH of the intestine and so prevents the colonization of fungus like *Candida albicans* (which causes thrush). When the percentage is better balanced, with seventy-five per cent of these beneficial bacteria, peristalsis is stimulated, flushing out toxic bacterial metabolites and waste products in the faeces, so checking putrefactive bacteria. It is possible to alter this balance with a thorough bowel cleanse (see p.131) coupled with sup-plementations of acidophilus (for suppliers see Appendix) and a healthy lacto-vegetarian diet.

It is quite common for the elderly, who generally have a tired, worn-out stomach lining resulting in achlorhydria (under-secretion of hydrochloric acid), to have too many of the bacterioids. Achlorhydria is also the result of consuming too much tannic acid in tea and coffee (yet another good reason to give them up) or of taking very hot or cold drinks or foods as well as indulging in high-fat, high-protein diets which favour meat. Benign bacteria flourish in lacto-vegetarian diets high in fibre and whole grains.

Breast-feeding leads to a flora with a predominance of benign bacteria. During the process of birth the baby is exposed to micro-organisms from the mother's vagina and intestinal tract and afterwards obtains these from the environment from being handled. The bacteria which colonized the skin and the mucosal surfaces of the upper respiratory and gastrointestinal tracts mark the beginning of a life-long symbiosis between the human organism and the indigenous flora.

Bottle-fed babies have a much higher density of bacterioids, clostridia and Lactobacillus acidophilus with few benign bacteria. Breast-fed babies

have acidic stools with a pH ranging from 5–5.5 which increases their capacity to resist infection by pathogenic bacteria. Bottle-fed babies have a faecal flora closer to those of adults in its consistency and odour with a pH of 6–7. So breast milk clearly comes out tops as far as healthy bacteria is concerned as well as having other immunological properties and breast-fed babies maintain a stronger component of benign bacteria as they grow up than their bottle-fed cousins. It seems that breast feeding is the first and most vital factor in the balance of desirable bacteria in the colon.

HOW TO IMPLANT BENEFICIAL BACTERIA

It is possible to balance your intestinal bacteria by eating lots of live yoghurt daily, by which I mean 12 oz (360 g). Anything added to the yoghurt except a well ripened banana will destroy much of the benign bacteria in it, so it must be eaten plain. Bananas, provided they are well ripened (the way to tell is to choose those with brown freckles all over their skins) are the only fruit known actively to encourage the growth of beneficial flora in the colon.

The problem with both bananas and yoghurt for some people is that they create a lot of mucus and 12 oz (360 g) of yoghurt is quite a lot to get through in one sitting. The alternative is to take acidopholus, a freeze-dried form of benign lactobacillus, in the form of one or two products called respectively Superdopholus and Probion. There are many other forms of acidopholus on the market but I have found these to be infinitely superior (see Appendix).

If overgrowth of the yeasts and fungal colonies in the intestines is the problem then an Argentinian tree bark called Pau d'Arco has long been used by the Inca Indians in Southern Peru to introduce a whole spectrum of complex biochemical properties based on its active ingredient lapachol into the intestine. Drink 2 cups of Pau d'Arco tea daily for its fungicidal properties.

The regulatory activity of the faecal microflora has been shown to have a greater effect on bowel function than the addition of dietary fibres. It is not uncommon for me to encounter patients who have been stuffing themselves to the gunnels with bran and to be achieving nothing other than an irritable bowel and lots of flatulence. Acidophilus improves transit time through the gastrointestinal tract, which prevents auto-intoxication ('self-poisoning').

Eli Metchnikoff, the first person to appreciate the medical benefits of fermented milk, observed, 'Not only is the auto-intoxication from the microbial poisons absorbed in cases of constipation, but microbes themselves pass through the walls of the intestine and enter the blood.'

Constipation is the hub of the mechanism in many disease processes. Toxins and micro-organisms pass through the intestinal wall into the body causing an endless array of disturbances. When the body absorbs poisons from the waste decaying in the colon the end result is self-poisoning. Meat, fish and eggs provide the most harmful metabolites, which on entering the bloodstream create a toxic load for the cells throughout the body and in particular the liver. This self-poisoning causes fatigue, poor concentration, irritability, insomnia, headaches and muscular aches, and leads to degenerative diseases.

BRAN

One of the obvious solutions to constipation is to increase the fibre in the diet and stop refined carbohydrate foods. Wheat bran is not the best solution as many people are wheat intolerant. Recently, it was discovered that 4 out of every 100 blood donors had laboratory evidence of an allergy to gluten in wheat. Gluten is also in rye, oats and barley. It is possible to get rice bran but far better to take flax-seed or psyllium husks, the outer seed coats of plantain (see Appendix). Alternatively try the following laxative gruel.

3 parts comfrey root	3 parts marshmallow
3 parts linusit gold or	root
psyllium husks	1 part lobelia
3 parts liquorice root	

Mix with fruit juice and sweeten with honey if desired. Take one tablespoon at a time or more as needed. The flax-seed or psyllium husks act as bulk, the liquorice root is a mild laxative, the marshmallow root is to assist clearance where hard stools are prevalent, the comfrey root heals and rebuilds weaker areas in the colon and gives lubrication while lobelia acts as an accentuating herb. For anyone where constipation has been a longstanding problem a thorough bowel cleanse is advisable.

DR CHRISTOPHER'S HERBAL COMBINATION TO AID IMPROPER BOWEL FUNCTION

This is a unique and unbeatable formula for treating all bowel problems and is also helpful as part of the treatment for haemorrhoids. It is the aim of this formulation to restore normal bowel function, *not to create a dependence* as most laxatives do. A combination of herbs cleanses the liver and gall bladder, starts the bile flowing, and stimulates peristalsis so that layers of encrusted ancient mucus can gradually slough off as the bowel is rebuilt, resulting in a perfect assimilation of food. It clears out the bowel pockets and diverticula, healing any inflamed areas and relaxing any areas of tension.

1 part bayberry bark	*1 part lobelia*
2 parts cascara sagrada	*1 part red raspberry*
1 part cayenne	*leaves*
1 part fennel	*1 part turkey rhubarb*
1 part goldenseal	*root*

Combine all the herbs, which should be finely powdered, and fill size '0' gelatine capsules with them. If lobelia is unavailable, substitute ginger.

I cannot emphasize enough that this formula produces a very individual result and therefore the dosage must be monitored and adjusted according to individual response. As there are no two people alike in age, size or physical constitution (and certainly people's bowels are as different as their fingerprints), you will have to regulate the dose of this formula according to your own needs. I would suggest that you begin by taking 2 capsules 3 times a day, with meals, or if you don't eat 3 times a day take 2 capsules with every meal that you do eat in order to achieve a bowel movement for every meal ingested. If you get diarrhoea cut down – if you can't get a bowel movement then raise the dosage until you can. Some of my patients have had to take as many as 15 capsules with each meal for the first few months of this formula. No matter. This is exactly how it should be and simply means the person concerned is chronically constipated and it is taking some time before the body releases its accumulated faecal matter.

The bits of encrusted mucus that emerge may look very odd. You may see nuts and seeds, which have been lodged in the colon for months or even years; traces of barium meal (if you have ever had one); bits of what looks like rubber tyre, tree bark or coloured Vaseline jelly. Alternatively bowel movements may emerge smelling particularly foul or may emerge accompanied by a great deal of rumbling or flatulence. Don't be alarmed by any of this. *Do not* taper off the formulation so much you lose the momentum and so the continuity of this elimination. A thorough bowel cleanse for a constipated person takes from 9 months to a year but it can take even longer.

It is essential to combine this gastrointestinal cleansing with a diet which is totally free of dairy products, eggs, meat and all refined foods for at least the first 6 months of a bowel cleanse. It is simply a waste of effort to put items which cause constipation in one end while you continue to try and pull impacted faeces from the other.

To determine whether the process is at an end and your colon is perfectly clean, go on a carrot juice and purified water fast for a day. Try to drink at least 8 large glasses of carrot juice and plenty of water on top of this. The resultant faeces should emerge looking bright orange-brown. If they are a mixture of brown and orange-brown this means there is still some old encrusted matter emerging and the process needs to be continued. If they are completely brown it means you have got a very long way to go.

Fasting for one regular day a week together with taking enemas morning and evening greatly helps this bowel cleansing process.

N.B. Omit the goldenseal from the bowl cleaning formula after 2 months and replace it with equal parts of wild thyme and garlic. Goldenseal destroys the B vitamins if taken long term. This formulation should not in any case be taken for longer than 1 year.

HERBAL FORMULA FOR CHRONIC CONSTIPATION

I label this affectionately my TNT formula and use it only when patients are chronically constipated in order to get them off to a flying start with their bowel cleanse. It should not be used for longer than 2 months. Equal parts of:

agrimony	garlic
alfalfa	ginger
cape aloe	senna pods
cascara segrada	wild yam root
cayenne	

Combine all the herbs, which should be finely powdered, and fill size '0' gelatine capsules with them. Take them in the same way as you would Dr Christopher's formula but begin very cautiously, even in cases of chronic constipation, as it is a much more powerful formula. Start with one size '0' capsule before each meal or adjust according to individual response.

OTHER AIDS

Take alternate hot and cold sitz-baths daily.

For a spastic colon apply a hot castor oil poultice to the abdomen nightly, all night, for 6 consecutive nights weekly. Keep it as hot as possible with a hot water bottle at least for the first few hours.

Fast on apple juice or grape juice for 1 day regularly every week, choosing the same day each week. Both juices must be freshly pressed. Take nothing else, including herbs, except mineral water and take a warm catnip enema morning and evening on this fasting day.

Increase abdominal strength with yoga exercises and get plenty of daily vigorous exercise every day, walking, swimming, horse-riding, hill climbing.

Visit the toilet after every meal to ingrain the reflex of opening the bowels.

Don't drink with meals. Aim to drink 8 large glasses of liquid daily.

DIARRHOEA

Diarrhoea is caused by a substance irritating the colon so badly that

peralsis goes into overdrive in an attempt to expel it. In some cases the build-up of old faeces trapped in the colon becomes so large that these themselves induce a state of continuous rapid peristalsis, which results in chronic diarrhoea. In other words severe constipation can show itself as diarrhoea. It may therefore be helpful to describe what the ideal bowel movement is, especially in view of the fact that I have found many of my patients are hopelessly embarrassed about actually inspecting their bowel movements.

WHAT IS THE IDEAL BOWEL MOVEMENT?

1. The faeces should be buoyant when passed. If they sink they are heavy with mucus.

2. They should emerge easily, all in one piece and almost immediately you sit down on the toilet. As they float they should begin to break up. If it takes you more than 5 minutes to complete a bowel movement you are constipated.

3. Faeces should be lightish brown in colour. If their colouring resembles that of the food you have been eating (for example greenish-brown after lots of green vegetables), you have not digested the food properly. If they look yellow or chalky you have a problem with bile secretion or the production of digestive enzymes.

4. They should not smell foul, though they will have a slight odour. If you go on a fruit fast for a week and the resulting faeces smell only of the fruit you have eaten, you can be confident that you have a clean colon.

5. They should be four-fifths as bulky as the food you have ingested and they should not be compacted.

6. They should emerge unaccompanied by foaming, gurgling, flatulence and general orchestration.

It is quite normal to have a bowel movement 3 times daily as long as the stool is formed and does not contain undigested food particles. Chronic or recurrent diarrhoea may be the result of long-term antibiotic use and its after-effects, irritable bowel syndrome, intestinal parasites, food intolerance, digestive-enzyme deficiency, candidiasis, food poisoning, heavy metal poisoning, prolonged stress, severe B-complex deficiencies or excessive vitamin C or zinc, pancreatic or adrenal malfunction, anaemia or colitis.

ACUTE DIARRHOEA

Fast on purified water with a squeeze of fresh lemon juice in it and take a warm camomile enema unless colitis is suspected. If colitis is suspected omit the enema. Also drink as much blackberry leaf tea as you can manage and either way ensure you take plenty of fluids to avoid dehydration and the constant loss of electrolytes. Once cleared in 2 or 3 days time go on to eating well ripened mashed bananas with yoghurt for a further day and then gently go back on to a normal healthy diet.

If the diarrhoea is extremely bad take two size '0' capsules of blackberry bark every second hour interspersed with two size '0' capsules of equal parts of goldenseal and echinacea every other hour so that some medication is being taken every hour in all. Continue with this pattern until the diarrhoea is completely under control.

If the diarrhoea lasts longer than 2 to 3 days it may be the result of colitis, irritable bowel syndrome, or coeliac disease – so seek further medical help.

INFANTILE DIARRHOEA

Any diarrhoea in infancy which doesn't clear up in 24 hours needs immediate and urgent medical attention. Causes may include over-feeding, the mother's poor diet if she is breast feeding, teething, or a bacterial or viral infection or intestinal parasites like giardia, threadworms, ascaria and amoeba which are now endemic in the UK. (1 in 5 British schoolchildren is infected with parasitic threadworm.)

Feed the baby on purified water, home-made barley water and home-made potassium broth with plenty of garlic in it. Also give sips of raspberry leaf infusion with a pinch of cinnamon in each cup and if in doubt seek immediate professional medical help. Parasitic diarrhoea certainly requires the help of a medical herbalist conversant with such matters.

BARLEY WATER

Pour 1½ pints (900 ml) of water over 1 oz (30 g) whole barley grains and boil until the quantity is reduced to half. Add the zest and rind of a lemon for flavour. Strain and drink at room temperature.

POTASSIUM BROTH

2 large potatoes scrubbed, chopped and sliced	*1 clove of garlic*
1 cup shredded carrots	*1 chopped onion*
1 cup shredded or chopped celery including the leaves	
1 cup of any other available vegetable including beet tops, turnip tops, parsley or a combination of all three	

Put all the vegetables into a saucepan covering with 3 pints (1800 ml) water and simmer slowly for half an hour, tightly covered. Strain and drink the liquid only.

TRAVELLER'S DIARRHOEA

Certain famous allopathic anti-diarrhoea remedies are now banned in Japan and Sweden after they have been found to cause severe eye and nerve damage. A much safer way to prevent diarrhoea when travelling abroad is to take two tablets of betaine hydrochloride after each meal (for suppliers see Appendix). Hydrochloric acid effectively kills any malign bacteria in the stomach and prevents infection. Alternatively, eating raw garlic daily is an excellent preventative and to a lesser extent undiluted lemon or lime juice taken on an empty stomach has an antiseptic sterilizing effect.

DIVERTICULITIS

Nearly 30% of people beyond middle age in the western world suffer from diverticular disease. It is almost unknown in undeveloped countries. It occurs where there is a weakness in the colon wall which can develop into a pouch called a diverticulum. The pouches are most commonly found in the sigmoid colon – that is the last section of the colon before it reaches the rectum – they become filled with bacteria and consume a large amount of B vitamins and blood loss may also occur. Once inflamed any fibrous indigestible material like seeds or skins from fruit can cause intense pain in the lower left hand side of the abdomen (often mistaken for appendicitis) occasionally accompanied by nausea, vomiting and a blown-up abdomen. Constipation or diarrhoea may alternate.

The solution is a high-fibre diet, but where there is inflammation the initial approach must be a low-fibre one until the inflammation has subsided. Fast on a single fruit or vegetable juice until all the painful symptoms have decreased consistently. Then gently begin to add baked or steamed root vegetables, well ripened mashed bananas, and papaya. Move on to puréed stewed fruit and then cautiously on to grated raw foods avoiding pips and skins. Then introduce whole grains which must be well chewed, and steamed fish. This whole process generally takes between 6 and 8 weeks. Three cups of slippery elm gruel daily will help to heal the intestinal walls. Also take the following formula:

3 parts camomile	2 parts marshmallow
1 part ginger	1 part turkey rhubarb
1 part liquorice	1 part wild yam

Make a decoction and drink 3 cups daily with meals.

If pain is acute apply a castor oil compress to the abdomen leaving it on for between 2–4 hours, and take hot and cold sitz-baths daily.

Once the diet has been adjusted go onto the diet prescribed for constipation and follow through with Dr Christopher's bowel tonic. A high fibre approach may result in flatulence and some pain initially but the body will soon settle down. Remember cellulose actively encourages friendly bacterial development, which in turn produces several of the B complex vitamins in the intestines. Raw sprouted alfalfa is particularly helpful for deodorizing diverticulum.

DUODENAL ULCERS

These are the result of gastric overacidity, and executive stress in the under-35s plays a large part in them. This used to be a male prerogative but duodenal ulcers are becoming more apparent as one of the penalties hard-working female executives are now paying for their stressful jobs.

Raw freshly made cabbage or potato juice is particularly helpful for duodenal ulcers. In order to make it you will need a proper juicer and good quality white or green cabbage or potatoes well scrubbed with their skins left on. Juice them separately or in equal proportions and because the final result will taste rather nasty mix it with celery or cabbage juice in half and half proportions. In other words one glass may consist of ½ part of carrot juice, ¼ part cabbage juice and ¼ part potato juice. Aim to drink it the moment it has been pressed and take 4 or 5 glasses (8 fl oz/250 ml) daily.

A SPECIAL DIET

Before breakfast take a glass of this juice. Breakfast itself should consist of bulgar wheat which has been soaked overnight in a slow cooker in some water so that it is soft, crunchy and palatable. If desired soak it overnight in vegetable juice. Add a tablespoon or two of linseed if the bowels are cositive and sweeten if desired with a teapoon of honey or spice with a few pinches of cinnamon. Sit down and chew this mixture extremely well so that each mouthful is a fine slurry before swallowing it.

Lunch

Begin with a good strong vegetable soup with about ¼ pt (150 ml) of raw cabbage juice or raw potato juice added to it once the soup has been taken off the boil. Follow this with unpolished rice, or cracked wheat, buck wheat, or millet, together with steamed vegetables and salad dressed with lemon juice or whey concentrate (for suppliers of whey concentrate see Appendix).

Supper

Take white meat or steamed fish and have as many vegetables lightly steamed as desired, concentrating particularly on dark green leafy vegetables. Do not eat any fruit at all but aim to drink plenty of freshly pressed fruit juice.

If strictly adhered to this diet will heal duodenal ulcers within 4 or 5 weeks. A cure depends fundamentally upon the ingestion of raw juices

and because they do not taste very palatable it is best to mix cabbage and potato juice in soup or with other stronger tasting juices like carrot juice. Never mix fruit and vegetable juices together. The two are incompatible and will ferment causing flatulence.

Also take 1 teaspoon of the following finely powdered herbs mixing with a little vegetable juice before each meal equal parts:

comfrey	*marshmallow*
liquorice	*slippery elm*

ENTERITIS

An inflammation of the intestine, usually the small intestine, due to a viral or bacterial infection. Fast on purified water with a squeeze of lemon juice as long as the acute stage of the infection lasts and take the following decoction:

2 parts comfrey root	*1 part goldenseal*
2 parts marshmallow	*1 part wild yam*
2 parts slippery elm	*1 part yarrow*
1 part echinacea	

Drink four wine glasses daily.

Once the worst is over drink slippery elm gruel with well ripened mashed bananas incorporated into it for one or two days then gently go back onto carrot juice, stewed apples, avocados, steamed potatos and root vegetables steamed. Gradually introduce other steamed vegetables, tofu and steamed fish and only when entirely comfortable introduce raw fruit and vegetables.

GALL STONES

If the bile duct from the liver is blocked sudden jaundice may ensue but gall stones generally are the result of bile stasis so the gall bladder is only partially emptied. This thickened bile combined with a faulty high cholesterol diet may induce small cholecuistitis (inflammation of the gall bladder) where gall stones get stuck in the neck of the gall bladder causing biliary colic which is very painful.

Surgery *never* helps either to correct the cause of gall stones or the disease and only serves to denude the body of a useful organ.

Over 90% of gall stones are made of cholesterol and the phospholipid concentration in the bile of gall stones patients is lower than normal. Two tablespoons of lecithin granules daily will help to increase phospholipid concentration and so work towards dispersing and preventing the formation of gall stones, provided it is coupled with cholic acid (a constituent of normal bile).

The pill doubles the chances of gall stones simply because it decreases the vitamin E content in the body so providing there is no history of rheumatic fever (in which case vitamin E is contraindicated as it may raise the blood pressure and burden the heart) in the family begin with 400 IUs of d-alphatocopherol acetate vitamin E daily and over a 3 month period raise to 1000 IUs and maintain this daily dose. (IUs is simply the measurement of international units.) D-alphatocopherol acetate is the preferred form of vitamin E as DL-alphatocopherol acetate is synthetic and so only half as potent.

Diet should be lacto-vegetarian with an emphasis on vegetable juices and raw and lightly cooked vegetables – plenty of fresh pears, grapes, apples, and grapefruit (which are particularly cleansing fruit for the gall bladder) as well as low fat yoghurt and cottage cheese and a complete avoidance of meat and saturated or denatured fats like margarine.

In acute attacks fast on diluted grape juice only and apply cold milk compresses to the liver. These are easily made by dipping a cotton cloth into cold milk. Renew these hourly and secure them with warm woollen blankets. Sip camomile tea and dandelion leaf tea.

THE REMOVAL OF GALL STONES

First ascertain their size by X-ray. Very large stones can become impacted in the duct necessitating surgery. Such stones can be dissolved with supplementation of choline, inositol, biotin, lecithin and the B-complex vitamins – but this must be done with the guidance of a medical herbalist experienced in these matters. Camomile tea is also said to dissolve gall stones to some extent.

If the stones are no bigger than your thumb nail you are safe to go ahead with an olive oil flush.

Fast for 3 days on grapefruit and grapefruit juice, eating and drinking as much of both of these as you like. On days 2 and 3 also drink at least 1 cup of slippery elm gruel made with water. On the fourth day continue with the grapefruit and also eat a large raw mixed salad with nuts at lunch and drink lots of juices and herbal tea. Dandelion root and parsley tea, beetroot, apple or black cherry juice are particularly recommended.

At 7 o'clock take 4 tablespoons of olive oil immediately followed by 1 tablespoon of freshly pressed unsweetened lemon juice. It is best to try to take the oil in one quick swallow holding your breath (and your nose too if it helps!) in order to reduce the sense of smell. Lemon juice 'cuts' through the taste of olive oil and stops any feeling of nausea. Distract yourself with some favourite music or a good television video while doing this.

Repeat this dosage every 15 minutes until you have drunk 1 pint (600 ml) of pure olive oil and ¼ pt (150 ml) of freshly squeezed lemon juice (six or seven lemons in all).

For those patients who find it truly horrendous drinking olive oil in such large quantities, I advise they sip it through a straw so that it does not contact the lips. I have found that this helps to control nausea considerably. After each dose of oil lie down on your right side with your knees tucked up and your hips elevated and stay in this position if you can for at least 2 hours unless actually sitting up to drink the olive oil and lemon juice.

N.B. If you vomit any olive oil continue to take the remainder but do not go back to the beginning.

Go to bed with a warm castor oil compress applied to the liver and if you do require further liquid take only herbal teas or water.

The following morning get up and take a chicory enema which will help to stimulate elimination. The stones that you pass with each bowel movement will vary in size, colour and number. Patients have brought into me stones the size of peas made of green bile pigment. I have seen bright red ones made of bilirubin. They range in size from gravel to beans and seeds and if stored in a jar you will find they will dissolve within a couple of days. In order to retrieve them (and this is for your own interest only) it is necessary to wash the bowel movements with running water through a sieve.

If you find your stomach swelling up with wind rub it gently or rock in a squatting position moving backwards and forwards. If you get nauseous sucking a cube of ice often helps.

N.B Calcarious stones cannot be removed by this method and hydrangea root will need to be used for this. During the course of a 3 day apple juice fast soak 2 oz (60 g) of hydrangea root in 2½ pt (1.5 litres) of apple juice. Keep the mixture covered in a cool room and stir or shake it several times a day. On the fourth day heat it to a rolling boil and then set aside. Once it is cool continue the fast but also take 1 oz (30 g) of this juice (strained) each waking hour until it is all used up.

I have used this method many times with patients with a great deal of success and although it does take a bit of courage it is extremely successful. Once back on a good diet it is important to take a daily dose of olive oil as part of the diet and a delicious way of doing this is to mix it up as part of a salad dressing with lemon juice, a touch of honey and rough grain mustard. A no fat or very low fat diet actually causes gall stones by decreasing bile flow so allow the bile to become concentrated. For continuing gall bladder maintenance take the adult formula recommended for jaundice (see p.148).

GASTRITIS

This is inflammation of the stomach lining without peptic ulceration. If left untreated it can evolve into a severe problem, so seek an accurate diagnosis from your doctor.

If pain radiates right through to the back, or if there is vomiting or severe abdominal pain, seek medical help immediately. If you suffer from weight loss, vomiting, constant diarrhoea or chronic constipation or pain is severe or persistent seek medical help urgently. What manifests as indigestion can, happily rarely, be cancer of the stomach, angina or pancreatitis.

Gastritis is made worse by smoking, alcohol, tea and coffee, spicy and fatty foods, sugar and other refined carbohydrates.

A good all-round remedy for gastritis is equal parts of:

comfrey leaf	*liquorice*
goldenseal	*calendula*

Make an infusion and sip a cup before each meal.

HAEMORRHOIDS AND ANAL FISSURE

This condition is a very painful one and surgery does nothing to prevent a recurrence. It only creates yet more scar tissue. An anal fissure, a split in the anus, is even more painful and because of its location can take a long time to heal.

DIET

Prevent constipation at all costs with a mainly raw diet high in fibre and drink plenty of liquids between meals, but not with meals. Sit on the toilet in the correct way (see p.128). Do daily abdominal strengthening yoga exercises and slant board exercises.

SLANT-BOARD

A slant board is simply a strong piece of wood big enough to lie on and positioned so that one end is supported several inches off the floor. Lie with your head at the lower end. Begin with a 3 in (7.5 cm) slope but increase this gradually as you get used to it to about 2 ft (60 cm). These exercises help to correct any prolapse in the body whether it be of the uterus, stomach, colon, bladder or anus and they are also useful for other problems including eye, ear and sinus.

Caution: A slant board should not be used by those suffering from hypertension, stomach ulcers, TB, appendicitis, abdominal cancer, those with a tendency to haemorrhage, or during a particularly heavy period.

1. With your head at the lower end of the slant board, breathe in slowly, raise your arms and stretch them above your head, reaching right back so that you touch the floor with the back of your hands behind you. When you get there breathe out and hold for a few seconds. Now breathe in again and bring your arms back. Rest them by your sides. Repeat this 10 times. On a 3 in (7.5 cm) slant you won't slide off but once you reach 2 ft (60 cm) you'll need to tuck your feet under a wide band of webbing or leather secured round the foot of the board to stay in place.

2. With your arms by your sides, breathe out fully and suck your stomach muscles in so that you feel as if your abdomen is touching your spine. Hold for a few seconds and snap out, at which point you will automatically breathe in again. Relax. Repeat 10 times.

3. Give yourself a stomach massage following the path of the colon from right to left, or if this is initially too strenuous, try rolling a small ball (about the size of a tennis ball) over your lower colon pressing deeply as you follow its path in a big clockwise circle.

4. Hold onto the side of the board firmly with your hands, slowly bend your knees so that they are resting on your chest. Don't worry if you can't do this fully at first – it will come in time. Now turn your head from side to side (5 times to each side) while holding this position. Then, if you can, lift your head slightly and rotate it, first clockwise, then anti-clockwise (3 times each way), then slowly replace your legs so that they are lying flat on the board.

5. Lift your legs vertically. You can bend your knees slightly if this makes it easier. Rotate one foot outwards in a circle 10 times, repeat with the other foot, then both together.

6. You will need to rest after the last exercise because it is quite strenuous. When you have got your breath back, lift your legs up again, this time keeping them as straight as you can at the knees. Bring them up to a vertical position both together. You may need to grip onto the board hard with the side of your hands to support yourself. Now lower your legs slowly back to the board. Repeat 4 times.

7. Cycle with your legs in the air working up to 25 rotations as a maximum.

8. Now relax and as you get your breath back squeeze all the muscles in your face hard, then let them go; as you do so you will feel the tension flooding from your face. As your breathing slows down to normal, feel the tension seeping out of your body. It sometimes helps to imagine it draining

*out of the top of your head. Rest and relax for a minimum of
5 minutes, letting the recharged blood circulate into your head. Get
up slowly.*

*A slant board must be long
enough for you to stretch out
and strong enough to support
your weight.*

To relieve pain sit in a hot sitz-bath on folded towels (see p.66) with four
drops of cypress oil added.

In acute cases where the haemorrhoids have prolapsed use cold sitz
baths with 4 drops of geranium oil added or insert an ice suppository.
Make a funnel of stiff waxed paper about the size of a tampon evenly rolled
so that the hole at the top is the same size as the hole at the bottom and seal
it well on the outside with Sellotape. Insert it upright into a piece of
plasticine and fill it with water. Freeze. Carefully remove it from the
plasticine and unwrap the paper. Insert it into the anus for 1 minute only
repeating once more later in the day with a new suppository. Alternatively
apply ice-cold witch hazel on a compress for as long as necessary. In the
case of anal fissure inject 4 fl oz (120 ml) cold witch hazel into the anus and
retain for 10 minutes.

After every bowel movement sponge with water and pat dry with a
flannel. *Do not* use toilet paper. Having done this apply pilewort ointment
internally and externally with the little finger.

To stop the bleeding of piles drink a wine glass of very hot mullein tea
sweetened with a little honey 3 times daily.

To shrink haemorrhoids make a decoction of:

2 parts dandelion	1 part chicory
2 parts stoneroot	½ part liquorice
1 part agrimony	1 part turkey rhubarb

and take a wine glass 3 times daily.

To heal an anal fissure take 10 drops of tormentil tincture in water
between meals 3 times daily and insert a suppository of goldenseal powder

moulded into a pessary with coconut butter (see below). Do this nightly before going to bed and protect the pants with a press-on sanitary towel as goldenseal stains bright yellow.

TO MAKE A SUPPOSITORY

In a double boiler melt a small piece of coconut butter and once it is liquid, mix in an equal quantity of finely powdered goldenseal to form a thick paste. Decant the paste on to an oiled wooden board or a marble slab and roll out into sausage pieces the width of your index finger. With a sharp knife carefully cut the sausage into lengths as long as your index finger. Store these on an oiled plate in the refrigerator until they are solid. Each suppository can then be individually wrapped in a little greaseproof paper and stored in a cool place.

HIATUS HERNIA

With a hiatus hernia the sphincter or valve between the stomach and the oesophagus is too high up in the chest so that acid refluxes up into the oesophagus causing heartburn, difficulty with swallowing, inflammation and possibly ulceration.

It can be caused by constipation, obesity, overloading the stomach persistently, a weak diaphragm or poor stomach tone, pregnancy, heavy weight-lifting, tight restricting clothes which cut in around the waist and hips, spicy foods, coffee and heavy smoking. The latter leads to a fall in sphincter pressure which then allows reflux to occur.

TREATMENT

1. *If constipation is a problem don't strain while sitting on the toilet (see p.127).*

2. *Avoid large meals, coffee, tea, alcohol, spices and refined carbohydrates and eat only when hungry. Don't drink with meals. Don't eat in the 3-hour period before going to bed.*

3. *Get a qualified yoga teacher to teach you some abdominal yoga exercises and do these daily.*

4. *Eat a diet rich in raw fruits, lightly cooked vegetables, wholegrains, nuts, beans and sprouted seeds and a modicum of white meat and fish but no red meat. Take flax-seed in juice 15 minutes before each meal, 1 level tablespoon per glass.*

5. *Lose weight if obese.*

6. *Stop smoking.*

7. *Chew well and slowly.*

8. *Do not wear corsets, tight jeans and belts and don't stoop – if you have to pick something up do so by bending at the knees while keeping a straight back.*

9. *For herbal formula see indigestion (p.146).*

10. *Raise the head of your bed 4 in (10 cm).*

HYPOGLYCAEMIA

There is a wide range of symptoms which may apply to hypoglycaemia and these need to be competently diagnosed by a medical practitioner familiar with this illness. Many do not even believe it exists. Symptoms may include any of the following: fatigue, irritability, indigestion, headaches, obesity, alcoholism, PMT, numbness, joint pain, nightmares, epilepsy, hyperactivity, anxiety, forgetfulness, breathlessness, migraine, vertigo, food cravings, blurred vision, a lack of sex drive, fainting and blackouts, angina, neuralgia, stomach cramps, depression, panic feelings, sweating, phobias, cold extremities, allergies, tinnitus and stomach ulcers. All this could be the stuff of a hypochondriac's dream! At some time in their lives most people experience one or more of these symptoms. This is usually due to transient hypoglycaemia which may be defined as a temporary or passing drop in blood sugar level. This is soon rectified by the body's own sugar regulatory mechanism. So once a balance is achieved the symptoms usually fade. If however there is a real long-term imbalance in sugar regulation the symptoms may well change but they will always return unless the imbalance is corrected. It would be helpful at this juncture to explain the mechanics of hypoglycaemia.

It is not a disease as such but a symptom of an imbalance in the blood glucose level showing as low blood sugar. There are three kinds of hypoglycaemia, severe, diabetic and reactive. Blood sugar level is normally confined witin a safe narrow range of variation by the hormone insulin secreted by the pancreas which reacts quickly to even the most subtle changes. Too much insulin results in too much sugar being driven into the cells and as a consequence a steep drop in blood sugar, which particularly affects the normal function of the brain.

Causes of hypoglycaemia include too much refined carbohydrate, chronic stress, food intolerance, thyroid problems, deficiencies of vitamin B complex, chromium, manganese, zinc, potassium and magnesium, skipped meals, excessive tea and coffee drinking, cigarettes and alcohol.

TREATMENT

Take 6 small meals of unrefined foods which are digested slowly. Avoid dried fruits and all fruit juices as well as salt, tea, coffee and alcohol and, of course, cigarettes. Eat fresh fruit with a small amount of protein like yoghurt and nuts. The only exception to this rule is bananas which are extremely high in sugar. Well-ripened ones may be eaten very occasionally once the treatment has continued for some months. Use only whole grain. Dairy products are fine if you do not have any intolerance and avocados and brewer's yeast are especially helpful. Natural honey needs to be used very moderately. A tub of yoghurt with 1 teaspoon of brewer's yeast is a good idea just before bed, to prevent blood sugar starvation while sleeping.

Fenugreek, dandelion root and liquorice are specifics for hypoglycaemia but *the prolonged use of goldenseal may actually cause hypoglycaemic symptoms*. Fenugreek must be used sparingly and warily and only for a short period of time. Never more than 3 wineglassfuls a day and it is to be taken not longer than 4 weeks at any one stretch. In the middle of a crisis drink a decoction of equal parts of gentian root and dandelion root. It tastes foul but works quickly to stabilize blood sugar levels.

Otherwise take 3–4 cups daily of a decoction of the following tea, and do not let it stand around or it will turn to an unappetizing jelly because of the mucilage of the fenugreek.

3 parts dandelion root	*2 parts mullein*
2 parts comfrey root	*1 part fenugreek*
2 parts gingseng	*1 part liquorice*
(Korean)	*1 part saffron*

After 4 weeks substitute 1 part of fenugreek with 1 part of kelp. Exercise initially should be gentle and sustained until a noticeable improvement is felt, at which time it should become gradually more vigorous. Gentle walking and lots of deep breathing are the best form of exercise at the beginning of treatment.

INDIGESTION *(Heartburn, Dyspepsia, Gastritis)*

Indigestion is a very vague term embracing any kind of abdominal discomfort after eating and is also called gastritis and dyspepsia.

It is one of the easiest complaints to rectify without resort to herbal medication if eating habits are altered. I abhor the use of commercial antacids. Made of sodium bicarbonate they are designed to relieve the excess acid which causes indigestion and heartburn by neutralizing the gastric acid in the stomach. But if used regularly, as they often are, they disrupt the natural acid/alkaline balance of the body causing alkalosis which can, if exacerbated by a substantial intake of dairy products, result in irreversible kidney damage. Indeed milk can actually increase hydrochloric acid secretion in some people which can make the symptoms worse. Many antacids contain aluminium, an excessive intake of which is extremely poisonous. Aluminium accumulates in the liver, interfering with its working, it affects the kidneys causing nephitis and degeneration and may cause non-specific joint problems by affecting bone metabolism. The last effect is because an aluminium overload also affects the central nervous system, particularly the parathyroid, influencing the degree to which it responds to low serum calcium by excreting parathyroid hormone.

TREATMENT

1. *Chew properly and thoroughly.*

2. *Do not take liquids with meals unless it is a medicinal herbal tea. Even soup needs to be drunk 15 minutes before or half an hour after any meal.*

3. *Avoid salt and all spices, sugar, tea, coffee, alcohol, soda, refined carbohydrates including sugar, fried foods and anything else which you know acts as a gastric irritant.*

4. *Do not eat excessively hot or cold foods.*

5. *Do not eat if distressed. If you are famished slowly sip a glass of vegetable juice at room temperature.*

6. *Do not eat if you are ill.*

7. *Eat in unhurried, relaxed surroundings. No arguments at the table.*

8. *Eat small meals and always leave the table feeling you have room for just a little more.*

9. *If food is eaten too soon after a previous meal the natural pace of the digestive process will be disrupted. So allow 2 hours after a fruit meal, 3 hours after a vegetable one and 4 hours after a combined meal of proteins, fat and carbohydrate.*

10. *I have often found correcting poor food combinations an excellent and speedy way to rectify indigestion (see* Food Combining for Health *by Jean Joice and Doris Grant, published by Thorsons, 1985). If this does not offer sufficient help also try separating out starches from citrus fruits.*

11. *Consider the possibility of food intolerance, especially dairy products and wheat (see allergy, p.248).*

12. *Consider candidiasis (see thrush, p.123).*

13. *Some indigestion in pregnancy is to be expected. So eat small meals and lots of green vegetables which are alkaline and help to* achieve the correct pH.

14. *Distortion of the thoracic vertebrae can affect the stomach. See an osteopath.*

15. *An iridologist will easily determine if your stomach is hypo- or hyperacid. Hydrochloric acid deficiency is a common problem especially in those over 50 and can be corrected by taking 200–600 mg of pepsin and betaine hydrochloride before each meal. I have found however that some of my patients react badly to the initial introduction of digestive enzymes and in these cases I begin by fasting them on freshly squeezed lemon juice, 1 fl oz (25 ml) to 8 fl oz (250 ml) water gradually increasing to half and half before introducing the enzymes (for suppliers of enzymes see Appendix).*

Hyperacidity can be corrected with the following formula.
Equal parts of:

camomile	meadowsweet
liquorice	sweet flag
marshmallow	

Take one cup 15 minutes before a meal. If you have high blood pressure omit the liquorice and substitute fennel or ginger instead.

If indigestion is acute fast on carrot juice only for 3 days. Try to drink at least eight 8 fl oz (250 ml) glasses.

JAUNDICE *(Hepatitis)*

The initial symptoms of jaundice may be hard to recognize, mimicking influenza with a general feeling of weakness and fever and headache. Certainly the liver may be tender and enlarged and the mood understandably depressed. There may or may not be grey faeces, dark urine, and yellowed, itchy skin or yellowed whites of eyes.

N.B. Serious cases may be fatal so if in any doubt seek medical help immediately.

Jaundice generally only occurs if overall resistance is low, so rejuvenate the liver with a high-protein nutrient-rich diet, excluding all meat and fish but including wheat germ, low fat yoghurt, buttermilk, tofu, brewer's yeast, lecithin granules (2 tablespoons daily), spirulena (4 teaspoons daily),

as well as plenty of green leafy vegetables for their chlorophyll content. A good juice to drink copiously would be:

8 fl oz (250 ml) carrot juice	2 fl oz (50 ml) parsley
6 fl oz (150 ml) nettles	2 fl oz (50 ml) watercress

Note that all nettles need to be picked by early summer and use only the green tender leafy tips. It is possible to freeze them without losing too much of their goodness. Simply ensure they are clean and bag them in plastic, sealing with a rubber band. If it is impossible to comply with this leave out the nettles and substitute celery juice instead in the same quantity.

The absolutely golden rule is to avoid all saturated fats and alcohol. Drink plenty of water, herbal teas and honey and lemon. Ensure your practitioner monitors ammonia build-up while you are on this diet especially if liver damage is severe.

Chicory enemas morning and evening will help to relieve the liver of bile – as will hot and cold compresses of feverfew or hot castor oil compresses placed over the liver area. Warm abdominal compresses of marigold petals are also helpful. In the case of children and babies boil up 8 oz (250 g) dried marigold petals for 30 minutes in a gallon (4.5 litres) of water and strain this into the bath. Top up with more warm water if necessary and allow the child to soak in the bath for a minimum of 20 minutes. In the case of a baby ensure the head is firmly supported of course. For children give a tea of:

3 parts barberry root
1 part wild yam

Sweeten with honey.

Dosage according to age (see p.74) but to be taken 3 times daily. For adults give equal parts:

agrimony	ginger root
catnip	parsley root
cramp bark	peppermint
fennel seed	wild yam

Two size '0' capsules of the finely powdered herb 15 minutes before a meal.

MALABSORPTION

A complete and thorough digestion of foods is vital if food is to be absorbed properly. It is not what you eat but what you assimilate that counts. The digestive process begins with the smell and anticipation of food which stimulates the production of pepsin in the saliva, an enzyme which breaks down starches, right through to the beneficial bacteria in the lower colon which prevent the colonization of fungus, assisting peristalsis and flushing out toxic bacterial metabolites in the faeces. If any one of the myriad digestive processes go wrong all sorts of distressing symptoms can result.

Malabsorption due to food intolerance is very common as is endocrine imbalance (as with hypoglycaemics and diabetes) which makes weight gain difficult. People who stay very thin in spite of eating like the proverbial horse are not necessarily to be envied because they are often absorbing very little food, thereby cultivating all sorts of future problems. Such people often have food appearing in bowel movements undigested and this is a sure sign of malabsorption.

TREATMENT

To be underweight is not as rare as you might suppose, confronted as we are with an avalanche of advice about melting the solid flesh. Nearly 30% of women in their 20s are underweight; 35% of women in their 30s. Not all of them have diagnosable anorexia nervosa by any means.

A word of caution here: if you are underweight according to the insurance charts, but look great, feel terrific and have bags of energy, you have got absolutely nothing to worry about. But if you tire readily, are highly strung and become easily ill, it is time you put on some weight. This means a diet rich in whole grains and pulses with a reasonable amount of cold pressed oils and natural sweets like halva and nuts and seed cereal bars. It is quality you want, not quantity, so do not get sidetracked by the banana split. Go for lentil soup with wholemeal bread and butter. Refined sweets and carbohydrates rob the appetite and displace the foods that really count. Half a cup of nuts daily will help you put on nearly a pound a week as they are 400 calories. Half a large avocado is 185 calories, and you can bump that up with a delicious vinaigrette dressing. Aim for 3⅓ oz (100 g) of protein and 2 oz (60 g) of fat from unsaturated sources like cold pressed oils as well as 60% unrefined carbohydrate.

Finally, if you are hyperactive, learn to calm down. It will help you digest your food properly. Do not neglect exercise; it will help you put on weight in the right places. The following formulation will also help with digestion and ensure the proper distribution of nutrients throughout the bloodstream:

3 parts papaya seeds	*1 part fennel*
1 part catnip	*1 part gentian*
1 part cayenne	*1 part wild yam*

Take two size '0' capsules at the beginning of each meal with sips of unsweetened pineapple juice. Also ensure your diet is rich in foods containing zinc. Natural sources of zinc include brewer's yeast, seeds (especially pumpkin and sunflower seeds), green leafy vegetables, and above all liver. Make it liver which is not groaning with secondhand antibiotics as is the case with ox and pig's liver. Organically reared chicken liver is probably your best source.

STOMACH ULCERS *(Gastric ulcer)*

The majority of these ulcers tend to occur in the part of the stomach that leads into the duodenum. Factors which cause stomach ulcers include delayed gastric emptying, over-secretion of hydrochloric acid, a deranged stomach lining and a wash-back of bile from the duodenum. They are certainly worsened by drugs, especially aspirin, and steroids, non-steroidal anti-inflammatory drugs such as Indocicl and cigarettes, alcohol and to a lesser extent tea, coffee, vinegar, spices and of course prolonged stress. Interestingly, people with an A blood group are more prone to stomach ulcers than anyone else and stomach ulcers are almost unknown in so-called primitive societies, which means an unrefined diet must surely play a large part in their prevention.

TREATMENT

This needs to be individually tailored but I have found that freshly juiced raw potatoes, ½ glass every 3 hours, are very helpful if the patient is not too emaciated. As potato juice tastes terrible by itself I would recommend that it is mixed with equal quantities of carrot juice to make it more palatable. Alternatively add it to a home-made vegetable soup once the soup has been taken off the heat and just before it is about to be served. Slippery elm gruel is also very soothing as is fenugreek tea which can be made a little more palatable with the addition of liquorice. Raw fruit and vegetables should be avoided initially as should fried or spicy foods, tea, chocolate, coffee, alcohol, red meat and refined carbohydrate and whole grain. Well-cooked millet is permissible and avocados, well-ripened bananas, yams and baked potatoes are particularly well tolerated. Once the condition begins to heal whole grains, raw goat's milk and raw eggs can be introduced gradually.

All the rules of proper digestion as outlined in indigestion apply here (see indigestion, p.146).

If you really want to take the bull by the horns Dr Christopher, my

teacher, has had great success using cayenne pepper to heal stomach ulcers. One teaspoon 3 times daily in freshly pressed vegetable juice. Dr Christopher tells a wonderful story about the husband of a student of his who kept taunting him about his profession whenever he saw him. This man suffered so much pain with his stomach ulcer that one night, finding the pain beyond endurance, he decided to kill himself. To his disgust when he opened the family medicine cabinet looking for something which would assist him to do so he found his wife had cleared it of everything except one jar of cayenne pepper. Imagining the pain of digesting something so fiery would probably kill him he mixed it all with some water and gulped down the lot. He then buried his head under a pillow to drown his dying screams and much to his amazement woke up the next morning feeling much better than he had done for many years. He continued to use the cayenne under his wife's supervision until the ulcer had healed completely.

I often relate this amusing story to my patients who are understandably dubious about taking cayenne pepper. Initially it certainly does taste a bit fiery (although not nearly as much as when cooked) but it is a taste the palate soon adjusts to and no, it doesn't hurt the stomach. (See contra-indication of cayenne pepper, p.78).

CHAPTER 7
URINARY SYSTEM

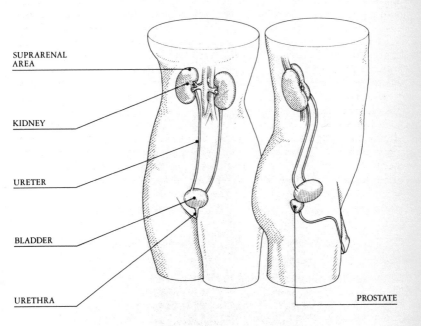

SUPRARENAL
AREA

KIDNEY

URETER

BLADDER

URETHRA

PROSTATE

CYSTITIS

Cystitis is a bacterial infection which inflames the bladder. Recurrent infections of the bladder are not uncommon especially in women. The short length of the female urethra and its proximity to the anus are part of the reason for this. But abnormalities in spinal structure can also cause reflex irritation and this should be checked. A prolapsed colon can put unnecessary pressure on the bladder.

AVOIDING CYSTITIS

1. *Drink plenty of fluid, at least 4 pints (2.5 litres) a day if possible.*

2. *Eat food which will encourage the health of the immune system, i.e. food that is 80% raw and consists of natural and unprocessed food, low in sugar, alcohol and animal fat.*

3. *Pay special attention to personal hygiene. After a bowel movement the anus should be cleaned from front to back so that no germs are carried towards the external opening of the bladder and this also applies after urination.*

4. *Don't use soaps, detergents and perfumed toiletries when washing the vaginal and anal areas. Plain water is good enough and running water is even better.*

5. *Don't wear nylon underwear, tights or trousers.*

If none of these measures helps, ask your practitioner to check for the possibility of chronic candidiasis (see p.123); also consider the possibility that you may be allergic to a specific food (see p.248).

TREATMENT

Follow a liquid fast for 5 days drinking apple juice, mineral water, and 3 cups of cider vinegar and honey mixed with hot water during the course of the day. Potassium broth and barley water is also helpful (see p.135).

Cranberry juice is particularly useful because it reduces the adhesion of bacteria to the membrane walls. Include 4 glasses of this a day during the course of your fasting.

After the fast go on to a vegan diet ensuring that your fluid intake is still high. The bowels must be opened at least once daily to ensure that there is no possibility of retaining toxins which can be recirculated into the blood and eventually have to be handled by the kidneys (see constipation, p.127).

Crouching over a wide deep bowl of steaming hot camomile and thyme infusion also helps. If this is uncomfortable place the basin underneath a chair from which you have removed the base. Surround yourself and the chair in a heavy blanket and keep as warm as possible. As the steam subsides keep topping it up with hot water and do this for 20 minutes twice a day. It may sound like a lot of trouble but I have found this even more effective than the usually recommended hot sitz-bath for pain relief. Hot compresses of parsley root and glycerine applied to the bladder and kidneys are also helpful.

Take as much as you can manage of the following tea – and not less than four cups daily:

4 parts marshmallow	1 part dandelion
1 part borage	½ part ginger root
1 part cleavers	1 part horsetail

If there is blood in the urine apply a poultice of cornsilk tassels to the kidneys and abdomen and add 4 parts of cornsilk to the formulation above.

Also take the antibiotic on page 28 as long as the infection lasts.

INCONTINENCE

Incontinence is an enormously widespread problem among the middle-aged and elderly but is one of those subjects that is simply not discussed. It can be caused by a number of physical and psychological factors including obstetrical trauma, poor pelvic floor tone, the neglect of pre- and post-natal exercises, obesity, swollen prostate gland and increased interabdominal pressure. As long as there is no organic defect or illness incontinence can be corrected herbally even if it is due to a loss of tone of the sphincter muscle of the bladder. The following is an excellent formula for incontinence; it needs to be taken over a period of several months to have a good effect.

Equal parts of:

agrimony	parsley root
goldenseal	sumach
horsetail	uva ursi
juniper berries	white pond lily
marshmallow root	yarrow

Take two size '0' capsules morning and evening with a wine glass of parsley tea.

Exercises that strengthen the pelvic floor also help and if you are pregnant these should have been explained to you by your gynaecologist. If incontinence is caused by any internal prolapse the slant board exercises

will help (see p.141). Swimming using the breast stroke will help build up pelvic floor muscles as will abdominal exercises and alternate hot and cold sitz-baths, this is particularly important after having a baby.

KIDNEY STONES

These stones are usually made of calcium oxalate but some stones contain urates, phosphates, or cystine and it is important that the practitioner treating them knows exactly what type of stone is present in order to ensure success. Certain stones are caused by kidney disease and there are many dietary factors that increase the risk of kidney-stone formation including refined carbohydrates, particularly sugar which can increase the absorption of calcium from the gut and elevate its level in the urine of certain prone individuals. It has been proved that vegetarians have a far lower chance of forming kidney stones due to the lower instance of uric and oxalic acid, both of which are involved in stone formation. People who consume large quantities of calcium containing antacids together with milk as they attempt to soothe indigestion or peptic ulcers can also be risking developing high blood calcium levels and so kidney stones. Alcohol, salt, and the oxalic acid naturally occuring in certain foods like tea, coffee, chocolate, peanuts, spinach, rhubarb and beetroot can also aggravate stone formation.

No matter what type of stone you have you should eat plenty of dietary fibre. Wheat and bran are both high in phytat which reduces calcium absorption. Eliminate intakes of animal proteins especially meat and cut out milk. (There are far superior sources of calcium including tahini, a sesame-seed paste readily available from health-food shops, sardines, millet, oats and all dark green leafy vegetables.) Avoid refined carbohydrates particularly those that are sugary. Ensure that plenty of mineral water is drunk. Reduce alcohol consumption and cut out salt altogether. Those with oxalate-containing stones or high oxalate levels in the urine should avoid food rich in oxalate acid, previously catalogued. In such instances B_6 and magnesium may also be useful. B_6 controls the body's production of oxalic acid increasing oxalate secretion while magnesium helps increase the solubility of oxalate in the urine.

EMERGENCIES

There is no worse pain known than a stuck kidney stone. Apply a poultice of hops, mullein and lobelia, as hot as possible, to the kidneys if pain is severe. Keep the poultice on with a hot water bottle and leave on for 1 hour. If after this time the pain still persists administer an enema of goldenrod tea. You are unlikely to be able to attain anything by mouth during the course of a severe attack. Sit in a hot sitz-bath for half an hour applying a cold compress to the wrist and another cold compress to the forehead. While doing so massage the stomach lightly downwards from the navel to the pubic hair line which will help to gently move the stone into the bladder. Then get out of the bath and apply a herbal poultice for a further hour, repeating this process until such time that the stone has passed into the bladder. If you feel like drinking take a little plaintain tea.

Please note all this treatment is best supervised by a consultant medical herbalist but I have detailed it clearly in case one is not available.

Follow-up treatment will include alternate hot and cold sitz-baths because the stone must not be allowed to remain in the bladder. This together with plantain tea will help to remove it and the only necessity for an operation is if the size of the stone defies natural physical measures.

A good general maintenance tea to be drunk as a preventative is equal parts of:

hydrangea	*stone root*
marshmallow	*wild carrot*

Drink 3 cups daily with meals. If there is even a hint of infection add 3 parts of echinacea to this mixture and increase the dose to 6 cups daily.

NEPHRITIS

Nephritis is a serious disease of the kidneys and requires the expert attention of a qualified medical herbalist well versed in its treatment. The worst cases I have tried to help are those which have been treated with almost non-stop courses of antibiotics over a prolonged period of time. There are many herbs which will actually irritate a diseased kidney, hence the need for expert help. Chronic cases may take 2 to 3 years to heal.

OEDEMA *(Water retention)*

Fluid retention in the body, particularly in the fingers, ankles and feet, is more likely to occur in women and is made worse by standing, sitting or lying down for long periods of time or by hot weather.

The long-term use of diuretics often increases fluid retention as the body compensates for the biochemical changes they cause. To my distress I often encounter patients who have been on them for many years but I do find that once they are weaned off them the fluid retention although initially worse, then settles down, particularly if salt and refined carbohydrates have been meticulously avoided. I have also found that some food allergies, particularly meat and dairy products, often produce significant fluid retention and of course an excessive intake of salt can also cause fluid retention. Oedema in pregnancy is often exacerbated by lack of vitamin B_6 and a therapeutic dose to correct this may be as high as 300 mg daily, but

do seek professional help to determine what your level of B₆ should be. Daily fomentations of ginger over the kidneys are also hepful as are hand and foot baths of equal quantities of dandelion and garlic.

An iridology test will determine the cause of the problem whether it lies in the kidneys, or in the liver's inability to handle toxins and so is diverting too many of them to the kidneys, or in the blood or lymphatic circulatory system. Protein deficiency can cause oedema but this is rare except under extreme conditions.

Certainly there are herbs which act as diuretics (the most effective being dandelion and yarrow) but nearly all water retention can be helped by a vegetable fast rich in potassium. The vegetables need to be juiced and can be taken for anything up to 3 weeks but such a lengthy fast *must* be done under appropriate supervision. A useful alternative is a water melon flush where nothing but water melon and its seeds are eaten for 3 days. I have used this treatment on oedemous patients with remarkable effect. Such a regime should then be followed by a balanced vegetarian diet until the problem has cleared.

Saunas and Turkish baths will help to reduce perspiration and alternate hot and cold sitz-baths are also useful. Vigorous skin brushing towards the heart is helpful.

Danielle Ryman, a well-known aromatherapist, recommends massaging the limbs with one drop each of petigrain, orange and rose essential oils mixed with 4–5 teaspoons of almond oil. She also advises adding this to the bath water.

CHAPTER 8
REPRODUCTIVE SYSTEM

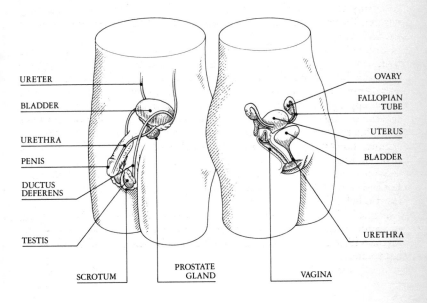

URETER

BLADDER

URETHRA

PENIS

DUCTUS
DEFERENS

TESTIS

SCROTUM

PROSTATE
GLAND

OVARY

FALLOPIAN
TUBE

UTERUS

BLADDER

URETHRA

VAGINA

BREAST FEEDING

You have heard it said before but I will say it again – breast is best. The only medical reason for a baby not being breast fed is if the mother has active TB, typhoid fever or malaria. Breast milk is germ-free, readily available, requires no preparation and comes at the right temperature. Most importantly, it is full of antibodies that protect the baby against disease and immunize her against infections. Breast-fed babies are less likely to suffer from allergies and the lactoferrin in breast milk stops the growth of certain malign yeast and bacteria in the baby. Breast-fed babies are less likely to become fat than their bottle-fed counterparts and suckling a baby produces oxytoxin which causes the muscles in the womb to contract and ao assists it back into place. There is now a suggestion that breast feeding lowers the incidence of breast cancer and will help you lose weight and get back into shape more quickly. Breast milk is also lower in salt and higher in vitamins A and C, and zinc and iron than cow's milk. It also contains a thyroid hormone which the baby is unable to produce for herself. It has been clearly shown that breast-fed babies have fewer gastro-intestinal, ear, respiratory, viral and yeast infections, less meningitis and more benign lacto-bacilli in their stores.

A further indisputable advantage of breast milk is that gentle, controlled medication for the baby can be given easily by giving the mother herbs – she will transport them in easily digestible form to her baby. I have used in precisely this way heart's ease and the calcium formula to cure cradle cap, catnip and fennel to soothe colic, camomile to soothe digestive upsets, and tormentil for diarrhoea.

Do remember that alcohol, nicotine, caffeine, opiates, tranquillizers, quinine, antibiotics and laxatives, as well as vitamin C, all pass through into breast milk in small amounts. Barbiturates, aspirin, iodine, bromides and ergot all flood into breast milk copiously.

Good milk is thin and flows easily. It should smell good, be pure (almost bluish) in colour and taste sweet. To test your milk, put a little on your finger nail and tilt the finger upwards. If the milk does not trickle down easily it is too thick. Herbs which improve the quality of milk are marshmallow and borage. Try the very young leaves of borage as a delicious alternative to cucumber in your salads, and the beautiful blue flowers can be used in the same way. Herbs which increase the flow of breast milk are fennel, cinnamon, anise, blessed thistle, vervain, fenugreek, goat's rue and caraway.

TO THIN BREAST MILK

Drink 2 fl oz (60 ml) cider vinegar mixed with a tablespoon of honey in hot water twice daily and eat hyssop, thyme and borage in salads. If they are only available dried make teas of them and drink 1 wineglass 3 times a day.

TO THICKEN BREAST MILK

Eat lots of soupy grains (such as green and orange lentils) and lace them liberally with garlic and onions. Add blessed thistle, comfrey and red clover blossom to the diet. The flowers of red clover make an unusual and tasty addition to salads in the summer.

INABILITY TO PRODUCE BREAST MILK

False unicorn mixed with other galactagogues (substances that produce milk secretion) is believed to encourage the flow of breast milk. Certainly a baby's frequent sucking action helps. I am also told that Sicilian women who have never had babies sometimes induce a flow of milk by putting a drop of goat's milk on to the nipple whenever the baby is about to give up sucking at the non-productive breast. After persisting with this for 2 weeks their own breast milk begins to flow. It is certainly worth a try if you are apparently unable to breast feed but very much want to do so.

CERVICAL DYSPLESIA (Abnormal cell development)

A cervical smear detects all changes in the cervix including dysplesais some of which may become cancerous in future. So any such problem needs to be treated as a matter of urgency. Between 30% and 50% of women with cervical dysplesia later graduate to cervical cancer. However, pre-cancerous lesions can be reversed with natural therapy and I have also had some success with cancerous ones. I put the patient on a 6 months' regime of raw food in which fish is allowed only twice weekly and 8 fl oz (250 ml) of freshly squeezed carrot juice is taken daily.

Make vaginal boluses using coconut butter and in each bolus put five drops of cypress oil. Insert one of these every night and douche the following morning with equal parts of infused goldenseal and yellow dock. Take 20 drops of the following tincture 3 times a day. Equal parts of: dandelion, garlic, burdock, yellow dock, red clover.

I would advise professional herbal medical supervision even for mild cervical dysplasia and certainly, of course, for cancerous dysplasia, together with regular monitoring from your specialist or doctor.

ENDOMETRIOSIS (Cysts in womb)

The blanket that lines the uterus in which the fertilized egg is planted is called the endometrium. Inadequate hygiene before, during or after love-making (for example, a dirty finger, or one that has been previously inserted into the anus and not washed, inserted into the vagina), childbirth, abortion, uterine curettage and carelessly inserted forceps are all means of introducing harmful bacteria into the endometrium. A poor diet and lifestyle, a wrongly positioned womb, retained placenta, lead poisoning and blood disorders also leave the uterus vulnerable to infection.

Endometriosis begins when small nests of cells stray into the pelvis, ovaries, fallopian tubes and bladder, forming tiny cysts. They bleed with the rest of the endometrium with each menstruation but are not evidenced until the cysts are stretched and swollen which may take as much as 10 or 15 years.

Endometriosis affects 5–10% of women between the ages of 25 and 45, and symptoms include chronic lower abdominal pain, dysmenorrhoea, pain after love-making and infertility.

Douche every day with equal parts of goldenseal, echinacea and squaw vine, retaining the douche for as long as possible, 20 minutes is ideal. Also take the following formulation:

3 parts echinacea	*1 part liquorice*
1 part blessed thistle	*1 part marshmallow*
1 part cayenne	*1 part parsley*
1 part goldenseal	*1 part squaw vine*

Take two size '0' capsules of the finely powdered herbs with each meal. If the condition does not improve considerably in 6 months seek the advice of a professional medical herbalist.

It may sound strange, but the absence of ovulation and menstruation will effect a cure in many cases. This means that if you are a young woman intending to have a family at some point the solution may well be the simple one of getting pregnant. If the problem recurs, you could consider spacing children closer together rather than waiting. In other words, endometriosis can be alleviated by interrupting normal ovarian function, and it is for this reason that it is often spontaneously improved once the menopause starts. Above all, remember that complete recovery may well be possible if the disease is diagnosed and treated early. So do not hesitate to seek the advice of a gynaecologist if in doubt. The blood-filled sacs can easily be detected by fibre-optic examination or laparoscopy.

GENITAL HERPES

Cold sores on the mouth are classified as the Herpes Simplex Virus Type 1. A closely related virus, Herpes Simplex Type 2, can affect the vulva, cervix and upper vagina. The distinction between the two viruses lies mainly in the area they infect, but many scientists now feel that differences between type one and two are diminishing.

Most genital herpes is caused by contact with a type 2 virus and is picked up during sexual intercourse. But it is possible to transmit the type 1 virus from a cold sore on the mouth to the genitals during oral sex. Type 1 virus is not implicated in the development of cervical cancer (as type 2 is), but the physical symptoms can be just as upsetting as those of type 2. They may begin with fever, swollen and tender lymph nodes,

excruciating itching, and painful blisters along the vulva which
graduate to inflammation around the urethral area, making urination excessively painful. In infections with Herpes Virus Type 2
the cervix may become red, irritated and ulcerated, resulting in
discharge and vaginal spotting. If you have had no previous encounter
with any of the other herpes viruses like shingles or cold sores, you will
not have acquired appropriate antibodies. Under these circumstances
getting Herpes Virus Type 2 can be very bad news.

For treatment see cold sores, p.89. Apply the tincture recommended
there directly to the affected area after a cold shower. Patients complain
that this stings but say it is preferable to the constant itching. Also take
60 drops of the tincture in a little water 3 times a day with meals.

If pain during urination is excruciating, spraying cold water on to the
vulva area from the shower head while urinating will help. Otherwise sit in
a bowl of cold water while urinating. Cold yoghurt compresses applied for
10 minutes at a time 6 times daily over the affected area may give some
relief.

All women who contract genital herpes should have a cervical smear at
least once yearly and be honest with any prospective sexual partner. Men
with genital herpes should be equally honest of course. The fact that the
ignorant public still see herpes as a penalty for sexual freedom has led to
unnecessary feelings of guilt among many who have become infected
without being promiscuous. Sexual and physical contact should be avoided
while the virus is still active.

IMPOTENCE

I hate labels. Frigidity, nymphomania and impotence are vague terms and
do not have any precise meanings. However, once a woman is labelled
frigid, or a man impotent, or worse still such terms are self-inflicted the
person concerned naturally becomes anxious, inadequate, helpless and
hopeless. No woman is frigid and no man impotent. All men, given the
time, the patience, and the counselling can maintain an erection and
control ejaculation. Similarly, a woman given understanding, sympathy
and gentle coaching through exploratory exercises by herself, and then
with her partner, can not only enjoy sex, but can reach orgasm without too
much difficulty.

The only real prerequisite is loving your partner. If you don't, or your
partner does not excite you sexually, nothing on earth is going to solve
your problems and save the situation. No amount of sexual counselling,
sexual therapy, experimentation and exercises will mend the rift between
you if love and feeling are gone.

During the sexual excitement phase a woman's uterus, vagina, clitoris
and vulva fill with blood and swell until they reach a state of vasocongestion,
swelling which often causes tension and pressure. Some doctors have

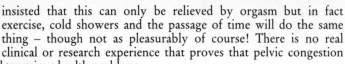

insisted that this can only be relieved by orgasm but in fact exercise, cold showers and the passage of time will do the same thing – though not as pleasurably of course! There is no real clinical or research experience that proves that pelvic congestion can lead to serious health problems.

So let's scotch the myth that women must have an orgasm in order to be healthy and if they don't something is wrong.

But if it is orgasms you want, bear in mind that the single most common cause for a woman failing to reach orgasm is inadequate stimulation, although there are other possibilities – underdevelopment of the endocrine and nervous system, diabetes, fear or ignorance, or immaturity of the female or male genitalia.

Impotence in men has many causes but is often related to an enlarged prostate, so if this is a problem, see it as a warning of incipient prostate enlargement and get this checked. Other factors such as very bad vitamin deficiencies or heavy metal poisoning may affect sexual performance. Remember too that many prescription drugs have impotence or frigidity as a side-effect; they include Aldomet, Bentyl, Hydropes, Inderal and Reserpine.

Physical and physiological causes will of course need to be looked at individually. The following formula may help.

Equal parts of:

cinnamon	*prickly ash bark*
damiana	*sarsaparilla*
liquorice	*saw palmetto*

Take two size '0' capsules of the finely powdered herbs with each meal daily for six months only. If you have high blood pressure leave out the liquorice, substituting the same amount of ginger.

Women should add to this formulation equal parts of false unicorn. Damiana has a marked effect on the sexual system, while prickly ash bark will stimulate the blood circulation. Cinnamon is warming; sarsaparilla is an excellent blood-purifier; saw palmetto is rich in natural hormones; and liquorice will boost the adrenal glands and help to counteract stress.

Alternating hot and cold sitz-baths taken twice daily are excellent as are icy cold plunges up to the waist after a sauna.

It is advisable to detoxify the body so begin with an initial fast for 3 or 4 days on fruit or vegetable juices and follow this with a diet of fruit, vegetables, nuts, grains and seeds to further detoxify the body.

Avoid hormones in animal products. Modern meat rearing now involves administering hormones to animals in the form of ear implants. One of these hormones, zeranol, is a form of oestrogen made from fusarium. This hormone occurs naturally in crops cut in damp weather, and given our miserable climate the level of this hormone in our food can be quite high.

A large percentage of women in Britain are noticeably zinc-deficient and some animals ingest copper-containing formulae which makes this balance even worse because copper is antagonistic to zinc. A copper IUD is not advisable for this reason. A zinc deficiency can be responsible for impotence, infertility and low sperm count, and reduced sex drive. Because zinc supplementation can reduce copper absorption it should be taken one hour or more before or after mealtimes to avoid interaction with other dietary elements.

Anyone taking long-term steroids, penicillin or diuretics and all alcoholics need to have their zinc status regularly monitored.

INFERTILITY

I have worked with this problem in men and women very successfully over several years now. The final results, the safe delivery of a healthy baby, has generally provoked in the medical profession such dismissive comments as 'well these things happen and we don't know why', this even in the case of parents both of whom have been pronounced infertile and very often after many years of allopathic intervention in the form of operations or fertility drugs. My success is not unique (and indeed it depends on the total enthusiastic cooperation of both the man and woman in question) but is enjoyed by other practitioners trained in the same way as I have been. The general approach is simple: clean out the body of all toxins and make sure that assimilation of nutrition is at its best and most efficient. I would strongly advise that infertile men and women have an iridology test which will help to establish the possible causes of infertility which are particularly relevant to them. In my own experience I have found far too many infertile women think only of their reproductive organs when the problem is more likely to be one of auto-intoxication because another organ or system is malfunctioning.

If a woman has been trying unsuccessfully to conceive for more than 6 months and she is under 30, check (by using a temperature chart and detecting any change in cervical mucus) that sex is not taking place on infertile days in the month consistently. Bear in mind that anxiety about feeling infertile can inhibit conception. Having a holiday is a good way of helping both partners to relax. A woman's natural fertility will decline after the age of 30 but it is unusual not to be able to conceive a second or third child if the first conception and pregnancy was successful. The good news is that although precise causes of infertility in a couple are often difficult to establish at least 50% of infertile patients can be helped medically and my own experience shows that natural methods of treatment enjoy an even higher success rate.

With repeated ejaculations the number of sperm in the ejaculate decline. A high live-sperm count per ejaculate is known to be essential for conception to take place. So if the male has ejaculated several times over

the preceding few days conception is less likely to occur on the day the woman ovulates because the semen will contain insufficient sperm. For this reason it is probably best to abstain from sexual intercourse for 2 or 3 days before ovulation is expected to occur.

On the other hand it is not advisable to abstain too long since sperm can live in the male reproductive system for only about 10 days. Consequently the number of healthy sperm in the ejaculate is known to be reduced in men that have not ejaculated for more than a week.

If a woman stands up and walks around immediately after making love most of the seminal fluid will leak out her vagina. To give as many sperm as possible a chance of beginning their journey to the fallopian tubes into which the egg-cell will be or has been released, it is a good idea to lie quietly on the bed for 20 minutes or more after making love with the buttocks raised slightly on a pillow and the knees bent upwards. By using this position the semen will be encouraged to bathe the cervix.

In general my advice would be that both partners adhere strictly to a mucus-free diet for as long as necessary (for details of such a diet see p.255). In general you tend to find that thorough bowel cleansing for both partners is helpful. For women the following formulation is good for cleansing all the organs contained in the pelvic and abdominal area, for purifying the blood, regulating periods, reducing swelling and soothing any vaginal irritation, relaxing the nervous system and killing any parasites, it is also rich in iron, potassium and vitamin B and C. Infertile women should take extra vitamin E up to 1200 IUs a day, providing their blood pressure is normal and there is no history of rheumatic fever.

Equal parts of:

blessed thistle	goldenseal
comfrey	lobelia
dandelion	marshmallow
false unicorn	parsley
ginger	red clover blossom

Infuse and drink 3 or 4 cups daily. Dry skin brushing, a rigorous exercise programme, and individual attention to determine preventive measures (see Chapter 1) will all be necessary.

In some instances I have found it necessary to use vaginal pessaries of equal parts of the following herbs:

comfrey root	red raspberry leaves
goldenseal root	slippery elm bark
marshmallow root	yellow dock root

Insert a vaginal bolus every second day and on the night of the second day douche with equal parts of yellow dock root and red clover blossom tea used tepid, before inserting another bolus. Douche again 2 days later. Keep this up on a cyclical basis and on the seventh day rest and fast. In order to rid the body of a sufficient quantity of toxins it is often necessary to use this bolus following this pattern for between 6 weeks and 6 months.

Dr Christopher offers the following formula to assist the function of developing the hormone and oestrogen balance in both men and women. Equal parts of:

black cohosh	*liquorice root*
blessed thistle	*sarsaparilla*
false unicorn root	*squaw vine*
ginseng	

The dose for both men and women is three size '0' capsules of the finely powdered herbs morning and evening.

Dr Christopher also recommends the following formula as a prostate aid for men.

Equal parts of:

cayenne	*juniper berries*
ginger	*marshmallow root*
goldenseal	*parsley root*
gravel root	*uva ursi*

Three size '0' capsules of the finely powdered herbs morning and evening, each dose with a cup of parsley tea.

I must stress that none of this herbal treatment is effective unless it is accompanied by a wholistic natural health programme which needs to be individually determined by a medical herbalist familiar with the problem of infertility.

LEUCORRHOEA *(Vaginal discharge)*

This is called 'the whites' because it shows itself as a white vaginal discharge which causes itchiness and pain. Fast for 3 days on vegetable juices only and take half a cup of the following tea hourly:

2 parts blue flag	*1 part goldenseal*
2 parts sage	*1 part parsley*
1 part dandelion	*½ part cinnamon*
1 part echinacea	

Douche twice daily with equal parts of goldenseal, sage and comfrey,

adding a tablespoon of cider vinegar to the mix and retaining the douche as long as possible.

THE MENOPAUSE

Within the first 2 years of the menopause three-quarters of ovarian oestrogen production is lost, but some of the ovaries' work is taken over by the adrenal glands. If the adrenals have been exhausted by an overactive sympathetic nervous system, poor nutrition or a malfunctioning liver or heart, they are incapable of taking on this extra workload. So healthy adrenal glands are a prerequisite to a comfortable menopause and the following formulation will help.

Equal parts of:

borage	*gota kola*
cayenne	*hawthorn*
ginger	*liquorice*
ginseng (preferably Siberian)	*mullein*

Take a quarter of a level teaspoon of the finely powdered herbs mixed with a little sugarless jam or juice 3 times daily. If you have any problems with high blood pressure leave out the liquorice and ginseng and substitute equal parts of motherwort and cinnamon.

The good news is that intelligence and memory remain intact, and that many of the other symptoms of ageing can be alleviated, slowed or checked by a superabundance of vitamins, minerals and enzymes in a particularly conscientious diet. This includes the rigorous avoidance of anything with chemicals in it, as well as meat, tea, coffee and sugar and an extremely moderate consumption of alcohol. Fertile eggs, yoghurt and buttermilk should be the nearest you get to an animal.

Eating less and, particularly, fasting actively slows down the ageing process and accelerates the repair process in the body. I undertake one long fast yearly, usually a 3 week one and several shorter ones of 4 to 7 days and they are times of self-enjoyment I look forward to.

AVOID HORMONE REPLACEMENT THERAPY

Too many of my patients come to me believing that their menopausal discomforts can be relieved by synthetic oestrogen and find, to their disappointment, that the moment they stop taking it the symptoms reassert themselves in no uncertain terms. This is because hormone replacement therapy is too often used prophylactically to prevent symptoms. The truth is that really healthy women seldom experience menopausal difficulties. So the secret of a trouble-free menopause is to get yourself into really good shape well before it starts.

In Britain oestrogen and progestogen are prescribed in a pattern that mimics a woman's hormonal output during the menopausal cycle, but synthetic oestrogen increases the need for vitamin E; and even Premarin, fondly billed as the 'natural' form of oestrogen (presumably because it is collected from the urine of mares), is just as capable of causing dangerous blood clots as the synthetic oestrogen. Gall stones are much more common among women who take hormone replacement therapy, and it is definitely not advisable for those with high blood pressure, a past history of thrombosis of any kind, diabetes, or chronic liver disease, or for smokers or those with a family history of heart disease.

Foods which are particularly rich in natural hormones include seeds and sprouted seeds, whole grains, royal jelly, bee pollen, bananas, carrots, potatoes, apples, cherries, plums and garlic.

OESTROGEN-RICH FORMULA

Equal parts of:

blessed thistle	pasque-flower
elderflowers	raspberry
false unicorn	sage
lady's slipper	wild yam
liquorice	

Take two size '0' capsules of the finely powdered herbs with a cup of sarsaparilla tea with each meal. This formula will also help after a hysterectomy and is generally beneficial throughout the menopause.

The normal course of the menopause is for menstruation to become erratic with longer and longer gaps between periods, or simply for periods to become lighter and shorter until they eventually stop. Sometimes menstruation will stop suddenly once and for all but this is very rare.

Please note that it is never normal to have frequent heavy periods or to pass blood clots during the menopause. Pain, spotting in between periods and after love-making are equally unacceptable. In an emergency if you are haemorrhaging, use a warm infusion of cayenne as a douche and put one teaspoon cayenne in a cup of warm water and drink it quickly. Consult your doctor immediately if any of the above conditions apply to you.

NIGHT SWEATS

A very simple but effective solution that I have found to work extremely well with my own patients is either 3 drops of essential oil of sage taken with honey and hot water just before bed, or 10 drops of the tincture of sage taken 3 times a day. Dilute the tincture in a little water.

VAGINAL CHANGES

The inside of the vagina is lined with flattened mucus epithelial cells, some 30 deep, that are continually shed, rather like skin cells. In the case of the vagina, harmless resident bacteria help decompose the cell detritus and in doing so manufacture lactic acid, which protects the vagina against harmful bacteria. Hence the vagina is generally able to look after itself without much conscious help.

But as oestrogen levels fall the vagina changes dramatically. The cells of the lining thin, dry out and are unable to fend off invading bacteria, so offensive vaginal discharges are much more common during the menopause and afterwards. This can then cause pain with love-making and can naturally put a woman off sex. The synthetic hormone creams do nothing to restore the vagina to its former state and remember that such creams are easily absorbed into the bloodstream. Vitamin E taken internally and used externally in vaginal boluses (using coconut butter as a base) helps, as does KY jelly or saliva.

The good news is that frequent intercourse keeps the vagina youthful. It seems that lubrication has much less to do with the intensity of stimulation than with its duration, so if you find yourself getting into difficulties, share this invaluable piece of information with your partner. However, experimenting with such advice must be done gently. In the post-menopausal woman whose clitoris is relatively more exposed because of labial atrophy, this exquisitely sensitive area will become more vulnerable to direct stimulation during intercourse. Any stimulation which is too intense, far from being exciting, can be distressing and painful.

MENSTRUATION

AMENORRHOEA (Lack of menstruation)

This is when you do not menstruate at all. Periods may fail to appear for all sorts of reasons other than pregnancy – stress or physical illness, extremely strenuous dieting or a fruitarian diet or jogging too much. It is now recognized that some women who jog strenuously and regularly, fail to ovulate. In particular, it is common for the periods that follow the menarche (beginning of menstruation) to be irregular and the bleeding short or lengthy. Ovulation is inevitably a bit hit-and-miss during these irregular cycles, which can go on for up to 6 years until the body settles down to its normal hormonal cycle (generally between 24 and 34 days, 28 days being average). Uterine tonics like rue, southernwood, false unicorn or blue cohosh can help the body to attain its natural cycle more speedily.

These will help in adulthood too but a woman may need something stronger to bring on menstruation. A cup of an infusion of equal parts of pennyroyal, parsley and tansy drunk 3 times daily on an empty stomach between meals is very effective. It should be unsweetened. But some of these herbs are abortifacients so seek the professional guidance of a medical herbalist and be sure you are not pregnant before taking them.

If the problem is more deeply entrenched try the following formula on a regular basis for 6 months:

2 parts catnip	1 part pennyroyal
2 parts tansy	1 part rosemary
1 part chasteberry	½ part cinnamon

Take two size '0' capsules of the finely powdered herbs with each meal with a wineglass of a tea made with raspberry and squaw vine mixed in equal parts.

> N.B. Because this formulation contains tansy which is potentially toxic it must never be used in pregnancy and its use is not recommended for the untrained. Therefore take this formulation under the supervision of a medical herbalist.

Adjust the diet to include plenty of hormone-rich foods like banana, whole grains, sprouted seeds, bee pollen, royal jelly and natural liquorice.

DYSMENORRHOEA *(Menstrual pain)*

Menstruation should not be painful. If cramping is severe it is because the uterus is heavily burdened with a highly toxic discharge and because calcium levels have dropped too low, causing muscle spasm and debility. The level of calcium in the bloodstream drops a week before menstruation and even more so at the onset of menstruation, so take the following calcium formulation throughout the month and just before menstruation is expected stick to warm foods only.

CALCIUM FORMULA

6 parts comfrey	1 part lobelia
6 parts horsetail	1 part marshmallow
3 parts nettles	root
2 parts kelp	1 part meadowsweet

Take two size '0' capsules of the finely powdered herbs with each meal.

Take warm sitz-baths or saunas to relax the uterus and ease the flow. Do not let your breathing become cramped and shallow. If blood is bright red it is indicative of poor assimilation of sugars and carbohydrates. If it is

dark red, stringy or smelly, it shows that the body is overburdened with putrefying protein and you should cut down on all meat, eggs and dairy products. The ideal colour of healthy menstrual blood is reddish brown.

Pain immediately before menstruation suggests that the position of the womb is abnormal. This is often seen in very thin women in whom the internal fat and ligament upon which the uterus is suspended has lost its tone. Let me clarify the concept of a normal position for a uterus. A uterus which is tilted towards the spine is called 'retroverted'. If it tips towards the pelvic bone it is called 'antiverted'. If it bends over itself it is called 'retroflexed' or 'antiflexed'. It seems to me there is a gynaecological obsession with uterine positioning, but a tipped uterus is not a 'condition' a woman needs worry about. Most women's uteri point in different directions at different times in their lives, but there are very few women who have a uterus tipped to such a degree that it causes pain or makes any difference in their ability to become pregnant.

If the uterus is truly out of position, slant board exercises (see p.141) will help this, as will the following exercises.

PELVIC-FLOOR EXERCISES

The pubococcygeal muscle is a cone-shaped hammock suspended from the sides and at the bottom of the pelvic bones, descending to the area between the legs. A weak PC muscle can cause menstrual problems, involuntary urination, a difficult pregnancy and delivery, infertility, painful intercourse, lack of sensation during love-making and difficulty in achieving orgasm, and can contribute to rectal, bladder and uterine prolapse. It is the one muscle in the body which is not exercised by gymnastics, daily living or any sport.

It doesn't matter what position you adopt – sitting, standing or lying. Slowly contract the PC muscle (i.e. as though you were trying to stop urination) until you are squeezing it as forcefully as you can. Then hold the contraction. Count to ten slowly. Relax the muscle slowly. Breathe naturally throughout. No clenched teeth or thighs! Repeat ten times. If you can't hold each contraction for ten do what you can and build up slowly. Do not let the abdominal muscles assist the PC ones. You will know you are cheating if you lightly place your hand on the lower part of the abdomen during the exercise and feel it tightening. To avoid this, spread your legs.

I would advise every woman to exercise this muscle regularly from her teens on. Not only is a well-toned PC muscle beneficial during pregnancy but it is insurance against prolapses and incontinence later in life.

If pain is before menstruation, but not immediately before, this suggests that the ovaries may be unhealthy, in which case hot sitz-baths should be taken on alternate nights of the week before menstruation is due. On the nights when you are not taking hot sitz-baths massage 2 drops of cypress oil into the area over each ovary and leave it on all night.

Eliminate all processed and refined foods and emphasize raw and sprouted seeds, nuts, raw organically grown fruit and vegetables, plenty of raw juices and supplementations of kelp, lecithin and cold pressed vegetable oils used uncooked as salad dressings.

If pain is felt during the menstrual flow it means your womb is inflamed and is crying out for help and at this juncture you will need the professional help of a medical herbalist.

Unhappily I admit too many women who have come into my clinic telling me about cysts 'the size of an orange' who have suffered in silence for years rather then get help. Most of them are beyond middle age and I suspect they have been brought up on the old-fashioned notion that a little pain with menstruation is natural and all part of a woman's lot. This is rubbish – menstruation should be comfortable and easy throughout life. If it is not, there is almost certainly something wrong, so do not ignore it, put it at the top of the list of urgent priorities.

DR CHRISTOPHER'S PERIODIC FORMULA

2 parts cramp bark	1 part blue cohosh
2 parts squaw vine	1 part cascara sagrada
1 part allspice	1 part pennyroyal
1 part beth root	1 part true unicorn root

Take two or three size '0' capsules of the finely powdered herbs with each meal throughout the month. As the effect is cumulative you will find that you will need less and less each month as the body learns to regulate itself.

METRORRHAGIA *(Bleeding between periods)*

This is spotting between periods. First investigate for possible cancer, fibroids, cervical lesions or any other cause of the problem before attempting the following therapeutic recommendations. Take hand or foot baths of equal parts of:

blackberry leaves	marshmallow root
garlic	sage
hawthorn	

Make sure that you have plenty of iron and calcium in your diet. If the condition persists in spite of an exemplary diet and exercise programme and the ingestion of this formula for several months, seek the advice of a medical herbalist bearing in mind the warning I have given at the beginning of this section, that is to have a full medical check-up to investigate any other possible cause for metrorrhagia.

MORNING SICKNESS

The fact that morning sickness can often be alleviated by a piece of dry toast or a biscuit suggests hypoglycaemia, although I am convinced that some morning sickness is the result of an inadequate diet before conception. There is some suggestion that increased levels of oestrogen also aggravate morning sickness.

Under all circumstances nausea needs urgent attention if dehydration is to be avoided, and if it continues until the fourth month it should be considered particularly serious.

A diet such as is recommended for hypoglycaemics, eating a little protein every 2 to 2½ hours, is advisable, and avoiding fatty, spicy and sugary food as well as coffee and alcohol helps. Vitamin B_6 supplementation can alter blood sugar levels although it is known to be helpful for morning sickness. Check with your medical herbalist or doctor before taking it as it is known to affect magnesium levels.

Eating a piece of wholewheat toast and sipping a cup of camomile or spearmint tea with half a teaspoon of ginger added before you attempt to get out of bed helps. Some women swear by sucking cherry stones or try the following morning sickness formulation, but do not stay on it too long as prolonged doses of goldenseal may cause the uterus to go into spasms. Use it only for 2 consecutive weeks before reverting to the above-mentioned teas.

1 part black horehound	*½ part goldenseal*
1 part clove	*1 part wild yam*
1 part ginger	

Take one size '0' capsule of the finely powdered herbs on rising and repeat later in the day if necessary.

There is a company that sells an elasticated wristband which contains an inverted rubber nipple that presses on two Chinese acupuncture points on the wrist which are said to control nausea (for supplier see Appendix).

POST-NATAL DEPRESSION

This has now virtually reached epidemic proportions. It seems that 1 in 10 mothers suffer from it, and the problem is so widely recognized that if a woman kills her baby within 12 months of its birth, the crime is not 'murder' – the term used instead is 'infanticide'. Post-natal depression can last for as much as a year, and one of my patients likened it to having flu permanently. The problem has been variously attributed to hormonal imbalance and lack of progestrone as well as high levels of stress, changes in lifestyle and social status, immediate separation from the baby after birth, an unexpected caesarean, over-sedation during the birth, lack of vitamin B and calcium influenced by lack of magnesium.

Whatever the combination of causes, communication is vital. There is an association specifically set up to help with this problem (see Appendix).

Keep your diet extremely nutritious and if you feel you may be lacking in any area of nutrition seek the help of a nutritional therapist urgently. Take 9 g of vitamin C daily or a dose that stops short of diarrhoea, and a strong B complex supplement with 75 mg of each B fraction in it twice daily.

Equal parts of:

cornsilk	pasque flower
gota kola	scullcap
lady's slipper	vervain
lemon balm	

Take three size '0' capsules of the finely powdered herbs with each meal. Dry skin brushing and barefoot walking morning and evening are also advised (see Appendix).

Depression can be greatly alleviated by purposeful action. Lean on those you love for support. They will be glad you do.

PREGNANCY

I was astonished to read in a little book published by the British Medical Association that, 'nothing very special is required for your diet in pregnancy. It is certainly unnecessary to add much to a diet that is normally well balanced.' A so-called well-balanced diet is extremely hard to achieve. The average Briton eats 4 lb (2 kg) of additives a year and supermarket produce is extremely likely to be deficient in vitamin B_6, magnesium, vitamin E, vitamin C, folic acid and trace minerals. Indeed a report in the *Sunday Times* (3 July 1983) stated unequivocally, 'anyone who eats the *average* British diet is in danger'. It has been proved that deficiencies of vitamins B_1, B_2, B_{12}, folic acid and vitamin A as well as a wide range of minerals are all associated with an increased tendency to produce congenital abnormalities. Because much of the crucial development of the fertilized egg into a baby takes place in the first 8 weeks of pregnancy it is essential that a pregnant woman's nutritional status is maintained at a high level at all times. By the time the foetus is 6 weeks old it will have stopped feeding off the amniotic sac and will be totally reliant on the mother for nourishment through the umbilical cord.

A need for calcium escalates rapidly during the last 3 months of pregnancy. A lack of it will cause leg and foot cramps, susceptibility to tooth decay (no doubt you have heard the quotation about a woman losing a tooth for every baby), headaches and sleeplessness. It may also lead to the baby having faulty bones and teeth.

It is difficult even in a healthy body to get calcium to pass into the bloodstream, and the problem is exacerbated by under-secretion of hydrochloric acid in the stomach. This generally is the result of years of faulty diet. Lack of fat also means that calcium is more likely to be discarded in the faeces. Bear in mind too that vitamin B_{12} needs to be combined with calcium during absorption by the body to be of any real value.

There is an equally popular myth that dairy products are the most effective source of calcium. They are *not*. An ounce (30 g) of hard cheese contains 230 mg calcium, compared to the 252 mg in 1 oz (15 g) watercress and 306 mg in 1 oz (30 g) kelp. Undoubtedly plants are by far the best assimilated form of calcium, and calcium needs vitamins A, C and D as well as phosphorus in order to function properly. Pregnant women need 2000 mg a day. Take the formula on page 171 throughout pregnancy, two '0' capsules with each meal, and during the last 3 months the dose should rise to three size '0' capsules with each meal.

The baby takes much of the mother's iron in the last 2 months of pregnancy and, like calcium, iron needs a healthy stomach excreting sufficient hydrochloric acid for its proper ingestion. A simple way to insure this is to sip a teaspoon of cider vinegar in water, half an hour before each meal, or to take digestive enzymes before each meal.

Iron should *always* be taken in its natural form in foods and herbs and is most obvious in herbs with very dark green leaves. The inorganic iron salts used in the 'enrichment' of food are known to lead to chronic disability and fatal disease in some people. Natural sources of iron are far better simulated in the body and in turn help with the assimilation of vitamins C and E. In addition natural iron has the added advantage of burning up accumulated poisonous waste, flushing it out of the body and unlike synthetic iron it does *not* cause constipation. Coffee or products with caffeine in them like chocolate, actively inhibit iron absorption.

If you are in any doubt about your iron intake from natural sources use the following formula, especially during the last 3 months of pregnancy.

---

3 parts yellow dock
1 part burdock
1 part gentian

Take two size '0' capsules of the finely powdered herbs morning and evening on an empty stomach. Do not drink tea, coffee or chocolate during the time you're taking this formula. Replace them with herbal teas and coffee substitutes.

THE PILL

Gross metabolic disturbances occur as the result of taking the pill, so discontinue it for a minimum of 3 months before conception and use other forms of birth control instead. Supplements may need to be taken to correct the nutritional deficiencies brought on by the pill. The elevated levels of vitamin A it produces need to be corrected. Vitamins B_1, B_2, B_6 and B_{12} which are all adversely affected by the pill need to be rebalanced. The requirement for vitamin C is greatly increased by use of the pill and plasma levels of vitamin E are lowered by it.

Besides taking nutritional supplements to correct the havoc created by the pill, also take Dr Christopher's periodic formulation to rebalance and retone the body gynaecologically (see p.173).

CONTRAINDICATIONS OF HERBS DURING PREGNANCY

These need to be strictly controlled in the first 3 months of pregnancy, and I will never put a pregnant woman through any kind of deep-cleansing programme. Herbs which should not be taken at any time during pregnancy include rue, pennyroyal, oregano, hyssop, myrrh, nutmeg, angelica, mistletoe, juniper, thuja, autumn crocus, barberry, goldenseal, mandrake, male fern, poke root, tansy, wormwood, southernwood, false unicorn (except to prevent miscarriage), false hellebore and celery seed. Culinary herbs which should be used only for flavouring in small doses include sage, thyme, basil, savory, marjoram and cinnamon. Blue cohosh is contraindicated, except during and just before labour.

TO EASE DELIVERY

Raspberry (both the fruit and leaves) is rich in citrate of iron and tones up the reproductive areas. Mixed in equal quantities with St John's wort, it will help to relieve the after-pains of birth. Massaging the lower back with one of the following essential oils – clary sage, ylang-ylang, rose, neroli or lavender – mixed with vegetable oil is very helpful. Use 10 drops of the essential oil to 1 teaspoon of the carrier base. One teaspoon of tincture of black cohosh in water or juice as needed during labour will facilitate a prompt delivery, and if uterine pushing is waning give one size '0' capsule of goldenseal every half hour as a safe oxytoxic, that is it will stimulate the contraction of the uterine muscle. It is advisable to check your doctor's or midwife's attitude to herbs wherever you choose to give birth, and to do this in advance.

Massaging the perineum daily during the last few months of pregnancy with almond or wheatgerm oil will help to prevent tearing.

Fasting before birth may also be helpful. I have known athletes to fast before a big event, swearing that fasting enhances their performance by increasing their stamina and concentration. So fasting (on freshly pressed juices, herbal teas and honey) for 24 hours before labour and of course during labour sounds a reasonable idea (unless you are hypoglycaemic).

Equal parts of ginger and cayenne tincture during labour itself will help to reduce tension, equalize blood circulation and soothe the nervous system. It may be administered in milk to blunt the fiery taste of the pepper and can be taken as much or as often as desired. It is certainly wonderfully restorative.

The adrenal formula (see p.250) linked with B_6 will assist during the prolonged exhausting first stage of labour and will also help the baby, whose adrenal glands are working equally hard. Both the formula and B_6 will also help speed recovery if labour is difficult.

PRE-NATAL FORMULA

This is Dr Christopher's famous formula with which during his lifetime he facilitated many births. It elasticizes the pelvic and vaginal areas, strengthening the reproductive organs for easy delivery. Equal parts of:

black cohosh	pennyroyal
blessed thistle	raspberry leaves
false unicorn	squaw vine
lobelia	

Take two or three size '0' capsules of the finely powdered herbs morning and evening with a cupful of raspberry leaf or squaw vine tea, beginning six months before the birth, *not sooner*.

PREMENSTRUAL TENSION

The highest number of violent crimes committed by women take place in the premenstrual period 4 to 7 days prior to menstruation. These days are also the peak ones for women being admitted both to prison and psychiatric institutions. Shoplifting is 30 times more common premenstrually. There is also an increased percentage of female accidents and suicide attempts during these days prior to menstruation. Brainwaves in the premenstrual period are increased in frequency and amplitude compared to those of mid-cycle, which is proof, if proof were needed, of a further indication of true psychological alteration.

The symptoms of premenstrual tension fall into two categories, physical and emotional. Many of the physical changes are the result of a shift in fluid balance in response to progesterone, which is produced in large quantities following ovulation. Common physical changes include swelling of the breasts, feet and hands, haemorrhoids, weight gain, migraines, backache, cramping, painful joints, pimply blotched skin and lank hair, asthma, hay fever, hoarseness and red eyes. Common emotional ones include food and alcohol cravings, depression, fatigue and irritability.

The craving for refined carbohydrates and refined sugar increases by two and a half times in premenstrual sufferers. It seems it is not the hypoglycaemic state itself that causes premenstrual tension because its symptoms disappear soon after food is eaten and never last for days on end. What hypoglycaemia does is to overburden the adrenal glands as they struggle to stabilize drastically fluctuating blood sugar levels. Distressed adrenal glands burn up a great deal of vitamin B complex and vitamin C. A typical kind of diet that produces hypoglycaemia initially is composed of highly refined carbohydrates which are leached of their B complex vitamins in the course of refining. These vitamins are essential for carbohydrate metabolism. So a woman tucking into sweet foods in excess gets trapped in a vicious cycle producing hypoglycaemia and adrenal exhaustion. This is why B complex and B_6 have been so successful in treating some cases of premenstrual tension. The adrenal glands also act as a back-up for the ovaries producing about 20% of the total oestrogen.

Interestingly, many premenstrual tension sufferers consume up to four and a half times more dairy products than other women. Saturated animal fats inhibit the formation of PGE_1, which is an anti-inflammatory prostaglandin which is known to be deficient in premenstrual tension sufferers. Evening primrose oil or its newer counterpart, blackcurrant oil, enhances the production of PGE_1. Vitamin E oil is also useful as an inhibitor against the formation of a PGE antagonist derived from the arachidonic acid found in animals.

The intensity of the emotional shift with premenstrual tension varies from woman to woman and month to month and much depends on how you feel about menstruating. Do you regard it as unclean, secret, embarrassing or difficult or as a special time to be acknowledged and honoured? Much depends on your attitude (which will partly be determined by your upbringing) and the degree of hormonal shifting in the critical days before a period.

TREATMENT

Good diet is a prerequisite for wholistic help with premenstrual tension and coffee, tea, cola products, chocolate, salt, alcohol, cigarettes and food heated in processed oil should be excluded from the diet. Meals should be taken little and often and should be high in unrefined carbohydrate with adequate protein. A total abstention from alcohol at this time is advised as is plenty of rest. It also helps to talk about your feelings and keep a premenstrual chart so that any untoward symptoms do not catch you or those you love – who get the brunt of your irritability – by surprise.

Supplements taken throughout the month on a daily basis should include 1000 IUs of vitamin E (as long as you do not suffer from hypertension or a rheumatic heart complaint), as well as 300 mg vitamin B_6, a strong B complex tablet, and six 500 mg capsules of evening primrose oil

daily. Vitamin B₆ should be increased to 500 mg the week before a period. Take all supplements with meals which will enhance their assimilation.

General exercise will help to stimulate and regulate the hormonal system and reduce stress levels.

Fluid retention is the major cause of physiological symptoms so avoid all foods containing salt, including dried fish, dried meats, soya sauce, hot dogs, pickles, anything containing monosodium glutamate, cheese, bacon and other pork products, any canned foods, salted butter, salted nuts and beer. Drink copious amounts of dandelion root decoction, at least 4 cups daily.

The following formulation is a general one designed to help water retention, cramping, nervous tension and nutritional and metabolic strain in the body.

3 parts dandelion root	1 part lady's slipper
2 parts horsetail	1 part motherwort
1 part borage	1 part scullcap
1 part cinnamon	1 part wild yam
1 part kelp	

Take one size '0' capsule of the finely powdered herbs hourly with sips of sarsparilla tea. Once the premenstrual tension has eased, reduce to three size '0' capsules three times daily with meals throughout the month.

PROSTATE PROBLEMS

Sixty five per cent of men over 60 suffer from a prostate problem and the truth is that it is entirely preventable.

PROSTATE GLAND MAINTENANCE

Avoid undue abstinence from sex or sexual intercourse without the natural conclusion of orgasm. Petting and withdrawal without orgasm will lead to a prolonged engorgement of the prostate gland and may result in functional and occasionally even structural damage.

Walking is the best possible form of exercise for keeping the prostate gland healthy. Aim to walk for an hour a day.

The diet should have an emphasis on raw seeds, especially pumpkin and sunflower seeds. They are high in protein and unsaturated fats and pumpkin seeds contain a male androgen hormone which is known to be beneficial to the prostate gland. Both seeds are also high in zinc and essential fatty acids and lack of these is known to be a contributing cause of prostate disorders. The diet should contain plenty of raw vegetables and fruits that are high in vitamin E and also wholewheat bread and wheatgerm as well as lecithin (available form health food shops) and natural sources of

vitamin Ɖ. Avoid coffee, alcohol and strong spices which are
known to be contributory causes of predisposition to prostatis.

When going to the toilet void all urine completely. Be careful
not to strain but continue even if it takes a minute or longer until
no more spurts can be obtained. By doing this bladder tone can be
maintained.

The following exercise is a good way of keeping the prostate gland in
good condition. Lie down on the floor flat on your back. Pull your knees
up to your chest as far as possible then press the soles of both feet
together. Maintaining this position lower the legs towards the floor as far
as possible with a forceful movement. Repeat 10 times or as many times as
possible.

A normal-size prostate is about the size of a walnut but, when it
becomes inflamed and swells, it puts pressure on the urethra and you may
notice a deep, dull ache in the lower abdomen close to the rectum, get
chronic backache, pain during ejaculation, see traces of blood in the urine
or semen, or notice that it is taking longer than usual to empty the bladder.
Any retained urine will cause cystitis, which in turn affects the kidneys and
leads to a backlog of urinary waste in the bloodstream. A swollen prostate
if neglected can become cancerous.

The prostate also secretes hormones which are fed into the bloodstream
and are a contributive factor to general health and well-being. So the herbal
approach to this problem is necessarily two-pronged: one to help the
hormone balance and the other to cleanse and maintain the bladder and
kidneys and reduce the swelling.

RETAINED ENEMA

You can reduce the swelling by mixing together equal parts of cold pressed
safflower, olive and sesame oil, measuring out 2 tablespoons in all, and
squeezing 10,000 IUs of oil-based vitamin A and 1000 IUs of vitamin E
into the oil. Put the mixture into a small bulb syringe and squeeze it into
the rectum just before bed, retaining it until your next bowel movement.
Do this nightly, remembering to rest on the seventh day until the swelling
is alleviated.

In addition to the pumpkin seeds previously mentioned which are rich
in vitamins A, B, E, F, zinc, iron, phosphorus and calcium as well as a male
adrogen hormone (aim to eat at least a heaped handful of these daily), take
1000 IUs of vitamin E daily working up to it gradually, and take another
dose of A and D for one month only, 25 000 IUs of vitamin A and
1000 IUs of vitamin D. Take two teaspoons of bee pollen daily, which is
rich in natural oestrogens.

Avoid alcohol, spices and sugar absolutely and follow a mucus-free diet
preceded by 4 or 5 days of internal cleansing on a fruit juice fast. A mucus-
free diet will consist of fruits, dried and fresh but not tinned or frozen,

vegetables fresh and preferably raw but frozen is permissible, nuts, whole grains preheated in a slow cooker (see p.255) and seeds.

SITZ-BATHS

This is especially helpful in acute cases. It relieves congestion in the pelvis and so helps with the pain. Use alternating hot and cold sitz-baths in either camomile or lemon balm. Sit in the hot bath for 15 minutes and the cold one for 2 to 3 minutes. If the pain is acute use ice-cold retention enemas of well strained camomile tea.

Take the following formula. Equal parts of:

buchu leaves	*goldenrod*
echinacea	*juniper*
ginger root	*marshmallow root*
ginseng	

Take two size '0' capsules in the morning with a cup of parsley leaf tea and two at night.

TOXAEMIA

This is very serious and must be treated immediately. Symptoms include oedema of the feet, legs, hands and face, hypertension and protein excreted in the urine. In an emergency fast on watermelon or boiled brown rice, chew several cloves of raw garlic during the fast and drink a tea made of equal quantities of red clover blossom, ginger, comfrey and dandelion root – 6 wineglasses daily. Contact your doctor immediately for further help.

Once the situation is back under control avoid all dairy products, spices, salt, red meat and alcohol and eat an abundance of raw fruit and vegetables.

TRICHOMONAS

Trichomonas can live outside the human body in any warm and wet environment and so can be picked up from things like wet bathing suits, underwear, towels and face cloths. It can be spread from the rectum to the vagina if the anus is wiped from the back to the front, through anal intercourse followed by vaginal intercourse without proper washing in between. Symptoms include itching and inflammation of the vulva and the entrance of the vagina, burning sensation on urination and a greenish-yellow very nasty smelling vaginal discharge.

N.B. It is possible for men to have trichomonas lodged in the urethra and normally this does not cause any problems. However, it still needs to be treated because it can be passed back and forth with sexual contact. Men and women can both take internal treatment. Chew one clove of garlic 3 times a day or if this is considered too antisocial take 2 garlic tablets 3 times a day with meals. Women only should also peel the fine skin off the clove of garlic without nicking it and wrap it as it is in a strip of gauze about 9 in long so that there is a long tail hanging from one end. Dip the garlic in its bandage in olive oil and insert into the vagina as neatly and as deeply as possible. Leave in as you would a tampon and change the clove 2-3 times a day. In between changes douche with thin live yoghurt. Continue with this treatment until such time as the vagina feels completely comfortable and there is no more discharge.

CHAPTER 9
NERVOUS SYSTEM

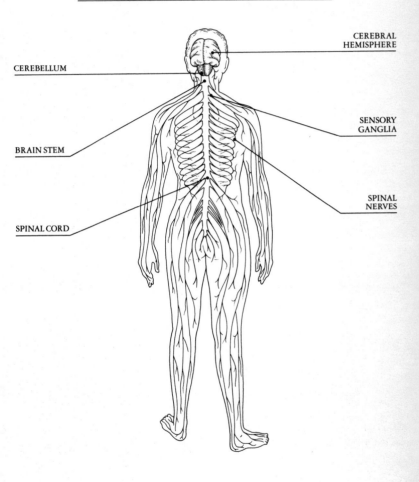

CEREBRAL
HEMISPHERE

CEREBELLUM

SENSORY
GANGLIA

BRAIN STEM

SPINAL
NERVES

SPINAL CORD

AGORAPHOBIA AND CLAUSTROPHOBIA

Agoraphobia, an abnormal fear of open or public places, and claustrophobia, a dread of being confined in closed rooms or small spaces, are often the result of an early traumatic experience. Both conditions need counselling and sometimes desensitization therapy helps.

All the tenets that apply to stress are also valid here (see stress, p.193). At the Department of Molecular Biology in Philadelphia (University of Pennsylvania at Philadelphia) agoraphobia has been very successfully treated with 2 tablespoons of linseed oil with each meal. On this principle evening primrose oil and sunflower oil which are rich in essential fatty acids may also be of use.

A hypoglycaemic diet which excludes gluten may be wise. Gluten contains neuroactive peptides which are suspect as far as any cerebral allergy is concerned.

I have also found the Bach Flower Remedies helpful for these conditions, so seek the advice of a practitioner who is conversant with them.

DEPRESSION

The mentally ill occupy as much as one third of hospital beds. You are more likely to suffer from depression if any of the following factors apply: isolation, no close friends to confide in, having no work outside the home, poor housing, bad financial problems, looking after toddlers at home full time, and losing your mother at an early age. The roots of depression spring from not being in control of your life. Feminist sociologist Pauline Bart defines depression as a response to powerlessness. She believes that society sets women up for depression by encouraging or forcing them to 'put their eggs in one or at most two baskets – the mother role and the wife role'. When they lose one or other of these roles many women respond with a loss of identity and a sense of powerlessness and uselessness. Depression can apply equally to career women crippling themselves in the attempt to be superwomen. People who retire unwillingly are notoriously prone to depression.

However, there may be physical causes of depression including an underactive thyroid, vitamin deficiencies, heavy metal toxicity, food intolerance (especially wheat), hypoglycaemia, chronic candidiasis, and endocrine imbalance.

TREATMENT

The following nervine formula helps.
Equal parts of finely powdered:

blue vervain	raspberry
hops	valerian
lady's slipper	

Take one size '0' capsule every waking hour as needed, and once the worst of the depression is over reduce the dose to two capsules three times daily with meals.

Physical exercise helps. One of the most common signs of depression is fatigue. Make your exercise regular, vigorous, enjoyable and – given time – it will revolutionise your physical and mental well-being.

Fighting back helps. If your rights or dignity are being trampled on summon the energy to stand up for yourself. Say what you mean. Show your feelings. Purposeful activity helps – ensure that it is something you really enjoy that will give you a sense of accomplishment.

Somerset Maugham once observed: 'It is a funny thing about life: if you refuse to accept anything but the best, you very often get it.'

Depression put in that positive context can be seen not just as struggle and pain but as an opportunity for enlightenment and growth, as an ideal means to build on strengths and understand weaknesses.

N.B. If depression is extremely severe seek immediate medical help without hesitation.

DIZZINESS

(See high blood pressure and other illnesses related to dizziness, p.108).

HEADACHES, MIGRAINES AND MIGRAINOUS NEURALGIA

Headaches are simply severe pain in or around the head. Migraines involve head pain which is recurrent with gastrointestinal and visual disturbance. Migraines are generally preceded by some warning symptoms, including fluid retention, mood swings, fatigue or food cravings. Migrainous headaches appear in clusters with 1 or 2 attacks daily for several consecutive days over a period of a few weeks. The patient is then often free of symptoms for several months. Pain tends to centre around one eye only and on the same side of the face. There may be a watery nasal discharge or water running from the eye.

TENSION HEADACHES

Stress can rapidly turn painless muscle tension into a headache. If the stress persists toxins will accumulate in the neck and shoulders and the final result may be osteoarthritis.

People who cup a telephone between the neck and shoulder while writing exacerbate this problem. A few big slow half-head rolls, sitting upright with the shoulders relaxed, helps here. To do these drop the head.

Chronic headaches can also be the result of liver congestion, poor circulation, constipation, hypoglycaemia, food intolerance, sinusitis, arthritis,

spinal lesions, anaemia, the side-effects of a lumbar puncture, meningitis, a brain tumour, high blood pressure and eyestrain. Some, as you can see, are serious, others need only minor correction.

N.B. Check them all out by consulting a doctor before resorting to self-medication with herbs. A severe headache with vomiting for example may be the result of intracerebral haemorrhage which is an emergency.

Dandelion and culver's roots help if there is liver involvement; peppermint if there is a stomach upset; goldenseal or fringe tree if it is bilious; a combination of camomile and peppermint for a sick headache with a nervous stomach; betony if there is vertigo; black cohosh if the headache is of menstrual origin; lavender for pain in the temples; lemon balm or marjoram for nervous headaches; lime flowers for headaches which begin on the right side and then affect the left side where the head feels dull and congested; pulsatilla for a neurotic headache with menstrual disorders; red clover for headaches accompanied by confusion or a feeling of dread; and vervain for headaches induced by muscular tension. All can be taken as simple herbal teas. A good overall remedy is equal parts of:

> *camomile*
> *catnip*
> *peppermint*

Drink a cup as often as needed.

There are some herbs which cause headaches in some people, like valerian (see depression, p.186) and ginseng, and I have had some patients react badly to garlic and thyme.

MIGRAINE

Recent studies have shown that 93% of children with severe frequent migraines have recovered on a restrictive diet and it is worth following a diet which excludes all caffeine (including tea), sugar, yeast extracts, liver, sausages, broad beans, cheese, pickled herrings, all pork, sauerkraut, oranges, bananas, wheat, milk and food additives for four weeks to see what happens. These foods don't have a common denominator. They are simply known to exacerbate migraines in certain people. Adults should also stop the contraceptive pill, smoking and alcohol.

If none of this helps try cutting out television, avoiding cigarette smoke and perfumes, following a hypoglycaemic diet (see p.146) and get an osteopath to check your spine.

Herbs which help include violet, peppermint, lavender, feverfew, rosemary, valerian root, vervain, dandelion, motherwort, centuary, ginger root, scullcap and chicory root. Drink a cup as an infusion or decoction if you suspect a migraine is building (but see warning below).

Lobelia is useful as an emetic as vomiting will often stop the onset of a migraine dead in its tracks (for its use see the section on first aid, p.232). An enema of chicory root will often help in the early stages.

Ginger is interesting because it is taken as an antiplatelet aggregatory and is excellent as a tea to prevent migraines. It seems the blood platelets of migraine sufferers spontaneously clump together more than normal between attacks. If you have the kind of migraine which is relieved by a hot water bottle placed on the face or head, use herbs which will assist to expand blood vessels in the head like peppermint, lavender, rosemary or feverfew. If it is relieved by icepacks use valerian, scullcap or motherwort. A good remedy on a preventive basis is equal parts of finely powdered:

agrimony	motherwort
ginger root	vervain
lemon balm	

Infuse and drink three wineglasses daily.

MIGRAINOUS NEURALGIA

This generally responds to the same type of treatment as migraine. If it does not, write down everything that you have eaten and drunk in the 24 hours that preceded the cluster attack and avoid these items if possible for several months to see if by doing so you reduce their frequency.

HYPERACTIVITY

The causes of hyperactivity are legion but it is becoming clear that food allergy is a major one as are reactions to salicylates, chemical exposure, nutrient deficiencies, hypoglycaemia, candida, parasitic infection, heavy metal toxicity, antenatal lack of oxygen, alcohol consumption, toxaemia and smoking, underlying physical illness, a bad reaction to drugs and even environmental lighting and radiation, including television watching.

TREATMENT

It is as well to ensure there is no underlying medical condition present first and then try an exclusion diet under the supervision of a medical herbalist, naturopath or orthomolecular therapist experienced in this field. If treating a child for hyperactivity remember such a diet is taxing on the child and should *not* be attempted without professional help.

If this does not turn out to be the answer check the other factors and introduce vigorous daily exercise under supervision; no television; saunas under supervision, once or twice weekly; massage along the spine using an

infusion of poppy petals once or twice weekly; and morning and evening hand and foot baths of red clover or lime blossom or camomile.

Parents are often understandably distressed by this behavioural disorder and will need as much help as the child.

INSOMNIA

The average time people sleep is 7½ hours but statistically 3 hours on either side is within the normal range. As you age you need less sleep. Sleep problems can often be connected with nervous-system depressants like alcohol, barbiturates, opiates and benzodiazepine tranquillizers like Librium and Valium, as well as nervous system stimulants like caffeine and amphetamines, anti-high blood pressure medications, hormones including thyroxine, cortisone and oral contraceptives, ulcer medications and anti-depressants. Excessive salt intake and nicotine can also affect sleeping patterns.

I have found the quickest and most effective way to administer herbs to combat insomnia is through the skin and in herbal teas. Camomile, catnip, lavender, lime blossom, woodruff and vervain all work particularly well in warm bath water or in hot foot baths. In tea form a mixture of Earl Grey and hops is quite palatable but I have found that hop pillows which traditionally induce sleep often cause stupor, dizziness or streaming eyes so a woodruff sleep pillow is preferable and smells sensational! Lavender tea should be drunk sparingly, no more than 2 cups a day. Its oil, applied directly to the skin without dilution, can cause convulsions. Lemon balm needs to be used fresh. The dried leaves are a dusty, flavourless disappointment. Catnip is helpful for allaying nightmares and works well on fractious babies. The ageing flowers of lime can be poisonous so be sure of your sources. Pulsatilla works best for the kind of insomnia induced by a bad menopause. Scullcap is particularly helpful for those who wake up in the night suddenly, full of unnamed fears and premonitions of calamity. Valerian taken orally by itself tends to depress the nervous system which can cause depression and headaches. In over-large doses it causes severe headaches, mental agitation, heaviness and stupor. There are some who find it unexpectedly stimulating because their digestive enzymes are unable to transform valerian oil into the calming principal valerianic acid. I prefer to use it in foot baths only but if administering a hot tea try to use the fresh root covered with 1 pint (600 ml) of freshly boiled *but not boiling* hot water and allow to steep as it cools for 24 hours. Prolonged heat (i.e. a decoction) dissipates the essential oils which are the principal healing ingredients.

A good combination tea which tastes quite palatable is:

3 parts wood betony	*1 part lemon balm*
1 part catnip	*1 part vervain*
1 part hops	

Take 1 or 2 cups before bed.

OTHER AIDS

It is pointless telling someone to relax when they simply do not know how to. Yet relaxation is possible to learn, just as it is possible to learn to read or ride a bike. The choice of methods is wide and not all methods are suitable for every person. Meditation, yoga, self-hypnosis, visualization, autogenics, biofeedback; keep trying until you settle on a method that is right for you. Do not be discouraged that you are not instantly brilliant at it. After all, could you learn to play a musical instrument in a week? The secret is to find a method that you like and persist with it.

Experiments in America have proved that paradoxical intention is often very helpful for chronic insomniacs, that is doing the opposite of doing what you want to make happen. Insomniacs were told to stay awake as long as possible to note their insomniac thoughts and one woman reduced her wakeful period from 90 minutes to 5½ minutes! Presumably trying to stay awake eliminates anxiety about not being able to fall asleep.

Other rules which help include:

1. *Go to bed only when tired.*

2. *Once in the bedroom no television, reading, and try not to worry.*

3. *If you do not fall asleep quickly get up and go out of the bedroom and do something until you really feel ready to try again.*

4. *Set the alarm for the same time every morning* including weekends.

5. *Do not overeat at supper and certainly no cigarettes, alcohol, stimulant drugs, refined carbohydrates or sugar.*

6. *Exercise during the day helps as do alternate hot and cold showers, especially on the head, and skin brushing but do not try any of these just before bed as they will act in the opposite way and keep you awake.*

Withdrawal symptoms from Diazepan, Mogadon and Lorazepan can cause severe temporary insomnia.

A zinc deficiency which causes sleep disturbances is quite common in young children and 1 mg of zinc per kilogram of body weight is often found to help. Babies sleep much better where there is repetitious and moderately loud noise level up to 75 decibels, which is about the level inside a jet. Total silence actually induces shorter naps and more time spent crying.

NERVOUS BREAKDOWN

For treatment see depression (p.186) and stress (p.193), and once recovering, see convalescence (p.235). I have also found the Bach Flower Remedies very helpful here.

NERVOUS TICS

Trigemminal neuralgia is often called 'tic douloureux' and is characterized by an involuntary muscular spasm or twitch of the face but these can occur eleswhere in the body (for treatment see neuralgia, p.192).

NEURALGIA

This painful inflammation of the nerve sheaths usually affects the trigemminal nerve of the face but can occur elsewhere in the body where there is direct or indirect pressure on the nerves. Spinal or cranial manipulation may be indicated or massage or posture re-education may be helpful and your medical herbalist or naturopath will be able to determine this. B_{12} deficiencies can lead to neuritis and a diet which balances the acid/alkaline ratios in the body is required (see rheumatism, p.209).

Heat applied externally is very soothing. Use Epsom salts and/or mustard baths or make a poultice of clay mixed with hot water and add one teaspoon of St John's wort oil or one of equal parts of linseed, hops and lobelia. Keep it hot by placing a hot water bottle over it. Alternatively use peppermint, wintergreen or Olbas oils externally or Tiger Balm ointment or cayenne tincture, but do not get any of these near the eyes, nose or insides of the ears or mouth.

The following formula taken internally helps.

black cohosh	ginger root
cayenne	wild yam
devil's claw	

Three size '0' capsules, three times daily with meals.

NEUROSIS

What the term neurosis means is an inefficient way of thinking and behaving and symptoms may range from anxiety, compulsion, depression, phobias, obsessions or defence mechanisms all of which induce psychological pain or discomfort.

Of course any relevant background factors need to be considered and appropriately treated separately. In herbal terms those herbs which act as nervous restoratives or relaxants need to be individually prescribed. The

Bach Flower Remedies are also useful for treating the patient as a whole.

Nervous restoratives include oats, damiana, vervain, Korean ginseng, gota kola, squaw vine, lady's slipper, St John's wort, rosemary, scullcap and lavender. Nervous relaxants include lobelia, black cohosh, blue cohosh, valerian root, raspberry leaves, camomile, lemon balm, lime flowers, catmint, motherwort, passionflower and wild yam. Their work in the body can be facilitated by circulatory stimulants which include all the hot spices.

A good general nerve tonic would be equal parts of the following finely powdered herbs made into a tincture:

black cohosh	lady's slipper
camomile	lemon balm
damiana	scullcap
ginger root	vervain

Dosage: 1 teaspoon in hot water between meals.

PARKINSON'S DISEASE

This is a serious degenerative disease which I have found it possible to help, but not to cure, with a diet of fruit, vegetables, nuts, grains and seeds, 70% of it raw. In addition some periodic lengthy elimination fasts on juiced organic vegetables and sprouted seeds ranging from 3 to 14 days in length. Such an approach certainly improves overall health.

Sometimes heavy metal detoxification is necessary and a careful investigation of any possible food intolerance. Forceful alternate hot and cold showers over the head help as do saunas followed by deep muscle massage. Orthomolecular therapy (treatment with high doses of certain vitamins) is often necessary and I nearly always give a lecithin supplement. The herbs I use include ginseng, damiana, prickly ash, ginger, lobelia, cramp bark, alfalfa, bayberry and Irish moss according to individual need.

An antispasmodic formula of a tincture made from equal parts of:

black cohosh	myrrh
ginger root	scullcap
lobelia	valerian

sometimes helps. Ten drops in hot water every half an hour until muscle spasm has eased or 15 drops in hot water three times daily.

STRESS

Valium is the largest-selling prescriptive drug sold in the world today and women-users outnumber men by a very large margin. 'Stress' is such a

loose definition of a wide range of physical symptoms that anti-stress drugs can be prescribed for virtually any reason (and judging by the number of my patients who take them very often are). Physical symptoms of stress, apart from fatigue, may include weakness, sweating, trembling, breathlessness, choking, fainting, hypertension, palpitations, digestive upsets, over-dependence on alcohol, drugs or tobacco, loss of interest in sex, insomnia, or simply a succession of mysterious aches, pains and niggling little discomforts. Allopathic prescriptions merely mask the symptoms but do nothing to deal with the social, emotional and physical conditions which are the cause.

It is now well known that anti-anxiety drugs are addictive and here herbs can play an invaluable part in helping the patient to withdraw from them – coupled with counselling, a good diet, plenty of exercise, the support of friends, and stress-management techniques like meditation, yoga, self-hypnosis, visualization, autogenics or biofeedback.

A prolonged dose of any of the benzodiazepines will produce withdrawal symptoms if stopped, doses in excess of 40 mg taken daily for three months will produce these symptoms, and I have observed some very sensitive patients experience the same symptoms on smaller, shorter term doses. Benzodiazepines include chlordiazepoxide, diazipain, nitrazepain, flurazepain, chlorazepate, lorazepain, oxazepain and ternazepain under such familiar trade names as Librium, Valium, Mogadon, Dalmane, Tranxene, Adivan, Serenid and Euhypuos. Withdrawal symptoms include anxiety, problems with breathing and occasionally convulsions and severe emotional and perceptive change such as seeing glittering lights, unsteadiness and experiencing noises and sensations of motion while resting. Diazepan, Mogadon and Lorazepan withdrawal can cause temporary but quite severe insomnia.

Weaning long-term users off Ativan, Serenid and Euhypnos, which are stronger, is harder than getting people off Librium, Valium, Mogadon, Dalmane and Tranxene but herbal remedies will act as a useful bridge as the dosages of the chemical medicines are very slowly and gently reduced. Herbs will actively tone, strengthen and nourish a battered nervous system which has hitherto been exposed to the heavy chemical stress of allopathic tranquillizers. Both valerian and scullcap initially replace the benzodiazepine effects whilst strengthening the nervous system, so helping to ease withdrawal symptoms. *They are not recommended for long-term use.* After 3 months switch to alternative herbs like camomile, catnip, hops, lavender, lemon balm, lime flowers, pasque flower, red clover, rosemary, vervain, motherwort, woodruff, oat and the ginsengs which all have a useful part to play as adaptagens or for the broad support the body needs during the process of withdrawal. All of these are more easily digested in tea form.

N.B. If you have been taking any of the allopathic tranquillizers for longer than two months it is unwise to try and wean yourself off them without the support and advice of a qualified medical herbalist. If you have been taking tranquillizers for less than two months stop them and use the following formula instead.

NERVE TONIC

Equal parts of:

black cohosh	lobelia
ginger	mistletoe
hawthorn	mugwort
hops	scullcap
lady's slipper	valerian
lemon balm	wood betony

Make a tincture and take 2 to 3 teaspoons 3 times daily, preferably stirred into a hot drink.

There is now a specific withdrawal pack of tranquillizers which you can get on prescription from your doctor and is designed to wean long-term users off drugs in 6 weeks. Do ask your doctor about this.

CHAPTER 10
GLANDULAR SYSTEM

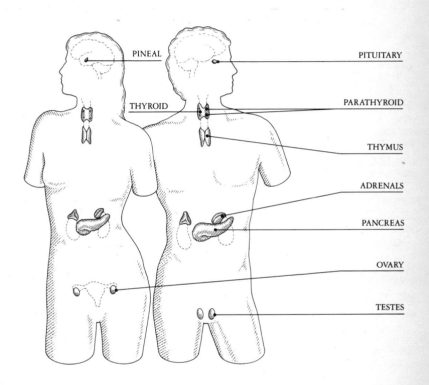

PINEAL

PITUITARY

THYROID

PARATHYROID

THYMUS

ADRENALS

PANCREAS

OVARY

TESTES

DIABETES MELLITUS

Diabetes has now become a raging epidemic in the western world and is indirectly responsible for 1 in every 8 deaths in the United States, and 1 in every 3 cases of blindness. It is undoubtedly one of the insidious diseases of our civilization. Studies of various populations prove that the incidence of diabetes rises with the consumption of sugar and refined carbohydrates. Of all diabetics 80% are, or have been at some time in the past, obese. Stress and adrenal exhaustion play a part in diabetes as does liver damage or toxicity and spinal lesions in the middle of the thoracic area are common in diabetes.

Interestingly blood sugar levels react differently for different people in response to the same food, though allergy must be considered as one of the factors in diabetes.

The basic problem with diabetes is that the level of glucose in the blood is higher than normal while being at the same time low inside the cells. This is brought about by the progressive inability of the pancreas to secrete the hormone insulin on demand. Using natural methods to help diabetes has proved successful but much depends on the severity of the case in question and the length of insulin dependency. Of all diabetics 20% survive on dietary management alone, but all diabetics need dietary advice.

DIET

The diet should be a natural one high in fibrous carbohydrates. Any fats eaten should be unsaturated or vegetable. Red meat is forbidden and chicken and fish may be taken only twice a week. Rely instead on vegetarian protein like soy. Fresh fruits are permissible in moderation although fresh fruit juice is not and all fruit must be eaten with a little protein to slow its digestion. Vegetables that are particularly recommended include Jerusalem artichokes, Brussels sprouts, cucumbers, green beans, garlic and avocados. Fruits recommended include grapefruits and bananas. All oatmeal products are highly recommended, including oatbran. The diet should be 80% raw. Natural supplements including spirulena, brewer's yeast and wheatgerm are particularly helpful. A potassium broth taken regularly throughout the day will help to restore mineral and electrolyte loss.

The pattern of meals should be the same as for hypoglycaemia (see p.146).

Other herbs and foods which are known to help because of their hypoglycaemic action (that is, they will lower blood sugar levels) include allspice, barley, bugleweed, burdock, cabbage, carrot, ginseng, lettuce, nettles, olive, onion, papaya, peas, spinach, sunflower, sweet potato, turnip, dandelion, string beans (one cup of string bean tea is equal to at least one unit of insulin). The recommended dose is one cup of string bean

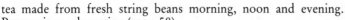
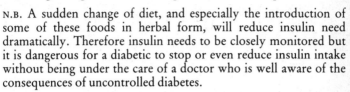

tea made from fresh string beans morning, noon and evening. Prepare it as a decoction (see p.58).

Dr Vogel recommends drinking 1 pint (600 ml) of fresh whey daily till the thirst abates. The bitter herbs like chicory, dandelion, endive, fenugreek, goat's rue and fringe tree bark also help.

> N.B. A sudden change of diet, and especially the introduction of some of these foods in herbal form, will reduce insulin need dramatically. Therefore insulin needs to be closely monitored but it is dangerous for a diabetic to stop or even reduce insulin intake without being under the care of a doctor who is well aware of the consequences of uncontrolled diabetes.

DR CHRISTOPHER'S PANCREATIC AID

Dr Christopher has used this on many diabetic patients and reduced their need for insulin over a period of 2 or 3 years.

Equal parts of finely powdered

cayenne	*liquorice root*
cedar berries	*mullein*
goldenseal	*uva ursi*

Dosage: 2 or 3 capsules depending on weight, to be taken with each meal.

OTHER AIDS

Take a very hot shower on rising especially over the pancreas and make it as forceful as you can.

Apply a castor oil poultice to the pancreas daily as hot as possible.

Use dry skin brushing twice a day to improve the metabolism and circulation followed by alternate hot and cold showers.

Hard exercise outdoors such as jogging, swimming or digging the garden will actually reduce the need for insulin.

Diabetes is more prevalent in soft water areas so drink lots of mineralized water which contains chromium and other trace elements. The absorption of chromium from chromic chloride is extremely poor, less than 1%. In order for chromium to be biologically active it must be combined with nicotinic acid (vitamin B_3) and several amino acids. This composite compound, called the Glucose Tolerance Factor (GTF) binds with insulin to improve the utilization of insulin by cells 10 times. Chromium GTF is found in high concentrations in brewer's yeast (its GTF activity is higher than any other food) and 30 tablets daily are recommended.

> N.B. Fasting is inadvisable under any circumstances for diabetics.

Avoid all mental and nervous stresses and strains. Such strains exhaust the adrenal glands and considerably slow any healing as far as diabetes is concerned.

GOITRE

This is an enlargement of the thyroid gland showing a swelling around the front of the neck and is generally due to iodine deficiency. Watercress and seaweed are rich sources of iodine. Certain foods classified as small goitrogens actually *inhibit* the utilization of iodine including peanuts, soy flour, Brussels sprouts, cauliflower, cabbage, kale, broccoli, turnips and kohlrabi; and vitamin E deficiency reduces iodine absorption by 95%.

Some countries like Switzerland and Australia actually add synthetic iodine to salt in the erroneous belief that this will solve the problem, failing to appreciate that it is natural sources of iodine which are needed. In those people whose thyroid secretion is already excessive iodine salt can lead to palpitations or worse still Basedow's disease (exophalmic goitre), besides which salt is harmful and should not be added to the diet at all.

Dr Vogal, an internationally revered Swiss naturopath, recommends cabbage and clay poultices prepared with oak bark decoction and alternately applied to the front of the neck. By alternately he means one warm poultice to follow the other once it has cooled down.

Specific foods which are helpful include: bladderwrack, dulse, kelp, garlic, brewer's yeast, watercress, unsalted sea food, egg yolks, and mushrooms. An excellent well rounded herbal formula is equal parts of:

bladderwrack	kelp
bugleweed	nettles
dandelion	parsley leaf
Icelandic moss	watercress
Irish moss	

All herbs to be finely powdered and three size '0' capsules to be taken with every meal.

PANCREATITIS

This is an inflammation of the pancreas and can be acute or chronic. It is associated with alcoholism, trauma or infection or injury to the bilary tract so treat with the diet advised for an inflamed gall bladder (see p.138).

Seek the advice of a medical herbalist as this is a serious condition and needs expert individual attention. Fringe tree bark has often been found to be specifically helpful for this condition.

SWOLLEN GLANDS

These can occur wherever there are lymph glands, in the groin or behind the knees, in the throat and in the armpits, and show a distressed lymph system no longer able to cope. Go on a 3-day fast of fruit juices followed by a diet of fruit, vegetables, nuts, grains and seeds, 80% of it raw to cleanse the lymph system. Dry skin brush daily followed by a hot then cold shower. Ensure you are not constipated. When well enough take up some form of exercise that will help pump lymph effectively around the body. Trampolining is best but also consider skipping or swimming.

Take the following brilliant formula. It is Dr Christopher's and I have used it successfully many times.

3 parts mullein
1 part lobelia

Make an infusion and drink half a cup 3 times daily until the glands are back to normal. Save the residual herbs for a poultice and apply it as warm as possible to the swollen area before bed, leaving it on all night. Alternatively apply a hot compress of the tea to the area as above.

CHAPTER *11*
*M*USCULAR AND
*S*KELETAL SYSTEM

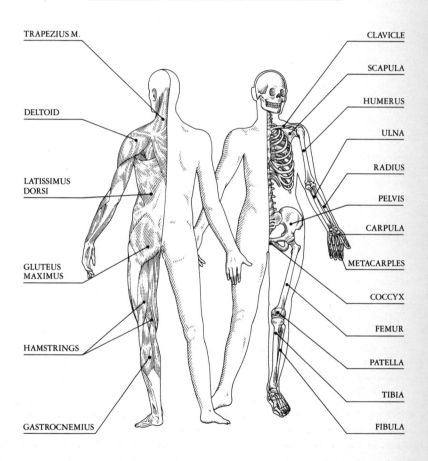

TRAPEZIUS M.

DELTOID

LATISSIMUS
DORSI

GLUTEUS
MAXIMUS

HAMSTRINGS

GASTROCNEMIUS

CLAVICLE

SCAPULA

HUMERUS

ULNA

RADIUS

PELVIS

CARPULA

METACARPLES

COCCYX

FEMUR

PATELLA

TIBIA

FIBULA

BURSITIS

This is the name for an inflammation of the small water-filled cushions which buffer the larger tendons and bones. Popularly known as Tennis Elbow, Housemaid's Knee, Tailor's or Weaver's Bottom. The condition can set in slowly or be the result of a direct trauma like a heavy knock.

If the attack is acute and caused by trauma use ice compresses (see p.62) leaving them on for 40 minutes at a time and repeating every 3 hours for the first 48 hours. Obviously the joint must be immobilized and rested so that any activity which may have caused it such as tennis, kneeling doing housework, fishing or hammering, is stopped. After the first 48 hours use alternate hot and cold compresses of diluted anti-spasmodic tincture (10 drops for 4 fl oz (120 ml) of water). Finish with the cold compress. Comfrey leaf poultices may be used as an alternative or hot Epsom salt packs if there is no swelling.

Vitamin C is known to help to protect against connective tissue injuries so take this to the point just short of diarrhoea.

If the pain is chronic and long established treat as for arthritis and rheumatism. Also massage using Red Tiger balm oil. Take the anti-spasmodic tincture on page 193 to ease the pain and inflammation. Add 10 drops of this tincture to 1 cup of comfrey tea and take 4 cups daily.

A recent study suggested that injections of vitamin B_{12}, 1 mg injected intramuscularly daily for 7 to 10 days and less frequently thereafter, is of value in acute bursitis. Seek professional help for this.

Alternatively bromelain (which is naturally present in pineapple and papaya) in very high doses has been used as an anti-inflammatory by some nutritional therapists and is said to be very effective for bursitis. However, high doses can cause gastrointestinal upset so this needs to be medically supervised. A bromelain supplement should not be used at all wherever there is a history of stomach ulcers.

CARPAL TUNNEL SYNDROME

This condition is particularly common in women and may be exacerbated after carrying heavy shopping. Sometimes the pain and tingling in the hands and fingers which extends up the arm may wake them at night or be particularly difficult on waking in the morning. The tingling and discomfort is caused by a compression of a large nerve in the wrist which passes from the forearm into the hand through a funnel of tissues between the wrist or carpal bones and a band of fibrous tissue at the front of the wrist. Any swelling in this area compresses the nerve tissue at the wrist simply because the bones and connective tissues in this area are so compact. This in turn may produce pain and numbness in the fingers. Causes of carpal tunnel syndrome may include underactive thyroid, rheumatoid arthritis, sudden weight gain, pregnancy and direct trauma to the wrist. A number of studies have shown that it can occur as the result of vitamin B₆ deficiency so it is worth trying supplementation of this before going on to more radical measures. Take 200 mg a day for a minimum of 3 months, coupled with a strong vitamin B complex supplement and a mega multi-vitamin supplement. Consider the possibility of food intolerance and follow a lacto-vegetarian diet.

FIBROSITIS

Follow the advice for bursitis (opposite) as far as external treatment is concerned and the advice for rheumatism and arthritis (p.209) for internal treatment. All heat including infra-red and the heat from saunas and Turkish baths is very helpful for this condition.

GOUT

Gout is caused by the precipitation of insoluble crystals of uric acid into the joints which consequently become red, swollen and painful. It can be helped by a number of dietary changes including losing weight if the patient is obese, eschewing alcohol completely, and following a strict low uric acid and low purine diet, that is, avoiding all meat (especially organ meats), eggs, fish and dairy produce. The only wheat to be taken should be in sprouted form. Foods high in potassium are protective against gout and the potassium broth on page 135 is exceptionally helpful. Red sour cherries and strawberries are of specific value in gout. Cherries have a remarkable ability to alkalize the system and neutralize uric acid. When they are in season it is advisable to do a 3 to 4 day fast on them. You may notice, if you try this, a considerable worsening of the condition in the early stages of fasting. This is simply the uric acid, dissolved by the juices from the fruit, being thrown into the bloodstream for elimination and will clear up if the fasting is continued. A series of short 3 to 4 days fast is preferable to one long fast.

Interestingly it has been acknowledged that a high blood level of uric acid is associated with a high level of intellectual attainment. What is not established is whether the high level of uric acid in the blood contributes to the higher level in intelligence or the intense intellectual activity leads to the elevation of blood uric acid.

High doses of vitamin C (up to 4 g a day) assist the loss of uric acid through the kidneys, and zinc and magnesium are also advisable but should be taken under medical supervision.

Take the following herbal mixture: equal parts of celery, boneset, burdock root, Irish moss, alfalfa. Make an infusion and drink 3 cups a day. If the pain is very bad add half a part goldenseal and half a part thuja.

LUMBAGO

This refers to any pain in the lower back which is often symptomatic of deeper organic defects. A lot of back pain is the direct result of kidney and bladder weakness. The toxins which are generally eliminated through the kidneys, bladder and urine are deposited in surrounding tissue areas, particularly the spinal joints of the lumbar region. If back pain is coupled with inflammation nerves may become irritated resulting in shooting pains called sciatica (see p.210). Occasionally the problem can be the result of reproductive malfunction, rheumatism or back lesions. Whatever the cause the root of the pain must be sought and the appropriate treatment used, whether it be with herbs, osteopathy or acupuncture.

Often a warming and stimulating liniment will help. I have had very good results at my clinic with the following formulation: equal parts of essential oil of black pepper, camphor, ginger, St John's wort and camomile. Mix 1 teaspoon of these combined oils with 1 teaspoon of almond oil and massage into the area which is painful.

The following compresses are also extremely effective.

2 parts comfrey root	*1 part ginger root*
2 parts marshmallow root	*1 part wood betony leaves*
1 part dandelion root	

Make a decoction and soak a cloth in the strained mixture. Wrap it round the whole trunk extending from under the armpits to the pubic bone. Cover it with plastic to save leakage and retire to bed, protecting the sheet with plastic to prevent the mattress getting wet. The next morning unwrap yourself and sponge down with a half and half mixture of cider vinegar and warm water. Use this compress nightly until the attack of pain subsides.

Cut out all tea, coffee, cocoa, alcohol and salt to relieve any pressure on the kidneys. Take the following formulation:

4 parts dandelion root	*1 part marshmallow root*
2 parts meadowsweet	
1 part ginger root	*1 part scullcap*

If there is also inflammation add 4 parts echinacea and 1 part lady's slipper.

Make a decoction and take half a cup every 3 hours.

MUSCLE ACHES

If these are transient as the result of an acute viral infection (as with influenza) take equal parts of boneset and ginger. Put the finely powdered herbs into capsules and take one hourly with a warm drink. If the cramps are long established, investigate the possibility of chronic candidiasis, nutritional deficiency or circulatory problems. Food intolerance may also be a problem. Sometimes a potassium deficiency can be a major contributing factor.

Restless twitching legs at night can be due to an iron deficiency which may in itself be the result of excessive tea consumption. Sometimes a supplement of folic acid (5 mg daily) is helpful as is the formulation to assist the circulation on page 109.

MUSCLE CRAMPS

Muscle cramps can be quite debilitating and nutritionally are known to respond to moderately high doses of vitamin E, 600 IUs a day, vitamin B_6 100 mg twice daily, and foods rich in calcium and magnesium (see the formula on p.171). Occasionally food intolerance may be causing the cramp so this should be investigated. If the problem is one of circulation take the formulation on page 109. The following formula if taken for a minimum of 3 to 4 months is also helpful.

2 parts crampbark	1 part ginger root
1 part angelica	1 part prickly ash
1 part camomile	1 part squaw vine

Make an infusion and drink a wineglass half an hour before each meal.

OSTEOPOROSIS *(Decrease in bone mass)*

This abnormal porosity of the bones in elderly people is usually the result of the body's inability to absorb and utilize nutrients properly, coupled with excessive consumption of meat, post-menopausal hormone imbalances and diminished physical activity. Prolonged cortisone treatment blocks the bone-building activity and decreases the intestinal absorption of calcium, as do antibiotics. Those with rheumatoid arthritis which is being treated with steroids ofen have osteoporosis with spontaneous fractures.

Remember that the richest sources of calcium are kelp, all dark green raw leafy vegetables, sesame seeds, and sardines canned in their own oil. The magnesium, the calcium and the phosphorus ratio in all of these items is more favourable than in dairy or meat products and they are more evenly metabolized. The need for calcium increases in old age as the production of hydrochloric acid dwindles in the stomach, food is less thoroughly chewed because of poor teeth or dentures, and exercise tails off. Calcium deficiency will only show itself with X-rays after 30% of the bone is lost and therefore it is very important that women start ingesting easily absorbable sources of calcium in high quantity well before the menopause. They should not simply wait for the damage to be done.

DIET

Concentrate on dark green leafed vegetables, carrots, fruits and berries of all kinds, sesame and sunflower seeds, as well as an abundance of lactic acid, foods like sauerkraut and yoghurt. The best grains are oats, barley, buckwheat, millet and rice.

Because hydrochloric acid secretion diminishes rapidly after the age of 40, betaine hydrochloride tablets should be taken with each meal to assure proper assimilation, or alternatively take cider vinegar and honey in a little water before meals. Because most calcium is leached from the bones at night while the body is at rest via the bloodstream, it is advisable to take plenty of calcium-rich foods just before bed. Any acid medium such as cider vinegar and honey will increase calcium absorption. It is advisable to cut back on dairy products in order to establish proper mineral balance and to cut out meat altogether because it contains 20–50 times more phosphorus than calcium which aggravates calcium lost from the bones in order to keep a proper phosphorus/calcium ratio in the blood.

EXERCISE

This is vitally important as diminished physical activity and loss of muscle strength are contributing factors in osteoporosis. Skipping is especially recommended for its piezoelectric effect, that is its effect of generating electricity in the body. Do this in soft shoes which have a good ankle support.

HERBS

One of my patients was run over by a refuse collecting truck and had the majority of her ribs crushed and her spleen badly ruptured. She was already eating what in essence was a lacto-vegetarian unrefined diet, so I rushed a formulation over to her hospital as follows: equal parts of comfrey and horsetail, and ½ part lobelia. I asked her to take one capsule every hour with sips of nettle tea or cider vinegar and honey. Her healing was remarkable and stunned the doctors who were treating her. This is an excellent formula for mending broken bones and strengthening the thinning ones.

I would also advise a little sunbathing daily if the weather permits. Women should also take the formula to strengthen the reproductive organs on page 44, which is rich in natural hormones.

PLEURISY

Pleurisy is a stage well beyond an ordinary bronchial infection and therefore needs professional management, but in the meanwhile treat as for fever (see p.237). Pleurisy root and angelica are both specifics for this illness. The presence of TB may have to be considered as will the need for antibiotics.

Poultices are particularly useful for this illness. Use a poultice of equal parts of linseed and angelica with several generous pinches of cayenne pepper. Apply it to the chest as hot as possible and renew it as soon as it cools. But always seek professional help.

RHEUMATISM AND ARTHRITIS

For the purposes of wholistic treatment it is not necessary to differentiate between the various sorts of rheumatism and arthritis. It is, however, necessary to recognize that though the path to recovery is long and arduous (for in my experience it undoubtedly is), recovery the natural way is possible. Certainly allopathic medicine has been able to control the pain of arthritis and rheumatism but I have never encountered anyone who has ever done anything other than get worse on conventional drugs. One of the most commonly prescribed drugs, aspirin, reduces vitamin C levels, damages connective tissue and if taken in large doses can cause the lining of the stomach to bleed. It also causes an increase in uric acid levels, depresses the adrenal glands and in large doses can lead to paralysis of the respiratory centre. Its prolonged use can cause dizziness, severe respiratory distress and mental confusion. Its only positive use, apart from reducing pain, is that it is known to reduce the clotting of platelets, so that may be useful for the people suffering from strokes – at a push. However salicylate-rich foods will act equally well in this respect. For a list of natural salicylate-rich foods, see page 116. Cortisone, the other popular drug prescribed for arthritis, depresses the adrenal glands and causes calcium depression, which in the long term results in osteoporosis.

POULTICES AND COMPRESSES

Mustard packs, castor oil compresses, clay poultices, slippery elm poultices with lobelia and cayenne and pulped cabbage leaf poultices are all helpful.

SUPPLEMENTS

A copper bracelet is of proven value in the treatment of arthritis. Small quantities of copper may be absorbed into the skin from wearing such a bracelet and have anti-inflammatory effects.

B₃ (nicotinamide), between 1 and 4 mg daily, has been shown to be helpful.

New Zealand green-lipped mussel extract which is available in tablet form and is taken orally has been used with extremely encouraging results.

Vitamin E (up to 600 mg a day) has been shown to be useful.

Evening primrose oil with vitamins C, B₆, B₃, zinc and cod liver oil are known to be a good combination. B₅ (pantothenic acid) is particularly helpful for fragile adrenal glands. Take 2 g daily.

HERBS

A good general remedy for arthritis is:

2 parts dandelion root	1 part goldenrod
2 parts devil's claw root	1 part horsetail leaves
	1 part meadowsweet
2 parts nettles	1 part St John's wort
1 part agrimony	1 part sarsaparilla root
1 part burdock root	1 part scullcap leaves
1 part celery seed	
1 part comfrey leaves	

Take 3 cups daily. Devil's claw makes the tea slightly bitter, so if you can't manage the taste, leave it out and take devil's claw tablets instead, following the manufacturer's instructions on the container.

BAREFOOT WALKING

If you are able to, take a barefoot walk on grass while it is still wet with dew early in the morning. This will ground the static electricity in your body and help to regenerate your energy. If you can't walk, get someone to massage your feet daily with olive oil mixed with 10 drops of pine oil. After barefoot walking dry the feet vigorously with a rough towel and get straight back into warm footwear.

EXERCISE

Do some yoga daily or, if this is beyond you, do some simple stretching exercises or ask a physiotherapist to work out a pattern of individual exercises for you.

RELAXATION AND VISUALIZATION

This is a vital part of any programme for arthritis or rheumatism because I have observed that people with this disease tend to be those that lavish time and attention on other people but focus very little on self-care. Rheumatism and arthritis are closely bound up with stress, the type of stress that results from the exhaustion of the adrenal glands, and conscious relaxation will help to combat this. Visualization is simply the conjuring up of graphic mental pictures which gradually work towards correcting the negative mental aspects of any disease. Reading Carl Simonton's *Getting Well Again* (published by Bantam) will help you construct a visualization programme suitable for your own needs.

There are certainly better ways to cope with rheumatism and arthritis, and safer ones. I find an iridology test is essential to determine the cause which is as individual as the person with the disease. There is no magic solution. Everything depends on the patient. The time it takes to heal depends on how long they have had the disease and, if it is chronic, it may take a couple of years of dedicated application before any real results are seen.

DIET

One of the causes of rheumatism and arthritis is an accumulation of poisons or waste products in the affected tissue and a major contributing factor to this is an inappropriate diet containing foods that the body cannot tolerate or devitalized adulterated ones. Avoid all foods known to impede mineral absorption – this includes tea, coffee, bran and any form of flour. Plants of the solanacea family are known to affect some people adversely so avoid tomatoes, aubergines, pepper, paprika, tobacco and potatoes for several months and then reintroduce them and see if your condition gets worse. Sometimes an exclusion diet beginning with lamb and pears only for a period of up to 3 weeks is worth following to trace any food intolerance. Lamb and pears are believed to be the only two foods which do not cause food intolerance in anyone. Make sure, of course, the lamb is organic and the pears unsprayed. Foods can then be introduced one at a time to determine which are the culprits. Some people have received great benefit from beginning each morning with a glass of freshly pressed potato juice diluted with a little water. It tastes vile but often the effects are brilliant! Drink at least one mug of potassium broth daily. This is easily made by boiling unpeeled scrubbed potatoes, carrot, beetroot, celery, turnips, cabbage and their leafy green tops where appropriate. Half the quantity should consist of potatoes, the remainder of equal parts of the other vegetables. Drink the broth only. The rest of the family can eat the vegetables. Apart from these fluids ensure that you take 3 pints (1.5 litres) of purified water with a little cider vinegar or apple juice added. Citrus fruits have an alkaline reaction on the metabolism and so should not, contrary to popular myth, be avoided.

FASTING

Repeated vegetable juice fasts for 4 to 6 weeks using carrot, beet, parsley, alfalfa, potato and celery juices are particularly recommended but this must be done under supervision. Initially the condition may worsen as uric acid floods into the bloodstream. Don't panic, keep at it. Leave at least an 8-week break between fasts, going back onto the recommended diet.

HYDROTHERAPY

Hot and cold showers and skin scrubbing to stimulate the circulation should be carried out once or twice daily. If you are too poorly to do it yourself, get someone to do it for you. Take Epsom salt baths twice weekly (see Appendix). Massaging painful joints under water using baking powder is also helpful. Movement under water in a warm swimming pool is useful too, but remember to shower off well afterwards because the chlorine in the baths is intensely poisonous. Paraffin baths are also helpful but these need to be administered for you.

MASSAGE

A daily massage will soothe and help mobility. An excellent combination of oils includes olive oil, cayenne, marshmallow, marigold, plantain, chickweed and comfrey in equal proportions.

SCIATICA

This is characterized by intense pain and tenderness running along the whole of the sciatic nerve extending from the lower spine and pelvis down the outside of the leg to the ankle. If the spine and hips are misaligned a manipulation by an osteopath or chiropractor will be necessary. If there is neuralgia treat with the following antispasmodic drops: equal parts of lobelia, scullcap, valerian, myrrh, black cohosh, skunk cabbage, hops, half a part of ginger, half a part of liquorice. Make a tincture and take 10 drops every 15 minutes if necessary until the pain subsides. This tincture can also be massaged into the painful area externally. The application of ginger poultices over the lower lumbar area and down the leg is helpful too.

Ensure that there is no constipation and the kidneys are functioning well. For a good bowel tonic see page 33 and for help with the kidneys see page 34.

SHIN SPLINTS

I have seen more of these in my practice as aerobics has become increasingly popular. The muscle in the front of the leg below the knee swells as the result of excessive strain on the tendons in the legs. Immobilization for 48 hours is essential, coupled with ice packs. Anti-spasmodic drops are also helpful (see p.193). Thereafter apply alternate hot and cold compresses of comfrey. Take tincture of betony, 10 drops every hour if the pain is acute.

CHAPTER *12*
THE SKIN

ABSCESS

An abscess is a localized collection of pus whether it be on the finger as a whitlow, on the jaw as a gumboil, or on any part of the skin as a boil. It can also develop internally in the breast, kidney and brain, and nearly all of them need professional attention if they are to be drained and treated properly. Repeated abscesses are a sure sign of toxaemia or they may be tubercular and in either instance they need professional help. Where abscesses are chronic the approach tends to be one of deep internal cleansing with special attention paid to the glandular system coupled with external poultices and herbs calculated to cleanse the blood, liver and bowels. In this instance burdock, echinacea, Oregon grape root, yellow dock and red clover are particularly helpful.

ACNE

This is characterized by various skin changes ranging from blackheads through to pustules and papules. These are usually found on the face, though sometimes they extend to the shoulders, back, arms and chest. Their cause is hormonal and dietary which is why it is only generally a teenage scourge. However some teenagers never grow out of acne and suffer acne lesions all their lives.

DIET

A meat and dairy-free wholefood diet is advisable. There is no doubt about it – saturated fats aggravate the problem, so these must be cut out of the diet entirely. Cold pressed unsaturated vegetable oils are permissible in very small quantities, but these should never be heated, in other words foods should never be served fried. Iodine certainly aggravates acne so avoid this. This includes kelp as well as certain cough mixtures and tonics which are rich in iodine and iodized table salt.

VITAMINS

Acne is known to respond to treatment with zinc, vitamins A and B_6 and selenium. The dosage needs to be determined according to individual need.

HERBS

Herbs which will help to drain the lymphatic system, cleanse the liver and the bloodstream as well as the bowel are indicated. If the condition persists after adolescence hormonal adaptogens like false unicorn and agnus castus for women and ginseng and saw palmetto for men are indicated. A good overall formulation would be:

2 parts echinacea	1 part poke root
1 part dandelion	1 part yellow dock
1 part figwort	

The tea should be drunk 3 times daily and dosage should be according to age.

N.B. Do *not* expect rapid results with natural treatment. It takes at least 30 days for the skin being formed internally to reach the surface so it is self-evident that for true healing that comes from within persistence is necessary. Allow at least 2 months before expecting to see any results. If the bowel is congested take the formulation on page 131.

Avoid hot baths and instead take alternating hot followed by cold showers using a mild soap. Apply witch hazel or lemon juice directly to the skin. To bring out lesions steam the face over hot water mixed with 10 drops of thyme oil and then dab the spots with marigold tincture or cubes of ice after the treatment.

ATHLETE'S FOOT

Keep the feet scrupulously dry and allow them as much air and sun as possible, but be considerate about walking around barefoot in public places because athlete's foot is highly infectious. Soak your feet nightly in a decoction of equal parts of sage, red clover, and marigolds with a dash of cider vinegar. Having dried the feet thoroughly powder them liberally with arrowroot.

Alternatively use Tea tree oil to soak the feet and Tea tree cream rubbed in well between the toes afterwards.

It may be that the athlete's foot is the result of a chronic candidiasis infection (see p.123).

BOILS

Most of us have experienced a boil as the result of local irritation by a hair follicle or a splinter but repeated boils are generally the result of auto-intoxication; that is a body that is congested with poisons. Very occasionally diabetes or an allergy may cause boils.

Do not attempt to lance boils as infection can easily be spread and using the mixture on p.28 the body can easily deal internally with any pus. If they must be drawn apply a simple hot plantain compress to the boil.

CORNS

Corns are usually caused by badly fitting shoes, so first of all correct your footwear.

Macerate 1 oz (30 g) ivy leaves and the same quantity of celandine leaves in enough cider vinegar barely to cover. Leave to stand for a fortnight and top up with vinegar from time to time if necessary. Fork out some of the leaves and bind them into the corner of a piece of linament and bandage. Change the dressing twice daily. The corn will gradually get soft enough to lift out.

Alternatively apply a crushed garlic clove to the corn protecting the surrounding skin with Vaseline or Elastoplast. Secure it with a bandage or plaster and renew this poultice once a day.

DANDRUFF

In my experience the commonest cause of dandruff is incorrect diet coupled with excessive sebaceous gland activity. However, there is some recent feeling that it may be a fungal infection so the general programme for candidiasis is advisable as far as diet is concerned.

Use an olive oil shampoo to wash the hair, and nightly massage the scalp with tincture of rosemary. Follow this with a poultice of linseed oil, protecting the pillowcase with thick towels. Wash this out well in the morning. A final rinse for the hair should be 1 cup cider vinegar in a basin full of water. Repeat this treatment on a nightly basis until the dandruff has completely disappeared.

ECZEMA

This is characterized by inflamed, itchy red skin eruptions which sometimes contain small bubbles just beneath the skin surface which can break producing a weeping rash. The term dermatitis – which simply means inflammation of the skin – is almost interchangeable with eczema and even though allopathic medicine tends to grace it with different terms the differences are not important as far as a wholistic approach is concerned.

Contact eczema or dermatitis which tends to be very common in adults involves avoiding the factor which triggers it off, whether it be chemical, perfume, plant, metal or an item of clothing.

Nutritionally people with eczema are much more likely to have a zinc deficiency coupled with associated disturbance in the metabolism of essential fatty acids. Many of them are allergic to food such as dairy products, eggs, fish, food additives and sugar. If eczema started just after the child was weaned a mother needs to look back particularly carefully at recently introduced foods. Eczema in a breast-fed baby is rare but this may be the result of something that the mother is eating and this needs investigation.

An iridology test will determine whether the liver, kidneys or nervous system have been disrupted and need support. I have had very good success with herbs like burdock root, Oregon grape root, nettle, heart's ease, red clover and black walnut. Ideally these should be prescribed according to individual need but a good overall remedy would be equal parts of:

black walnut	nettles
burdock	red clover
heart's ease	

The tea should be taken 3 times a day before meals, dosage to be adjusted according to age.

An ointment made from 1 oz (30 g) powdered goldenseal root mixed with 9 oz (270 g) linseed oil is helpful applied externally. Alternatively use a marigold, comfrey or chickweed poultice applied ice cold for 1 hour and refresh as necessary. Do this twice daily.

N.B. Although I have been extremely successful in helping patients with eczema be warned that, in my experience, it always gets worse before it gets better and therefore be prepared for a flare-up in the first month or two of treatment.

Interestingly I have always found eczema and its distant cousin psoriasis respond well to a correction of essential fatty acid deficiency. Evening primrose oil is helpful whether it be used internally or externally as are sunflower, safflower, corn, soy and flax seed oil. Any of these may need to be included in the diet, raw and unheated.

HIVES (Urticaria)

This is generally an allergic reaction to food, chlorine, drugs, or an insect sting and it manifests itself as a very nasty, itching, weepy rash.

N.B. If there is severe anaphylactic shock and the patient has difficulty breathing or has fainted, immediate and urgent hospital attention is required.

If hives are chronic I always look to treating the kidneys and attend to adrenal exhaustion and liver congestion as well as lymph stasis. I also cut out all sugars and saturated fats from the diet and reduce the intake of carbohydrate.

A paste of sodium bicarbonate applied to the area locally is useful for itching and for larger areas take a chickweed bath at 104°F (40°C). Or apply cold chickweed compresses to the area affected. A tea of equal parts of burdock root, goldenseal and yellow dock root will relieve very severe itching. Bathe or sponge the skin with it.

IMPETIGO

This is a bacterial infection which produces yellow, crusting infected patches on the skin, generally in children, and it is highly infectious so scrupulous hygiene is of the essence. It usually only occurs when the person concerned is run down, so administer a strong mega-multi vitamin and mineral supplement and ensure the diet is rich in fresh fruits and vegetables. If necessary give doses of vitamin C which stop just short of the point of diarrhoea.

Apply garlic oil directly to the skin or a light spreadable cream made of marigold, echinacea or myrrh. Give the following formulation internally.

2 parts chapparal	1 part pasque flower
2 parts echinacea	1 part poke root

The dose is 1 cup 3 times a day for an adult. Alter the dose accordingly for children depending on age (see p.74).

INGROWN TOE NAILS

Cut the toe nails straight across, never round them at the corners. Mix alum powder with enough witch hazel to form a paste and spread over the ingrown toe nail. Cover with lint and a bandage. Renew twice daily until the swelling and pain are gone. As a preventative measure, scratch the top of the toenail with an emery board so that it is thin. Do this daily and the toe nail will grow out flat.

LIVER SPOTS

These are the large brown freckles which usually appear on the back of hands and seem to be the result of age and lack of vitamins E, C and B_2. Massage nightly with castor oil. Some of my patients have used this on a regular basis and achieved very good results.

PSORIASIS

This affects 2% of the human race and is characterized by the presence of red, scaly plaques which are found on the arms and legs, particularly the elbows and knees, the trunk and scalp. Psoriasis is not contagious but it is possible to pass it on to one's children. In my experience intensive tar, sulphur or X-ray treatment merely impede any possible healing of this very stubborn skin disease.

Naturopaths believe the most common factor seems to be a thinning of the small intestinal walls which allows poisons to enter the circulation system and the lymph thereby setting up irritations on the skin. This thinning may be the result of constipation, malabsorption of essential fatty acids, food allergy, improperly functioning kidneys or liver, previous immunizations or candidiasis. An iridology test is therefore particularly helpful to enable the practitioner to adopt an appropriate approach.

Emotional factors must not be ignored. Stress certainly makes this disease worse.

In my own practice I have found the use of a raw food diet coupled with lecithin supplementation particularly helpful, together with zinc, folic acid, and essential fatty acids. All animal products need to be strictly eliminated and prolonged supervised fasts ranging from 1 to 3 weeks produce excellent results.

Certainly sunbathing and sea water help to effect a temporary clearing and alternate hot and cold showers are useful. I advise the application of a castor oil poultice to the abdomen 6 nights weekly resting on the seventh. The colon needs to be strengthened and cleared with the formula on page 32–33, and this treatment should be coupled with fasting and enemas done on a supervised basis for 1 to 3 weeks periodically. A good overall formulation is a tincture made from equal parts of:

burdock	scullcap
dandelion	yellow dock
figwort	

Dosage: 20 drops of the tincture in water before a meal 3 times daily.

N.B. Psoriasis takes a very long time to clear so treatment must be long term.

SEBORRHOEIC DERMATITIS
(Malfunction of sebaceous glands)

This is characterized by a nasty red, greasy, scaly rash which is mildly irritating and usually found on the face, around the nose, chin and forehead, behind the ear, between the shoulder blades, over the breast bone, in the armpits, groin and under the breasts in women (see also cradle cap for babies, p.224).

It seems that mild forms are extremely common and vitamin B_6 and B_2 deficiencies are often present. Take a strong supplement of vitamin B complex. Also take two tablespoons of cold pressed linseed oil daily. Coming off the contraceptive pill helps. Avoid all refined carbohydrates initially, all fruits except for papaya, avocado and well ripened bananas. Ensure the diet is very rich in seeds, nuts, legumes and pulses, and vegetarian proteins like tofu.

Also take 20 drops of grindelia tincture in water 3 times a day and apply external poultices of an infusion of the leaves twice daily.

SHINGLES

This is an infection of nerve fibres produced by the same virus that causes chicken pox. It is characterized by the appearance of clusters of painful blisters wherever the branches of the affected nerves end, most often on one side of the face or on the side of the trunk. You have to be very run down to get shingles so look immediately to the diet. Move over to a vegetarian diet which is rich in whole grains. Massive doses of vitamin C which stops just short of diarrhoea are particularly helpful.

A useful overall remedy is:

2 parts echinacea	*1 part scullcap*
2 parts goldenrod	*1 part valerian*
1 part oats	

Make a tincture and take 20 drops daily in fruit juice. Also dab the affected area with equal parts of a tincture made from marigolds, lavender, goldenseal and myrrh. This will greatly relieve the itching.

Neuralgia will sometimes persist after the blisters have gone so continue to treat the condition as for neuralgia (see p.192).

CHAPTER *13*
CHILDREN'S *ILLNESSES*

Regard children's diseases as beneficial in so far as fevers involved dispose of pathological material within the system that would otherwise cause more serious conditions later on. Provided the child is healthy the disease will easily be overcome and the body strengthened as a result of doing so. It is essential to ensure that all childhood diseases are treated properly and not suppressed. Fevers destroy not only the poisons accumulated during the lifetime of the child, they also eliminate many of those toxins which have been brought over from the embryonic stage of development. Indeed, it is my experience that people who have never had any childish ailments are apt to succumb to all sorts of diseases later in life. So properly handled fevers are wonderfully curative in as much as they protect us from, rather than expose us to, diseases. Also having properly endured a childhood disease we tend not to get it twice because we build up antibodies to such illnesses as German measles and chicken pox viruses.

It must always be remembered that diet is the single most important factor that protects us or disposes us to childhood diseases. Give a germ lots of soil to flourish on and it will wreak all kinds of havoc – such soil being sugar and all other refined carbohydrates. I have no patience with parents who complain that their sick little mite will not under any circumstances eat green vegetables. Dietary habits can readily be instilled in a baby. Wean a baby on to green vegetables and fresh fruits, leaving the unprocessed cereals, especially wheat, till last and you should have no problems. My three-year-old goddaughter and her baby sister are simply not interested in junk food, not merely because they are never offered it (at least by their parents!) but because they do not like the taste of it, having been correctly weaned. A well-fed child will develop a strong, healthy reaction to any childhood disease and they tend to be over quickly. It is far better to develop a short-lived high fever with a good rapid rash development and heavy sweating than a mild fever, light perspiration, and a nearly invisible rash.

TREATMENT

Basic treatment for most childhood infections is simple. Nearly all children who are left to their own instincts will ask for only liquids, so offer only fruit and vegetable juices, home-made lemonade sweetened with a little honey but *no* sugar, plenty of mineral water and herbal tea.

Work with the fever by applying warm packs to the body using either compresses or poultices over the infected areas. Warm baths are also helpful. In both instances such gentle hydrotherapy encourages perspiration which is essential. At all costs the bowels must be kept open and working freely so herbal laxatives or small rectal injections of lukewarm herbal teas may be needed. The best ones to administer are catnip, camomile or horsetail. Rectal injections consist of only 5 fl oz (125 ml) of liquid whereas a full enema may consist of a pint (600 ml) upwards and is therefore a bigger undertaking.

N.B. Do not attempt to administer an enema to a child without medical supervision. Once learned they are very easy to carry out and in my experience very young children do not mind them at all providing one is quick and adept with them.

BEDWETTING

Do not give the child anything to drink after 7 o'clock. If she/he is thirsty, offer a really juicy piece of fruit instead. There must be absolutely no salt in the diet. Massage the kidneys daily with warm olive oil and encourage the child to sleep on one side, not flat on the back. A hand towel tied around the waist and knotted at the back helps here and is simpler than sewing the proverbial tennis ball into the pyjamas. Give 3 cups of equal parts of parsley and corn tassel tea daily. This is a particularly safe remedy for children because it won't irritate tender tummies or the urinary tract, so making the problem worse.

Foot baths of corn tassel also help (for correct administration see p.65).

There really isn't any need to worry about bedwetting unless it happens frequently after the age of 6 or 7, but do attend to *any* anxiety in the child as bedwetting is often the result of well disguised anxiety.

Cold sitz-baths, provided the child can be persuaded to take them, are particularly helpful for this condition. Five minutes, twice daily. Start with cool water and add iced water gradually if this is more comfortable and acceptable. Alternatively, if the cold sitz is too strenuous, try hot and cold sitz-baths (hot one minute, cold two minutes, repeating once). However, the cold sitz-bath is more effective.

Consider spinal lesions which may disrupt the normal flow of circulation to the bladder. An iridology test will show them clearly and referral to an osteopath is necessary in this case.

CHICKEN POX

Give the child a warm catnip tea enema (observing the provisions already mentioned in this chapter, see above or a herbal laxative (see p.32). Herbal tea such as catnip and peppermint, pleurisy root and catnip, raspberry leaf, yarrow or pennyroyal, elderflowers and peppermint, boneset, yarrow and echinacea will all induce sweating.

It is essential to avoid pock scarring. Try first to encourage the child not to scratch. Sponge the skin with herbal teas made as a double strength decoction of burdock root, goldenseal, or goldenseal and yellow dock root in case of severe itching. Ice cold witch hazel is also helpful dabbed directly on to the skin with a piece of cotton cloth. Afterwards dab the area dry and pat with a little arrowroot.

High doses of vitamin C have been known to help a number of viral infections including measles, mumps, shingles and chicken pox. Give a dose that takes the child just short of diarrhoea. Soluble vitamin C is usually more readily accepted (for supplier see Appendix).

Biochemic tissue salts are very helpful for treating children and ferrous phosphate is one I particularly like giving to feverish children because it assists in the oxidation of toxins. These are available from chemists. Ask your local chemist about the appropriate dosage.

CRADLE CAP *(Seborrheic Dermatitis)*

If the child is no longer breast feeding, check there are no dairy products in the diet. Give 4 teaspoons of a standard infusion of heart's ease (Viola tricolor) with every feed and ensure there is plenty of calcium in the diet, if necessary adding the following calcium formula sprinkled in oat or millet cereals.

4 parts comfrey	*1 part meadowsweet*
4 parts horsetail	*3 parts nettles*
2 parts kelp	

All herbs to be finely powdered. For babies under one year, half a level 5 ml teaspoon to be mixed into food once daily. For older children adjust dose accordingly (see p.74).

If the baby is still at the breast, ensure the mother drinks one pint of almond milk daily (soak 1 oz/30 g of freshly-grated almonds in 1 pint/600 ml of water for 24 hours and drink the juice). Add the remaining almond sludge to cereals or soups. Ensure the mother's intake of magnesium and B_6 are adequate.

Crush 100 mg B_6 to a fine powder and add 1 tablespoon of almond oil. Rub gently over the yellow crusty scabs. The almond oil may be substituted by St John's wort oil for even better effect. Alternatively, wash the head with a tepid standard infusion of meadowsweet flowers, but on no account use plain soap and water. It only makes the condition worse. In either case massage the oil into the scalp for 5 minutes and then leave it on for a further half hour. Brush the scalp well taking care not to cause bleeding or create inflammation and then rinse out the oil with a heavily diluted baby shampoo. Finish with a tepid rinse making sure there is no trace of shampoo left and repeat twice weekly until the condition is cleared (for suppliers of good shampoo for babies see Appendix).

CROUP

This is characterized by laborious and suffocative breathing and a harsh, brassy, crowing cough. It tends to get worse at night. It is a disease that is characteristic of children and rarely affects adults.

Keep the bowels working freely with mild laxative herbs like liquorice and turkey rhubarb. Stay on a fruit and fruit juice fast for a few days although slippery elm gruel is also helpful. Give equal parts of catnip and peppermint tea with 10 drops of lobelia in each cup – dosage according to age.

Keep the air moist with a good steam vaporizer. These are reasonably easy to order from electrical suppliers and come complete with instructions.

If an adult gets croup it usually spreads to the larynx so treat as for tonsillitis (see p.97).

MEASLES

This is common in childhood from 6 months to 5 years. Early on, when you are uncertain as to the nature of the illness, take a look at the mucus membranes on the inside of the cheeks near the molars at the back. If it is a case of measles you will discover, a day or two before the blotchy rash appears on the forehead and behind the ears, that there are bright red spots with small white dots approximately one-eighth of an inch (3 mm) in diameter. This is an unmistakeable sign of measles.

Hot ginger chest poultices applied in the initial stages of the disease will bring out the rash. Then apply hot compresses of wild thyme to the skin directly to draw out internal toxins.

The diet is as for chicken pox with fresh fruits and lightly steamed vegetables being introduced once the child is well recovered. Do *not* overfeed which may lead to complications including *otitis media*, a middle ear infection, and bronchopneumonia. Vitamin C will need to be taken to a point just short of diarrhoea and may have to be administered intravenously in very severe cases.

To ensure oral hygiene if the child is tiny wrap a clean cloth around your fingertip, dip it into diluted whey-concentrate (for suppliers see Appendix) and disinfect the gums and mucus membranes in the tongue which are nearly always furred. A small toothbrush dipped in the same solution can be used for bigger children.

A tea of equal parts of yarrow, pleurisy root and lady's slipper should be given to produce perspiration. It may be given freely.

Keep the room dark so that the eyes will not become irritated. If the child's eyes do become sore bathe them 2 or 3 times a day with a solution of freshly made and well strained tea of equal parts of eyebright, raspberry leaf and goldenseal. If the child is hyperactive or irritable give camomile tea freely. If itching is a problem treat the skin as for chicken pox (see chicken

pox, p.223). If the glands become swollen give a tea of equal parts of marigold and cleavers, the dosage according to age (see p.74). Also apply mullein and lobelia compresses externally as required.

The biotissue salt Kali-phosphate will help if there is any suggestion of lung or bronchial complications (ask your local chemist about the dose). A tincture of sundew is useful if a cough develops (again dosage according to age).

MUMPS

Complications are rare before puberty but because it is chiefly the parotid glands which are attacked, care must be taken that swelling of ovaries or testicles does not get out of hand, otherwise permanent sterility may result.

Treat as for chicken pox in terms of diet and bed rest. Treat swollen glands internally and externally with mullein and lobelia formulation (see p.97). Replace the external compress every half hour during the day and leave on all night.

Administer warm sitz-baths at 110°F (43°C) adding equal parts of an infusion of arnica and marigold to the water.

Particularly painful testicles will benefit from a warm poultice of St John's wort oil or a poultice of whey concentrate (for suppliers see Appendix). Ensure the feet are kept warm while the poultices are applied. If ovarian complications look possible administer one size '0' capsule of pulsatilla every second hour while awake. This is an adult dose. Adjust according to age (see p.74).

Gargling with whey concentrate or a tincture of thyme will soothe sore throats.

In all cases give the following formulation in addition to other suggested remedies:

2 parts echinacea	*1 part goldenseal*
1 part ginseng	*1 part yellow dock*
(Korean)	*½ part ginger root*

Of the finely powdered herbs, in the case of teenagers and adults take four size '0' capsules twice daily until completely recovered, including the period of convalescence but for not longer than three weeks in all. Alter the dose accordingly for children (see p.75). No coffee to be taken while on this remedy. For children under 10 omit the ginseng and substitute angelica root instead.

NAPPY RASH

Nappy rash can best be avoided by using a mild soap for washing and immediately after bathing try St John's wort oil. Alternatively make a cream of equal parts of lavender, camomile and balm of gilead in an almond oil base. Add 10 drops of each of these oils to 4 fl oz (100 ml) cream. Do not use talc to soothe nappy rash. It collects bacteria very efficiently and will make the situation worse.

SCARLET FEVER

This is an acute streptococcal infection of the throat and because secondary complications are a possibility (nephritis, middle ear infection, rheumatic fever) seek the professional help of a medical herbalist. Children may need to be treated in the short term with very high doses of vitamins C and A as well as zinc and anti-infective herbs together with gargles of Tea tree oil diluted in water.

WHOOPING COUGH

This is one of the most serious childhood diseases and treatment must be particularly vigorous and consistent to get the best results. Prevention is the obvious answer and it helps to avoid colds and stuffy damp rooms.

Keep the child warm and in bed. Fast on fruit juice, especially pineapple and citrus, for a few days then introduce potassium broth (see p.211), vegetable juices and fresh fruit. Overfeeding definitely makes the condition worse.

Apply a garlic foot compress (see p.61–3) and chest poultices of onion, horseradish or mustard (see p.60–1). Take care that they do not blister the skin by overlong contact. Maximum reddening of the skin shows the poultice should be removed.

Steam inhalation of Olbas will also help as does the following remedy. Equal parts of:

bayberry	*thymus*
hyssop	*turkey rhubarb*
raspberry leaves	

Decoct the first 4 herbs then pour this over the thyme and infuse for half an hour covered. Strain. Take one teaspoon or more as needed, depending on age (see p.74).

CHAPTER *14*
INFECTIONS AND INFESTATIONS

CRABS

Most people who have crabs know from the incessant itching of pubic hair that something is awry. The eggs take from 7 to 9 days to hatch and each crab is capable of laying 3 eggs a day.

Crabs are easily transmitted not only by sexual contact but by sitting on the same couch, using the same toilet, or sharing a bed with someone who has them.

To 3 fl oz (75 ml) olive oil add 10 drops each of rosemary oil and lavender oil, 12 drops of eucalyptus oil and 13 drops of geranium oil. Saturate the area infested (usually the pubic area although they can survive in any hairy part of the body) with the oil and cover with close-fitting plastic pants or wrap the area in cling film. Leave on for 2 hours. Remove over the toilet and shampoo. Comb through the hair with a fine-tooth comb to remove any eggs. Repeat the treatment after 3 days, and again after a further 3 days.

FLEAS AND LICE

I once owned a cat which was so rife with fleas that I was bitten from the knee down on a permanent basis. The moment we got rid of them on her she would go off hunting and come back infested all over again. Tincture of bay oil used externally is a good flea repellent. Sprinkle it around the house or rub it on to the skin.

It must be remembered that all these parasites cannot exist long with clean healthy cells so internal and external hygiene is vitally important.

Dr Christopher recommends for the treatment of head lice the following infusion:

6 parts hyssop	*½ part cloves*
1 part walnut leaves	*½ part ginger*
½ part cinnamon	*½ part lobelia*

Take half a cup 3 times a day internally. Make a compress over the head or any other areas infected and leave this on all night.

For quick relief bathe the head or body parts affected with undiluted-cider vinegar and garlic tincture or walnut tea.

Spray the room with a tea made with 6 parts of chapparal, 3 parts black walnut leaf, and 1 part of lobelia and to each pint (600 ml) of the spray add a teaspoon of lavender or mint oil. Linen must be changed and boiled daily and pay particular attention to the cleanliness of your clothes and towels.

After removing the fomentation every morning, comb your hair through with a fine-tooth comb (available from chemists). These are designed to remove the dead lice and eggs.

VIRAL INFECTIONS

There are some herbs that help to lessen the effect of viral infections. It must always be remembered that infections, with or of a bacterial, viral or fungal nature, will only occur when the body's defences are weakened. Such weakness need not just be the result of a neglected diet but can embrace drug therapy, emotional trauma or a pre-existing disease. A debilitating virus which threatens to drag on can be treated with the following mixture:

2 parts chapparal	2 parts goldenseal
2 parts echinacea	2 parts myrrh
2 parts garlic	2 parts poke root

Drink a cup of this mixture as hot as possible three times a day. It doesn't taste wonderful so decocting it in fruit juice may be helpful.

Also increase the vitamin C intake to a point just short of diarrhoea. Ensure you are getting plenty of B complex. Continue with the herbal medication for at least two weeks after you feel the virus has cleared up. It is often a good idea to go on a course of ginseng after a viral infection, particularly the sort that leaves you feeling very run-down and tired for weeks afterwards. Mix equal parts of Asiatic, American and Siberian ginseng and take 2 g daily for 3 out of 4 weeks. Do not continue this regime for longer than 3 months. The elderly are advised to take 800 mg on the same cyclical basis.

N.B. For children who are hyperactive and women with menstrual irregularities ginseng is contraindicated. Nor should it ever be taken with coffee or any product containing caffeine.

WORMS

Worms outrank even cancer as the human race's deadliest enemy. According to the World Health Organization every fourth person is infected by

worms and if one were to add worms picked up in the tropics including hook and whip worms then possibly every third member of the human race has intestinal parasites. These parasites range in size from microscopic single-celled creatures to 24 ft (7.3 m) tape worms. Some of my patients, during the course of a thorough bowel clean, are quite stunned to see worms come out of themselves, never having displayed the usual symptoms of anal irritation, dry lips during the day and wet at night, a little pool of spit dribbled on to the pillow at night, loss of appetite, irritability, dark circles under the eyes, frequent colds, anaemia, sudden loss of weight, weakness and lassitude.

As well as tape worms, round worms, thread worms, there are also hook worms, all floating around in a variety of unpleasant places, eager to crawl into a comfortable and nourishing body. You can ingest them by eating unwashed foods that have been grown on soil fertilized with manure that has not been properly composted. Soil in China and other parts of the Third World is fertilized with human excreta and when having a colonic irrigation administered after my return from China I was not therefore unduly surprised to witness two quite large worms beating a hasty retreat from my colon. These were in fact round worms. Such worms if left to breed (and a single female produces about 200 000 eggs each day) may become entangled in the intestines, blocking various organs or ducts.

In order to avoid them always wash your hands after going to the toilet, do not eat anything which has been composted in human faeces, and always wash all vegetables. Do not allow dogs to lick the face or hands. Field mice can be infected by excrement from dogs and this in turn can be transmitted to cats and from these to humans. The larvae of echinococcus can form small blister-like swellings in the human liver, as well as attacking the intestine. So do not allow cats who are infested with worms to sleep on the bed.

Tapeworms are acquired from poorly prepared pork (no wonder the writers of Leviticus banned pork products – a sensible precaution in the days before refrigerators) and from uncooked fish. They are the most difficult worms to get rid of and linger in the colon, slightly lowering iron absorption year by year but rarely going far enough to be fatal (obviously a parasite that actually killed its host would be rather self-defeating). Tapeworms can induce a particularly severe form of anaemia.

Hookworms tend to occur in tropical countries and are picked up by people walking barefooted in areas where faeces have been excreted from pigs, dogs, cattle and humans. I saw many people suffering from them during my childhood in East Africa. As with tapeworms, hookworms primarily cause anaemia but they can also lead to respiratory problems, nausea and diarrhoea.

Threadworms are the most common worm infestation and 65% of British schoolchildren are known to be infected with them at some time or another. They are spread by inhaling or ingesting their eggs and the female creeps out of the anus at night to lay her eggs externally. If the anus is then scratched the eggs lodge under the fingernails and can be passed on. A single female is capable of laying 10 000 eggs which can mature in 2 weeks. They can produce symptoms which appear to be like appendicitis. As with all other parasitic infestations threadworms develop best if the vitality is low and the diet is poor, particularly if it is rich in refined carbohydrates and sugar and low in fibre. If someone in the family has threadworms hygiene is obviously of the essence and all underwear, sheets and towels need to be boiled.

Treatment

Worms revel in a constipated colon and enjoy sugar and acid conditions. So a high fibre alkaline and sugar-free diet are the best means of prevention and cure. Foods which worms particularly dislike include garlic, onions, pomegranates, pumpkin seeds, cabbage, papaya, horseradish, figs and pineapple.

Dr Shook, my teacher's teacher, advises the following regime to get rid of both tapeworms and roundworms. Begin by eating all the foods that worms hate (together with other foods, of course) and drink a strong cup of wormwood tea in the morning and at night for 3 days using the usual proportions for an infusion. On the fourth day take a cup of senna tea to cleanse the bowel of the dead parasites. Add some liquorice to the tea to prevent griping pains and instead of wormwood any other anthelmintic may be used if it seems more appropriate. (Other anthelmintics include aloe, butternut, elecampane, hyssop and wormseed.) In fact wormwood tastes very bitter and it works just as effectively in pill form so avoiding the extreme bitter taste. Pomegranate seeds would be a tastier and more palatable alternative.

To assist tapeworm evacuation (and I know this sounds hilarious) sit on a bucket with some warm milk in it when it is time to empty the bowel. Cold air stops the tapeworm from leaving and warm air entices it out. It is vital to ensure that the head with its digestive suckers which look like 2 big eyes emerges, so inspect the contents of the bucket afterwards.

Threadworms need to be treated with garlic enemas or a peeled clove of garlic with the inner skin still left unbroken inserted directly into the anus at night. Rub garlic oil externally around the anus. Quassia tea made as a decoction in equal parts with liquorice should be taken internally, 2 teaspoons before meals 3 times a day.

Because the removal of worms is rather a tricky business you are advised to seek the professional help of a qualified medical herbalist conversant in these matters.

CHAPTER *15*
FIRST AID

Every responsible household should have a well-stocked first aid cabinet at the ready in case of an emergency. Accidents are the most common cause of death in the age group from 1 to 14. Yet most serious accidents can easily be prevented. People, particularly children, are more likely to have accidents when they are sick, tired, cranky, very excited, distracted, unhappy, jealous or worried. As far as children are concerned it is interesting to note that they tend to be prone to particular accidents. Research has proved that individual children are prone to certain types of accidents, some fall, some pinch their fingers, some get burned, some ingest poisons, in fact, a study carried out on poisonings shows that 25% of all children who ingest poisons will have a second episode of ingestion within a year. So the more parents understand their children's own tendencies the more effectively they can safety-proof their environment and work to educate their child. This section is not designed to qualify anyone in first aid and it does not have detailed instructions for bandaging, splinting, suturing or setting broken bones. All these can be learned at a first-aid class and everyone is urged to attend at least one. Most people are terrified at the mere thought of an accident occurring and wouldn't know what to do if one did occur. Learning the most effective way to respond to any accident will help to relieve much of this terror and attendance at a first aid course is the first step to doing this.

There are two accident situations in which prompt action is essential:

1. When a person has stopped breathing due to choking, electric shock or drowning.

2. When a person is bleeding severely due to a large cut or puncture wound.

If breathing has stopped resuscitation should begin within minutes and such resuscitation is taught at first-aid class.

If someone is bleeding severely a firm pressure should be applied directly. Only very serious bleeding from a major artery requires the use of a tourniquet and this is best applied by somebody properly trained in first aid because improper use can actually result in blood vessel and nerve damage.

The aim of this section is to deal with the most commonly occurring conditions as far as first aid is concerned and to offer advice on what to do until the doctor can be reached. Please note that most accidents are not serious and they rarely are true emergencies in the sense that it is important to act or get help immediately. In nearly every accident one has enough time to comfort the victim and calm them down (as well as calming down oneself of course), before you even evaluate the extent of the injury. In fact, calming down is the first important step in treating most scrapes, stings, bites, cuts, burns, bumps and falls. But there may be situations where you are far away from home, for example, when there simply isn't the time or the facility to look up medical treatment or situations such as severe burns, poisonings and head injuries and so some basic knowledge beforehand can be very useful. You are therefore advised to read this section through completely and memorize anything you feel may be important.

LIST OF ESSENTIAL HERBAL PREPARATIONS FOR A FIRST AID CABINET

Ensure you stock the following seeds in their whole form:

caraway
dill
fennel

Also ensure you have a small supply of each of the following herbs:

cayenne
chaparral
false unicorn
ginger
lobelia (obtainable only on prescription from a qualified medical herbalist)
slippery elm

Include the following tinctures:

arnica
cayenne
echinacea
goldenseal
lobelia
plantain

The most important essential oils are lavender, rosemary and thyme oils. A larger container of St John's wort oil and Tea tree oil are also useful.

Ensure you have a bottle of Rescue Remedy and a bottle of syrup of ipecacuana as well as some vitamin E oil in capsule form, a small jar of organic runny honey, several garlic cloves, comfrey ointment and marigold cream. Finally, a bottle of witch hazel is always useful for sprains and elder flower, peppermint and yarrow herbs should be kept at the ready for fevers.

Bites

Snake Bites

Red Indians applied crushed root of black cohosh directly externally to the bite and administered a few drops of the fresh juice internally.

However, as different snake poisons affect the body in different ways the most advisable course of action is to seek medical treatment immediately. If possible try to get an accurate description of the snake as this will affect the treatment.

Dog Bites

Apply bruised leaves of hound's tongue directly to the wound. Half of the people who get bitten by dogs are children under 5 and the dog is normally a family one or belongs to a neighbour. So always supervise small children when around dogs, including family pets or better still do not get a dog till the child is old enough to be trusted not to provoke an animal either deliberately or by innocent activities that might seem threatening to a dog.

Bruises

Apply a compress of tincture of arnica, prepared from the flowers externally every few hours. Do *not* use tincture of arnica internally. Homeopathic tablets of arnica at the dose prescribed on the container can be used internally.

Apply an ice-cold compress of witch hazel externally and renew as needed.

Burns

For first-degree burns (first-degree burns affect the outer skin only and many may cause redness, dryness, blistering and mild swelling) immerse the burn immediately in cold running water or rub it with ice cubes until all the pain has gone. This will stop blisters and modify any tissue damage. Alternatively when the first degree burn is very mild cut the juicy leaf of aloe vera open and apply the gelatinous contents directly to the burn. This is a useful houseplant which can be readily at hand and is easy to grow (for suppliers see Appendix) or rub in St John's wort oil (see p.70) or marigold cream.

For second-degree burns which involve the lower skin layers and may produce mottling, blisters or swelling follow the same initial step then spread the contents of a 1000 IU capsule of vitamin E over the burn or use several capsules if the area is large. This will protect the skin while you prepare a paste of equal parts of:

> *powdered comfrey root*
> *runny organic honey*
> *vitamin E oil*

Spread this evenly over the burn and *leave it on*. Do not attempt to peel it off. Simply apply more as the skin absorbs it and cover with gauze and a bandage. Continue to do this for a few days until all pain and swelling has subsided. If for any reason you do have to remove it (and try to avoid this) soak it off with a warm decoction of equal parts of echinacea and goldenseal. Keep the burn out of the sun for at least a year, and as soon as the skin is strong enough skin brush daily.

For acid burns flush the area immediately with 1 pint (600 ml) of cold water into which you have stirred 1 teaspoon of bicarbonate of soda. Apply poultices of non-alcoholic witch hazel till the pain subsides and then cover with vitamin E oil, replenishing this every hour.

Third-degree burns which involve the full thickness of the skin need immediate medical supervision, but taking powdered comfrey root internally, ten size '0' capsules daily, will accelerate healing. Continue soaking the area in ice-cold water on your way to hospital.

My American teacher got such a severe burn on his hand that the hospital suggested a skin graft. Apart from being totally devoted to natural healing he was well aware of the exorbitant cost of American hospitalization and so chose to heal himself by fasting on a gallon (4.5 litres) of carrot juice daily and by using the comfrey, vitamin E and honey poultice with a generous bunch of lobelia added to it. The initial extreme pain he tried to help by taking equal parts of valerian and wild lettuce but he said it was not very effective.

He now has no signs of scarring whatsoever on his hand.

A burned tongue may be cured by sprinkling a few grains of sugar on it, and repeating as often as necessary.

CONVALESCENCE

Mental and emotional healing is as important as physical healing and often the Bach Flower Remedies will be of great help here. Ask a medical herbalist who uses them for advice (see Appendix).

Ensure deep and restful sleep by taking lemon balm tea before bed, sweetened with grape sugar. This oxidizes in the system without any waste and does not leach calcium from the body.

Systemic treatment best suited to the individual, determined by an iridological examination, will lay the sure foundations for a speedy convalescence, but the following remedy will help generally.

Equal parts of:

angelica	gotu kola
alfalfa	Icelandic moss
ginger	scullcap

Take two size '0' capsules of the powdered herbs with each meal which should be light and exceptionally nutritious.

CUTS AND MINOR WOUNDS

Place the wound in ice-cold water to stop the bleeding and reduce inflammation or alternatively apply cayenne pepper directly externally which will do the same thing. Ensure the cut is absolutely clean. Proper cleansing is vital to help the wound heal easily and to prevent infection. If after a day or two the cut becomes tender and begins to swell or redden, indicating that it has become infected, there is a very simple remedy. If the infection is mild, soak the injured area in warm water for 15 minutes, 2 or 3 times a day. The warmth of the water increases blood flow which brings antibodies and white blood cells to the area. Tea tree or thyme oil applied directly to the wound will sting like crazy but will certainly stop infection. A poultice of powdered comfrey root will accelerate the healing or if the cut is very superficial use comfrey ointment.

Apply neat cayenne pepper over bleeding cuts, it sounds radical, and it certainly stings, but it works magically!

If a person cuts off a large flap of skin, such as a finger tip, pressure should be applied to the cut to stop the bleeding. The piece of skin should be put into ice-cold water or salt water (½ teaspoon of salt to 2 pints (1.2 litres) of water) and taken along to the doctor. Generally it is possible to stitch the flap back on.

If the bleeding is copious and difficult to stop take a ¼ teaspoon of cayenne in water, preferably warm, internally and apply a tourniquet externally. However the majority of cuts are minimal and rapidly heal by themselves. A cut will need attention by a doctor only if it is deep or doesn't stop bleeding readily or contains dirt or foreign bodies that cannot be easily extracted. You may consider a cut deep enough if it goes through the skin and is long enough so that the sides of the cut separate and do not stay together. When a cut is this deep shiny connective tissues or yellow globules of fat can be seen in the wound.

Whereas scrapes and minor cuts seem to be part and parcel of early childhood, puncture wounds and many lacerations can be prevented. Children should be instructed at a very early age in dangers and proper use of sharp objects like scissors, knives and tools. Puncture wounds are most commonly caused by nails in boards so any such boards with nails or tacks sticking out or sharp scraps of metal should obviously be removed from

areas where children play. Large scrapes are generally caused by falls on cement or gravel when children are running or riding bikes and in this instance it is advisable that parents exercise some supervision about where their children engage in such play.

DYSENTERY

If at all possible take an enema of thinned yoghurt and every half hour take 1 size '0' capsule of:

---

2 parts blackberry bark
1 part chapparal
1 part goldenseal

Once you can eat take only plain live yoghurt and rice for several days.

My American teacher who had a bout of dysentery in India accelerated his own healing by using the cold sheet treatment which involves taking a garlic enema, inducing a fever by sitting in a hot bath of diaphoretic herbs which will help you sweat freely and drinking diaphoretic teas, wrapping the soles of the feet in garlic paste and finally sweating it out wrapped in a sheet dipped in melting ice cubes and lightly wrung out and woollen blankets. To the layman such treatment may sound both hilarious and horrific but it is extremely effective. It is also very searching and powerful and so ought to be supervised by a medical herbalist (see Appendix). Garlic is particularly helpful as this is a bacillary infection, usually the result of food poisoning.

AMOEBIC DYSENTERY

This is the result of an amoebic infection and is confined to tropical and sub-tropical countries. This is difficult to treat but was very successfully curbed by American Red Indians with equal parts of tincture of:

---

echinacea
rhatany
wild indigo

Dosage: 20 drops in water every 2 to 4 hours depending on the symptoms of the patient. It probably owes it success to the emphasis on hepatic herbs as often follow-up treatment for the liver is necessary.

FEVER

The most important thing to remember about a fever is to work with it not against it. A fever is nature's way of offloading toxins and destroying pathogenic bacteria which only thrive in a body of normal temperature.

An elevated temperature slows down their reproduction to such an extent it will eventually destroy them.

When I am working with a fever I try not to let the temperature drop below 102°F (39°C) unless it has gone on for more than 3 days, or to rise above 104°F (40°C). If fever reaches 106°F (41°C) there is a possibility of brain damage, a prolonged fever can point to depleted energy reserves or a poor immune system unable to rally, and an inability to sweat demands immediate intervention. Sweating is nature's way of regulating temperature and offloading toxins.

N.B. A fever in a baby needs medical supervision as infants' fevers are notorious for escalating rapidly because their temperature control mechanisms are still unstable. Children also need to be carefully monitored as so much of their fever management depends on the condition of the child.

TREATMENT

Nothing by mouth except hot herbal teas. The most helpful are:

catnip	*lemon balm*
elderflower	*peppermint*
ginger	*verbena*

All act as diaphoretics, inducing mild sweating but a decoction of pleurisy root will induce really copious sweating. To eliminate mucus drink a decoction of fenugreek with 7 crushed peppercorns added to 1 pint (600 ml) of decoction.

To help body aches drink boneset tea or take two size '0' capsules of boneset every hour.

Diluted fresh fruit juices and honey and lemon are also helpful. My favourite mixture, which is pretty antisocial but effective, is a decoction of ginger root with plenty of honey and lemon in it, a crushed clove of garlic or a teaspoon of garlic syrup and a pinch of cayenne.

The idea of any diaphoretic herbal tea is to encourage sweating. It is vital not to become dehydrated and this particularly applies to children – so drink lots of mineral water.

Throughout a fever take a tincture of 5 drops of echinacea and 5 drops of goldenseal together in a little water every hour.

To reduce the temperature take body temperature baths (98.6°F, 37°C) for half an hour followed by a brisk towel rub and dry skin brushing if vitality is high. If low use a body pack or an Epsom salt bath with a teaspoon of mustard in it (see p.63) and keep covered with lots of woollen blankets.

Once the fever has broken sponge the body down with a half and half mixture of cider vinegar and warm water. Air dry the body naturally and put on clean cotton nightclothes and fresh bed linen to sleep.

FROST BITE

Rapidly warm up the area by take a warm bath of about 110°F (43°C). Take care not to overdo the heat or you will burn the frozen skin. Pat do not rub dry. Administer Rescue Remedy internally and externally if necessary every 15 minutes and seek immediate medical help. Generally there are few complications but if improperly handled the condition may lead to gangrene.

HAEMORRHAGE

As this is usually an emergency, I find cayenne pepper the most easily used remedy. Cayenne tastes hot so the idea that it will not be harmful is hard to grasp for the amateur but it is not irritating if uncooked and I have used it many times in all sorts of emergencies with great success. It gives speedy results. It normalizes internal and external circulation and so stops bleeding.

Take a level teaspoon in a cup of warm water, drinking it as quickly as possible. If necessary repeat every 15 minutes. It can also be used as a vaginal douche to stop uterine haemorrhage though it does sting!

HICCUPS

This tends to be a problem only when food is fermenting in the stomach causing gas to build up, or if you are full of phlegm. Ensure fruit and juices are not taken with any meals, though they may be eaten or drunk separately an hour or more after a meal. Make sure your food combinations are correct (see p.22). Meals should be eaten in a quiet calm atmosphere at a leisurely pace.

You will know the one about drinking cold water out of the wrong side of a glass. It often works. If it doesn't, try giving equal parts of fennel or anise or dill and roses boiled as a decoction, a teaspoon at a time. This is especially suitable for babies. Freshly grated coconut, if you have it to hand, mixed with equal parts of solid honey is good for toddlers. Make sure it is chewed well.

Adults might like to try a sturdier approach and eat a lemon wedge soaked in angostura bitters (everything but the rind). Alternatively sneezing can be induced by sniffing a small pinch of black pepper. As the last resort breathing into a paper (N.B. not plastic) bag often helps.

INSECT STINGS

Remove the sting by flicking it out with the thumbnail so the barb comes out cleanly without tearing the skin and if one is to hand, rub the area with a cube of ice. Alternatively suck up and spit out the poison. Rub a pulped

leaf or ivy, plaintain or a piece of raw onion on to the sting. Apply a salt water compress to which a little tincture of ivy or plantain has been added. Take 10 drops of plantain in water every 2 hours internally till swelling and itching have subsided.

INSECT STINGS IN THE THROAT

To prevent choking gargle frequently with 4 teaspoons of salt in a cup of water. If tincture of ivy or plantain is available add 10 drops to the water.

Once the poison has been partly drawn out by the salt water gargle apply a cabbage leaf poultice externally to the neck (see p.60).

REPELLING INSECTS

Rub in oil consisting of 2 drops of lavender and rosemary oils diluted in 1 teaspoon of almond oil. Apply it to any exposed flesh externally but avoid contact with mucus membranes. Citronella oil which is often recommended smells so nasty it acts as a human repellent not just an insect one!

Vitamin B_1 (200 mg) has long been acknowledged as an excellent insect repellent as it is excreted through the skin and disliked by insects. The length of its effect depends on your weight, digestion and whether the B_1 is a sustained release formula. Adults should not take more than 50 mg daily and this for not more than 8 consecutive weeks without seeking medical advice. It takes some 48 hours to begin to be effective.

ITCHING

Itching from mild poisons, ivy stings for example, where there is no blistering can first be relieved by holding the area under running hot water at 120–130°F (49–54°C) for a minute or so and then applying a tincture externally made up of equal parts of mugwort, comfrey root, plantain and white oak bark.

Vulval itching can be helped by a compress of plain live yoghurt applied on a sanitary towel or dabbing the area with tincture of goldenseal, but as this stains badly remember to protect the knickers with a press-on towel.

Rectal itching, if it is not the result of bowel or rectal disease or antibiotics, is often the result of a poor reaction to coffee, tea, cold drinks, beer, chocolate or foods containing sugar or tomatoes. Alternate hot and cold sitz-baths and then apply tincture of goldenseal to the anus.

NOSE BLEEDS

Clasp the nose between the thumb and index finger and squeeze just enough to stop the bleeding but not enough to cause pain. Breathe slowly

through an open mouth. Hold the pressure for a minimum of 5 minutes, uninterruptedly. Then insert a ball of well masticated yarrow leaf as high into each nostril as possible, but not so high it cannot be retrieved. Continue to breathe through the mouth until your nose feels comfortable, then gently extract the yarrow leaf.

POISONING

If the victim has swallowed a poisonous food (like a toadstool) induce vomiting as quickly as possible by giving 1½ fl oz (35 ml) of ipecacuana syrup to an adult or ½ fl oz (10 ml) to a child (1 level teaspoon is 5 ml). Do *not* use tincture of lobelia as I have sometimes seen advised. This will only speed up the digestion of any of the substance left internally. Also do *not* use salt water which may induce acute salt intoxication, producing such symptoms as irritability, appetite loss, coma and convulsions. Poison centres have reported fatalities after well-meaning helpers have administered salt water. Vomiting can be made easier and more comfortable by taking an emetic while standing, lowering the head and rubbing the waist and abdomen gently.

In the case of a child place the child over your knee in a spanking position with the head lower than the hips to help avoid inhalation of vomit.

Keep the patient calm. Hysteria merely accelerates the speed with which the poison invades the system.

Seek immediate medical help.

If the victim has swallowed a poisonous substance several hours before showing symptoms of poisoning do not waste time by inducing vomiting. Get to the hospital quickly.

If you do not know what the victim has swallowed and he/she cannot tell you or is unconscious, ring the hospital immediately on the emergency number. Describe if possible the container and give all the information you can. They will advise you what can be done immediately while you wait for an ambulance.

If the substance is caustic *do not* induce vomiting as it will only burn the oesophagus further. Plenty of milk will slow its absorption.

If the patient is getting drowsy give a double strength decoction of peppermint tea and keep him or her walking. If the patient is unconscious do not give anything at all. Aspirin and paracetamol do not initially induce coma but in large quantities they can damage the liver so act quickly and get the patient to the hospital.

TREATMENT FOR ALL FOOD POISONING

Administer an enema if the patient does not already have copious diarrhoea and if the food was eaten more than 4 hours previously. Syrup of ipecacuana or tincture of lobelia (1 teaspoon/5 ml) at a time can be given to induce

vomiting and clear the stomach but soothe the aching stomach afterwards with sips of very hot peppermint tea. The only other thing to be taken is copious amounts of mineral water served at room temperature with a squeeze of lemon juice in each glass, the more the better to combat dehydration.

Do not work against the body's natural defence process of unburdening itself by trying to stop the diarrhoea with kaolin and morphine for example. Once the patient is calmer and has stopped vomiting give equal parts of goldenseal and chapparal two size '0' capsules every four hours. Gradually introduce pure fruit juices.

SHOCK

I carry Dr Bach's Rescue Remedy, which consists of the tinctures of 5 different herbs, with me permanently and consider myself well equipped for any emergency with a bottle in my pocket. This deals with the emotional effects of shock which if not helped immediately can reverberate through the system for years, causing an insidious build-up of all sorts of psychological and physiological problems. When coupled with scullcap it is one of the best remedies for short-term stress. (One size '0' capsule of the scullcap should be taken hourly as long as the acute crisis lasts.)

The Rescue Remedy should be diluted, 4 drops in 2 fl oz (50 ml) pure spring water to which add a little brandy or, if you are allergic to alcohol, cider vinegar added as a preservative. Take 4 drops of the previously prepared mixture in 1 teaspoon (5 ml) water and hold it on the tongue for 30 seconds before swallowing. Repeat this at least 4 and up to 6 times daily. If the patient is unconscious, rub it into the lips or on the wrists. Rescue Remedy is available from some health food shops or by post (see Appendix).

Shock could be one of the main products of sudden and sometimes permanent cell changes in the body, and it is one of the major contributors in all disease, which is why I find the Rescue Remedy so invaluable. Have some on hand at all times. It comes in a tiny bottle with its own dropper and is easily slipped into a purse, pocket or the glove box of your car.

Alternatively take 1 teaspoon cayenne in hot water. In the event of a heart attack take 3 teaspoons of the powder in a cup of water drunk immediately and all at once. Then take 10 drops of tincture of cayenne in hot water every 15 minutes until normal colour returns and of course get medical help as quickly as possible.

SEPTACEMIA *(Blood poisoning)*

Treatment is by antibiotics (see p.28).

SPRAINS

No matter which joint is sprained apply an ice pack to the area immediately. A packet of frozen peas will do in an emergency, while you prepare a proper ice pack by crushing ice with a rolling pin in a plastic bag before transferring it into a pillowcase.

An alternative way to make an ice pack is to soak a hand towel in cold water, wring it out till it stops dripping and place it folded on foil in the freezer. Let it stay there until crystals form but the towel is not frozen solid. This way it conforms nicely to the injured area.

If massaging an area with ice on a regular basis (and this has been found to be very useful in 80% of patients suffering from chronic pain of various types ranging from lower back pain, rheumatoid and osteoarthritis and cancer, supplying relief for up to 3 hours) fill a polystyrene plastic cup with water, freeze it, then peel the cup to below ice level. You then have a block of ice and a cold-resistant handle. Keep the ice moving to avoid skin damage and stop the treatment the moment skin numbness occurs.

When treating a sprain secure the ice pack close to the body by wrapping round firmly in more plastic and refresh as needed. Leave this on for 30 minutes, elevating the joint to stop effusion. If the fingers and toes turn blue you have overdone it. Loosen the plastic bandage and gently rub the blue bits to restore circulation. Then apply a thin layer of bandage soaked in comfrey as a compress securing this with a stretchy elastic bandage. Leave this on for a day. Do not allow the patient to move. If necessary apply a sling to immobilize a sprained shoulder or enforce complete bed rest to heal back sprain.

Remove the bandage and compress and immerse the joint or part of the body concerned in a warm decoction of comfrey root or use a compress of comfrey root as hot as is bearable. Gently move the joint but not to the point of pain. If it swells again apply ice and a cold comfrey compress otherwise there is no necessity for any further bandages. Simply apply arnica tincture externally 6 times daily.

If in any doubt at all and you feel the joint may be fractured seek immediate medical help.

TEETH

TEETHING

Rubbing the gums with a little honey and a tiny pinch of salt may take away some of the pain, but generally you will find you will need stronger measures. Try letting the child chew on a piece of arrowroot, liquorice or marshmallow root. Not too much liquorice or the bowels get very loose.

The biotissue salt calcium fluoride alternated with calcium phosphate also helps. These are available in well-stocked chemists. If the pain is very bad rub two or three drops of essential oil of camomile on to the gums having first mixed it with a little hot water and honey as the taste is very powerful and allowed it to cool until it is lukewarm.

DIARRHOEA WHILE TEETHING

Mix equal parts of the following seeds:

anise	*dill*
caraway	*fennel*

Pound as finely as possible in a pestle and mortar. Add enough slippery elm gruel to mix to a poultice consistency and spread over the stomach. Give no other foods or drinks until the worst of the diarrhoea has subsided, except weak yarrow tea (½ oz/15 g to 1 pint/600 ml) – 4 teaspoons every 20 minutes. If the diarrhoea simply won't pass off properly, feed the child slippery elm made into a thin gruel with yarrow tea.

TOOTH ACCIDENTS

These often look horrendous and are more upsetting for the parent than the child. If the trauma is very severe, either breaking or loosening the tooth, the blood and nerve supplies may be severed which means that the tooth becomes dead. Such a tooth will become infected after varying amounts of time. Signs of infection include pain, unusual mobility or looseness of the tooth, or a whitehead on the outside of the gum. However after any accident a tooth can be darkened and become discoloured which is simply the result of blood entering the inner pulp of the tooth. This does not necessarily mean that the tooth is dead.

It is always advisable to call a dentist in the case of a dental accident and book in for an emergency consultation. If the tooth is still in the socket but severely displaced the dentist may want to realign it providing the child is brought in for a consultation immediately after the accident. If there are signs of infection the dentist may want to do root canal work, cap the tooth or remove it altogether.

Initially if there is active bleeding the person offering treatment should press a tissue directly over the area hard until the bleedings stops. Ice can be applied if it makes the recipient more comfortable. Should the tooth be knocked out or cracked, move freely or the gum swollen or bleeding phone the dentist immediately. Rescue Remedy is invaluable here to alleviate shock.

TOOTHACHE

First try using dental floss between the aching tooth and its neighbours because impacted food may have set up the pain. If this does not work apply an ice pack against the jaw on the infected side and if this makes things worse apply a hot water bottle.

If you see a cavity make sure it is clean (sterile cotton on the end of a toothpick helps here) then pack into the hole a piece of cotton cloth saturated with oil of cloves or garlic. Rub the surrounding gum with tincture of cayenne and repeat as necessary.

Also rub ice over the web of skin between the thumb and index finger on the same side of the body as the pain is. This is the acupressure point used to relieve toothache. Make an appointment with your dentist as soon as possible.

THREATENED MISCARRIAGE

Most miscarriages take place during the first 3 months and are due to foetal abnormalities or a defective implanting of the embryo in the womb. If there are any signs of a potential miscarriage get the patient to lie down and take Rescue Remedy. Telephone the doctor immediately, stay in bed, keep warm. Drink half a cup of the following decoction every half hour until the bleeding stops then reduce the dose to every waking hour for 3 days. Thereafter take one cup with meals.

6 parts false unicorn	*1 part cayenne*
2 parts squaw vine	*1 part cramp bark*
1 part blackcurrant	*1 part lobelia*
leaves	*1 part wild yam*

The beauty of this combination of herbs is that they will not interfere with the natural process of miscarriage and if the foetus is damaged or dead then it will ease its expulsion.

TRAVEL SICKNESS

The astronauts were given ginger to stop space sickness. To relieve travel sickness take a wineglass of fresh ginger hot tea or two size '0' capsules of powdered ginger as often as needed. This has been proved to be twice as effective as Dramamine.

A particularly effective cure for seasickness is 3 drops of essential oil of marjoram in a little honey water.

Pressure on an acupuncture point called nei-kuan helps relieve seasickness or travel sickness. This point is on the surface of the inside of both forearms, 3 finger widths away from the crease of the wrist and in the

centre between the two flex tendons (see diagram). Press this point with the tip of the thumb (short fingernails help here). Repeat as often as necessary. A specially designed wrist strap with a rounded plastic button that will do this for you is available and neck pads that apply light pressure to appropriate pressure points in the neck are increasingly available.

It helps to focus on distant objects while travelling in a car or train rather than on nearby ones moving fast. Ensure children, while safely strapped in, are elevated enough to see out of the window. On a plane sit on a seat over the wheels rather than in the tail which moves more than the rest of the plane. On a ship stay on deck as much as you can and keep busy.

The nei-kuan pressure point is 3 finger widths from the crease of the wrist between the two flex tendons.

CHAPTER 16
MISCELLANEOUS
ALCOHOL AND ALCOHOLISM

Most of us are aware of the long-term effects of too much alcohol – liver disease, high blood pressure, irritability, tremors, slurred speech, inability to think, depression, fatigue – but few are cognescent of the adverse effects it has upon both the body's metabolism and nutritional state. Obesity is common (a pint of beer is 250 calories), as are damage to the oesophagus, stomach and pancreas, increased risk of gout, and increased cholesterol levels. Alcoholism can also exacerbate diabetes, heart disease, it can damage the brain and nervous system and increase the risk of developing cancer of the liver, oesophagus, larynx and mouth. It is now known that women who drink in the weeks before and during pregnancy risk giving birth to children with facial deformities or mental retardation.

For some people there is no safe limit, however low, and some are actually allergic to alcohol either because of the additives in it or because they have a food intolerance to grape, grain, sugar or yeast.

It is increasingly acknowledged that alcoholism may be the result of a failure to absorb specific nutrients. Of all alcoholics 95% are hypoglycaemic which is not surprising when you consider alcohol gives an even quicker sugar boost than sucrose. However, alcohol addiction is very rare on a really good diet.

TREATMENT

If possible follow a two-week vegetable juice fast to normalize blood sugar and stop the physiological alcoholic addiction. Normally I do not recommend supplementation while fasting but in this instance I give B_6 50 mg and magnesium 200 mg with one strong B complex vitamin tablet daily.

This is then followed by a hypoglycaemic diet of high fibre, carbohydrates with adequate protein, divided into 6 small meals daily. All fruit is to be eaten with a little protein and fruit juice is banned. The malnutrition that inevitably accompanies alcoholism requires individual supplementation, usually a broad spectrum of high potency multivitamin multimineral supplements and emphasis on B_1, B_2, B_3 and B_{12}, vitamin C that stops just short of diarrhoea, calcium, zinc, magnesium and essential fatty acids and a glucose regulator like Spirulena provided the lymphatic system is not heavily congested.

DELIRIUM TREMENS

This is no joke and requires immediate attention. It is the result of coming off a high intake of alcohol abruptly and withdrawal symptoms include mental confusion, memory loss, hallucinations, shaking, sweating, insomnia, agitation, fast pulse and high blood pressure which may go on for 3 to 4 days. Such symptoms can be eased with equal parts of scullcap and lady's slipper brewed as a decoction, strained and sweetened with honey. A quarter of a cup to be taken hot every hour until the DTs subside.

OTHER AIDS

One cup of angelica tea using the roots and leaves as a decoction taken 3 times daily helps to create a distaste for alcohol.

Evening primrose oil, 500 mg taken 8 times daily, softens the effect of alcohol withdrawal. If liver function is seriously impaired give the following formula throughout the course of treatment:

3 parts agrimony	*1 part fennel*
2 parts dandelion root	*1 part ginger root*
1 part calamus	*1 part marshmallow*
1 part catnip	*root*
1 part cramp bark	

Three size '0' capsules of the finely powdered herbs to be taken three times a day half an hour before meals with a cup of dandelion root decoction.

N.B. An alcoholic must not be allowed even a teaspoon of alcohol as it will only restimulate the craving. Therefore it is wise to check all herbal and allopathic medication to ensure it does not contain alcohol. For example, many allopathic cough mixtures are alcohol-based.

ALLERGY

Over the last decade allergies have become very fashionable just as whipping out tonsils was *de rigueur* from the 1930s to the 1950s. Is it any wonder when you consider the plethora of chemically processed foods and other irritants our overburdened livers have to neutralize? The problem is that most allergy specialists tend to look at the difficulty myopically and have no wholistic tools with which to diagnose the original cause of the problem. this is where iridology comes into its own (see p.48).

Accurate diagnosis is obviously vital for the treatment of every illness but this is especially the case with allergies. An allergy may be the result of adrenal exhaustion, improper weaning, specific food intolerance, enzyme deficiency, poor elimination or a permeable bowel, chemicals, heavy metal poisoning, chlorinated or fluoridated water, drugs, radiation, sensitivity to inhaled substances, spinal lesions, immune system disturbance, intestinal infection, liver disorders, or it may be psychosomatic. You can readily grasp why, given the list of possibilities, accurate diagnosis is the essential first step. I have encountered patients who have put themselves, or worse still their children, on severe elimination diets, often on their doctor's advice, only to find they are not suffering from a food allergy at all and in the process of following the special diet they have become malnourished. This is particularly worrying in the case of children who need all the necessary nutrients *all the time* to continue to grow and develop normally. I have encountered others who have struggled with symptoms like migraines, mouth ulcers, fluid retention, depression and even in one case schizophrenia without realizing the root cause was an allergy.

A GENERAL TREATMENT FOR FOOD ALLERGY

Fasting

Fast for 5 days on vegetable juice using organically grown vegetables only. Carrot juice makes a nice bland base and you can add smaller quantities of other vegetable juices. A teaspoon of horseradish or garlic juice is particularly helpful if the nose and eyes are streaming. Add this to 8 fl oz (250 ml) of carrot juice. Aim to drink 1 fl oz (25 ml) carrot juice for every pound of body weight.

If poor production of digestive enzymes is the problem (see p.29 for further information) add 5 fl oz (125 ml) of pineapple juice to 10 fl oz (300 ml) of papaya juice and 1 teaspoon of sprouted alfalfa juice.

For general strengthening of the system take 8 fl oz (250 ml) of carrots, 4 fl oz (100 ml) of celery and 4 fl oz (100 ml) of beetroot with 1 fl oz (25 ml) of fresh parsley juice.

Generally, it is better not to fast on fruit juices as I have found they tend to aggravate the symptoms in a significant number of patients. I disapprove of water fasting for similar reasons. A water fast alters thyroid hormone function and increases the production of hormones like cortisol from the adrenal cortex making the patient temporarily and artificially well to such an extent that every food which is consequently reintroduced causes a violent reaction.

After the fifth day take one food back at a time beginning with other vegetables including sprouted seeds, then fruit, then nuts and grains.

Colouring and preservatives – leave any food containing these till last. They are the main offenders. Alcohol, chicken and hen's eggs, chocolate, tea and coffee, citrus fruits, cow – anything that comes from this, including its flesh, peanuts, pork, sugar, whatever its colour, wheat, oats, rye and corn, yeast.

When introducing grains test each one for 2 consecutive days as they can cause a delayed reaction. It is advisable to stay on an 80% imaginative raw food diet consisting of fruit, vegetables, nuts, sprouted grains and seeds for 12 weeks. If you cannot do this at least eliminate any food that causes a reaction until you have been through your healing process. It may then be possible to introduce small quantities of the culprit food sporadically once the whole body is stronger.

HERBS

The following formula will strengthen your adrenal glands and detoxify your liver.

Equal parts of:

---

barberry root
borage
cayenne
dandelion root
ginger
ginseng (preferably Siberian)
hawthorn berries
liquorice

Take half a level teaspoon of the finely powdered herb mixture in vegetable juice 3 times daily. If you have high blood pressure avoid the liquorice and substitute motherwort instead. A minimum course of 3 months is recommended. If further treatment is necessary seek the advice of a consultant medical herbalist.

OTHER GENERAL AIDS FOR ALLERGY SUFFERERS

In the meanwhile stop smoking, come off the contraceptive pill which is a major cause of stress. The hormones in the pill can have side effects including increased risk of cervical cancer, thrombosis, raised blood pressure, diabetes, migraines, oedema, fluid retention and increased weight, thrush and depression and its effects on nutrition are staggering. It increases the need for vitamins C, B_6, B_2, B_{12} and folic acid, E, K and zinc and affects the proper metabolism of B_1. It can also exacerbate food allergies. Eat only natural unprocessed foods and try to ensure your meat is organically raised, avoid allopathic drugs if you can, limit alcohol to moderate quantities with meals only. If you are asthmatic avoid wine altogether which may contain metabisulphite or yeast, both of which can trigger a reaction. Organic wine is available by mail order (see Appendix), but as with all wine it is fermented and will obviously contain yeast, so even this is best avoided if a yeast allergy is suspected, though it does not contain metabisulphite.

Ionizers sometimes prove helpful to people sensitive to inhalant allergens. Get plenty of sleep, sunlight and clean air and above all exercise, this will produce endorphines and enkephalins which heighten the sense of well-being and stimulate the metabolism.

If chronic candidiasis is the problem get this cleared (see candidiasis, p.123).

ALZHEIMER'S DISEASE

This is the technical term for pre-senile dementia and occurs between the ages of about 40 and 65. It is alarmingly on the increase and in the United States nearly a third of people in this age group are said to be suffering from it even if only in very mild form. Symptoms include memory impairment, a lack of orientation and personal neglect (of one's appearance and surroundings). The cause has not yet been pinpointed but slow virus infection, genetic factors and aluminium toxicity head the list. Certainly high levels of aluminium have been found in some of those people with the condition and aluminium produces changes in brain structure similar to those seen in Alzheimer's disease itself because it is neuro-toxic. Occasionally Alzheimer's disease runs in families.

Aluminium status must be determined by a hair analysis test. It is unwise to cook with aluminium tools or pans or to eat food out of aluminium cans. Supplements of calcium and magnesium together with vitamin C inhibit aluminium absorption from food and help reduce the accumulation in the body. The diet should be rich in fish oils and an evening primrose oil supplement should also be considered. 50 mg of elemental zinc and 3 g vitamin C per day should be taken. 1 mg of vitamin B_{12} injected intramuscularly once weekly is advised. This injection needs to be given by your doctor. Ice-cold showers run over the head specifically are helpful as is more physical exercise, particularly exercises on a slant board (see p.141) and the continued lively use of your mental functions is of paramount importance.

A diet which emphasizes plenty of fresh fruit and vegetables, vegetarian proteins and high fibre whole grains with several servings weekly of fatty fish (mackerel, salmon, herring, sardines) together with plenty of garlic and onions, a daily serving of lecithin, fresh wheatgerm, beans and peas is helpful. Salt, alcohol, coffee, sugar, margarine, fried foods and all red meat, cheese, cream and milk should be avoided. Buttermilk and low fat yoghurt are permissible.

JET LAG

The problem only arises on crossing one or more time zones when the body resists adjusting to new cycles of sleep and wakefulness. There are no jet lag effects on north–south flights.

Try to adjust as soon as you board the plane. If by your calculations it

will be night when you land pull down your window blind, wear a sleep mask and try to sleep if possible. Equal parts of scullcap and valerian, two size '0' capsules taken before your time on board the aircraft may help here. If you leave at night and will be arriving during the day try to keep awake, keep your eyes open and the seat light on trying to make it seem that you are already in the new time zone. Reset your watch immediately after take-off because it will help you get in tune with the new periods of day and night you will have to adjust to on arrival.

If you land in daylight do not give in to the temptation to go to your hotel and take a nap. This will only encourage your old rhythms to keep working. Stay outdoors if possible. If you are indoors keep the lights on and stay awake.

On arriving at night go straight to your hotel room and try and sleep if you can.

Diet is vital. Protein-rich foods can provide up to 5 hours of energy whereas the foods which are high in carbohydrates such as pasta, salad, fruit and rich desserts provide an hour's energy surge but then tend to make you drowsy. If you arrive at your destination in the morning after a long flight and need to get down to work without delay start with a high protein breakfast and eat a high protein lunch to keep you going through the afternoon. For dinner eat carbohydrates to ensure sleep.

MARIJUANA SMOKING

Even more damage is done to the lung of marijuana smokers than heavy tobacco smokers. Its long-term effects can result in constant fatigue, an inability to study, poor memory retention, constant and recurrent small illnesses especially genital herpes, cold sores and skin problems and lack of muscular co-ordination.

The canabinoid substances in marijuana suppress the immune system and strongly interfere with vital cellular processes. The characteristic smell of cannabis smoke is enough to produce the same effects in a habitual marijuana smoker even when all the known active constituents have been removed – which means it is psychologically as well as physically addictive.

A good formula to help you get off it is:

4 parts prickly ash	*1 part bayberry bark*
2 parts ginseng	*1 part Icelandic moss*

Put 4 oz (120 g) in 2 pints (1.2 litres) of water and stir well. Cover and macerate for 2 hours. Simmer for half an hour then strain. Add 1 cup of blackstrap molasses and cup of glycerine to the liquid and dissolve over heat while stirring. Cool, bottle and take 3 tablespoons 4 times daily between meals, the last dose to be taken just before bed.

MULTIPLE SCLEROSIS
(Disseminated Sclerosis)

Early symptoms of the disease can often be radically improved
with changes in diet. The longer a person has had the disease the less likely
a cure because the protective sheath round certain nerves becomes scarred
and calcified causing permanent damage. With prolonged and persistent
treatment I have helped patients achieve very long remissions but self-
discipline is of the essence.

A gluten-free and virtually dairy-free vegan diet without any saturated
fats is the first prerequisite. No tea, coffee, alcohol, salt, sugar or fried
food. No gluten-free substitutes for bread baking (brown rice and millet
are permissible) and obviously no additives and preservatives and no
smoking. This leaves fruits, vegetables, brown rice and millet, seeds,
yoghurt, lactic fermented food washed of its salt content, whey, cold
pressed unsaturated oils, nuts and nut butters, sprouted and raw seeds and
tofu.

Mercury poisoning can produce the same symptoms as multiple sclerosis
so it is necessary to check for this. Vitamin and mineral supplementation is
always necessary and this needs to be tailored to the individual needs of the
patient. The B vitamins especially vitamin B_{13} found in whey, and the
essential fatty acids are specifically indicated. The mistake patients make is
not taking enough. Evening primrose oil needs to be administered at a
minimal dose of 4½ g up to 6 g daily.

Glandular disturbances of the liver, pancreas, thyroid, adrenals and gall
bladder are often part of the overall problem of multiple sclerosis and can
be individually determined with an iridology test and corrected with the
appropriate herb. Nervous restoratives like oats, damiana, vervain, Korean
ginseng, gota kola, lady's slipper, scullcap and lavender may also be
necessary.

Cold baths on rising taken in warm surroundings are especially helpful,
preceded by vigorous skin brushing. Osteopathy with particular attention
to the third and fourth cervical vertebrae and dorsals 5 and 12 is nearly
always advised. Daily yoga is an excellent idea as is outdoor swimming
especially in the sea. Some of my patients have shown great improvement
with hyperbaric oxygen therapy. This involves sitting in the kind of
oxygen tent they put deep sea divers in for several hours at a time on a
regular basis.

SMOKING

I do not want to remake the wheel but let me give you some facts about
smoking you may not already know.

1. Cigarettes affect the circulatory system. The heart accelerates from

20 to 25 beats per minute after one cigarette and so needs more oxygen but the poisonous carbon monoxide from cigarettes actually forces the oxygen out of the bloodstream.

2. Cigarettes reduce blood flow to the hands and feet and it takes 6 hours after the last cigarette to get the blood flow back on an even keel. So if smoking is the first thing you do on rising and the last on sleeping your circulation will probably only be normal for about 2 hours a day.

3. Smoking depresses the immune system and this process takes 3 months to reverse once you have given up.

4. Thinning of the bones is aggravated and may even be caused by smoking.

5. Men who smoke get more problems with their prostate glands and women more severe menopausal problems.

6. Smoking inhibits the pancreas and may lead to hypoglycaemia.

7. Smokers' ulcers will heal more slowly, if at all.

8. Tremors in the fingers increase by 39% after only one cigarette.

9. Deaths from lung cancer in women will overtake deaths from breast cancer by the year 2000.

10. Passive smoking greatly increases the risk of lung cancer as well as heart disease, nasal sinus cancer and brain tumour. If you work an 8-hour day in the same room as someone who smokes 30 a day you will have passively inhaled 5 cigarettes. This is enough, in the case of a pregnant woman, to affect the foetus.

COMPROMISES

If you simply cannot give up try smoking your own smoking mixture using herbs that do not contain nicotine. Coltsfoot is a tonic expectorant and actually decongests the tar-laden lungs, or try rosemary, mullein, yerba santa or sarsaparilla, spiced perhaps with cloves or cinnamon, mint, liquorice or even rose oil.

I cannot pretend that a home-made smoking mixture (and there are some available in health-food stores ready made up) tastes anything like tobacco but at least it is not physically addictive. It can be used as an in-between step to wean yourself off the habit of smoking altogether.

Lobelia which contains lobeline, a substance similar to nicotine but without the same effect reduces the sensation of need for nicotine but does not provided the effects that lead to addiction. Lobelia is on the poisons list and is only available from a medical herbalist.

Remember any burning plant material contains smoke and tar so herbal cigarettes should not be smoked except as a halfway step to stop smoking altogether.

AVERSION THERAPY

Every time you feel like a cigarette chew a piece of calamus root or dab some of the powdered herb on the tongue. If you smoke a cigarette after this it will make you physically sick.

Alternatively restrict your smoking to an intensive one hour daily (enough to cause nausea in itself!) and take 15 drops of lobelia tincture in water half an hour before this session and 15 minutes afterwards. If you smoke more than 1 cigarette take 15 drops every 15 minutes after each cigarette. The result will be nausea or vomiting which mentally becomes enmeshed with smoking.

OTHER AIDS

A 2-week juice fast is helpful both to detoxify the body and overcome nicotine craving. Motivation for this however needs to be high.

Coffee and tea need to be cut down to only 3 cups of each or both before attempting to give up.

Stress levels can be reduced by plenty of exercise.

Oral gratification by chewing a piece of liquorice root, provided the blood pressure is not dangerously high, is also helpful.

A hypoglycaemic diet helps to smooth blood sugar curves and so strengthen will power (see alcohol, p.22).

Keep doses of vitamin C to just below diarrhoea level while giving up smoking. It is, among its many other assets, a good detoxifier and will help to combat the apathy and depression that may set in if willpower wavers.

THE MUCUS-FREE DIET

The purpose of this diet is to clean all the mucus out of the body and encourage the proper assimilation of food. This preventive procedure cleanses mucus not just from the organs which people appreciate obviously contain it like the sinuses, bronchi and lungs but from every other organ in the body, particularly the colon.

No salt, eggs, sugar or any products containing sugar, meat in any form, dairy produce in any form, flour and flour products are permissible. A little organic honey, real maple syrup or blackstrap molasses is allowed. A small amount of white fish or organic chicken may be eaten once a week if the person on the diet feels this is absolutely necessary, but even this is best avoided.

All food taken should be free of sprays and chemicals and 70–80% of it should be raw. If possible breakfast should be avoided and only freshly pressed vegetable or fruit juice served at room temperature should be taken. The eliminative functions of the body begin at 4 o'clock in the morning and continue until midday so eating will stop this process. However if you are very hungry you may eat presoaked low heated grains or fresh fruit. Such grains may be prepared by soaking them first for 20 to 30 hours in purified water, and heating them in a slow cooker at a very low heat with enough water to cover overnight. Bulgar wheat and millet taste particularly nice served in this way. Both may be served with a little olive oil sprinkled on them, and honey or a pinch of spice are also permissible. Lunch and supper should consist of home-made vegetable soups or broths followed by lightly steamed vegetables or any combination of salads desired, including plenty of freshly sprouted seeds.

Proteins and starches should not be mixed in the same meal. Fruit should not be served when any starches are eaten and it is best to eat fruit at the beginning not at the end of the meal.

There are several helpful books on the subject which outline diet in much more detail (see Appendix).

REVITALIZING SUPPLEMENTS

Cayenne pepper

Take 1 teaspoon of cayenne pepper 3 times a day. Start gradually with ¼ teaspoon in a little cold water or vegetable juice and rinse the mouth out afterwards with a glass of water. Add ¼ teaspoon to this dosage every 3 days until 1 level teaspoon 3 times a day is reached. A graduated dosage accustoms the system to the pungency of the herb. Do not take for more than three weeks without a break of a few weeks before resuming (see contraindications, p.78).

Honey and cider vinegar

Mix 1 tablespoon of honey with 1 tablespoon of cider vinegar in enough warm water to liquefy the honey. Take this amount 3 times a day with or between meals so that at the end of a day a total quantity of 3 tablespoons of each item has been drunk.

Kelp

Take 2 teaspoons of powdered kelp daily. Use it as a condiment sprinkled on salads or put it into gelatin capsules.

Blackstrap molasses

Take 1 tablespoon of blackstrap molasses 3 times a day. May be eaten directly off the spoon or stirred into hot water. Please clean the teeth afterwards as, if it is left in the mouth, it will eventually lead to the acceleration of tooth decay.

Try not to eat between meals, but if eating is necessary chew seeds either singly or a combination of equal parts of sunflower, sesame and pumpkin seeds. Do not eat after 8 o'clock at night. If hungry after this hour eat fresh fruit or drink fruit or vegetable juices.

APPENDIX 1

BOTANICAL INDEX

A

Abor Vitae
(see Thuja)

Absinthe
(see Wormwood, Common)

Aconite
Aconitum napellus

Agrimony
Agrimonia eupatoria

Alfalfa
Medicago sativa

Allspice
Pimenta dioica

Almond
Prunus dulcis

Aloe
Aloe vera

Angelica
Angelica archangelica

Anise
Pimpinella anisum

Arnica
Arnica montana

Arrowroot
Maranta arundinacea

Artichoke
Cynara scolymus

Ash
Fraxinus excelsior

Autumn Crocus
Colchicum autumnale

B

Balm, Lemon
Melissa officinalis

Balm of Gilead
Populus balsamifera

Balsam poplar
(see Balm of Gilead)

Barley
Hordeum vulgare

Basil
Ocimum basilicum

Bayberry
Myrica pensylvanica

Bay Laurel
Laurus nobilis

Bearberry
Arctostaphylos uva-ursi

Beebalm
(see Bergamot)

Belladonna
Atropa belladonna

Benzoin
Styrax benzoin

Bergamot
Monarda didyma

Beth Root
Trillium erectum

Betony
Stachys officinalis

Bilberry
Vaccinium myrtillus

Birch
Betula pendula

Black Cohosh
Cimicifuga racemosa

Black Horehound
Ballota nigra

Black Snakeroot
(see Black Cohosh)

Black Walnut
Juglans nigra

Blazing Star
(see Unicorn, False)

Blessed Thistle
Cnicus benedictus

Blue Cohosh
Caulophyllum thalictroides

Blue Flag, Blue Iris
Iris versicolor

Blue Rue
Ruta graveolens

Boneset
Eupatorium perfoliatum

Bog Rhubarb
(Butterbur)

Borage
Borago officinalis

Bouncing Bet
(see Soap Wort)

Bramble
Rubus fructicosus

Brooklime
Veronica beccabunga

Broom
Cytisus scoparius

Bryony, White
Bryonia alba

Buchu
Agathosma betulina

Buckthorn
Rhamnus cathartica

Buckwheat
Fagopyrum esculentum

Burdock
Arctium lappa

Butterbur
Petasites hybridus

Buttercup
Ranunculus bulbosus

Butterfly weed
(Pleurisy Root)

C

Calamus
Acorus calamus

Camphor
Cinnamomum camphora

Cape Aloes
Aloe ferox

Caraway
Carum carvi

Carrot, Wild
Daucus carota

Cascara Sagrada
Rhamnus Purshiana

Castor Oil Plant
Ricinus communis

Catnip
Nepeta cataria

Cayenne
Capsicum frutescens

Celadine, Greater
Chelidonium majus

Celery
Apium graveolens

Common Camomile
Chamaemelum nobile

Camomile German
Chapparal
Matricaria necutita

Chasteberries
Vitex Agnus-castus

Chestnut, Horse
Aesculus hippocastanum

Chervil
Anthriscus Cerefolium

Chickweed
Stellaria media

Chicory
Cichorium intybus

Chive
Allium schoenoprasum

Cicely, Sweet
Myrrhia odoratus

Cinnamon
Cinnamomum zeylanicum

Citronella
(see Stone Root)

Clary Sage
Salvia sclarea

Cleavers
Galium aparine

Clove
Syzygium aromaticum

Clove Pink
Dianthus caryophyllus

Clover, Red
Trifolium pratense

Cocklebur
(see Agrimony)

Coltsfoot
Tussilago farfara

Comfrey
Symphytum officinale

Cornflower
Centaurea cyanus

Corn poppy
(see Poppy Red)

Cornsilk
Zea mays

Couch Grass
Agropyron repens

Cowslip
Catha palustris

Cramp Bark
Viburnum opulus

Cranberry
Vaccinium macrocarpon

Cuckold
(see Burdock)

Cucumber
Cucumis sativus

Cudweed, Marsh
Gnaphalium uliginosum

Currant, Red
Ribes rubrum

D

Daisy
Bellis perennis

Damiana
Damiana aphrodisiaca

Dandelion
Taraxacum officinale

Deadly nightshade
(see Bella donna)

Dill
Anethum graveolens

Dock, Yellow
Rumex crispus

Dulse
Rhodymeria palmata

E

Early Purple Orchid
(see Orchid, Wild)

Echinacea
Echinacea angustifolia

Elderberry
Sambucus sp.

Elecampagne
Inula helenium

Elm, Slippery
Ulmus rubra

English Daisy
(see Daisy)

English Holly
(see Holly)

English Primrose
(see Primrose)

Eucalyptus
Eucalyptus globulus

European Cranberry bush
(see Cramp Bark)

Evening Primrose
Oenothera biennis

Eyebright
Euphrasia officinalis

F

Fennel
Foeniculum vulgare

Fenugreek
Trigonella foenum-graecum

Feverfew
Tanacetum parthenium

Figwort, Knotted
Scrophularia nodosa

Fireweed
(see Willow-herb)

Flax
Linum usitatissimum

Foxglove
Digitalis purpurea

Fumitory
Fumaria officinalis

G

Garlic
Allium sativum

Gentian
Gentiana spp.

Gentian, Yellow
Gentiana lutea

Geranium
Geranium spp.

Gill-over-the-Ground
(see Ivy, Ground)

Ginger, Root
Zingiber officinale

Ginseng Asiatic
Panax ginseng

Ginseng, Siberian
Eleutherococcus senticosus

Gispy Weed
Lycopus europaeus

Goat's Rue
Galega officinalis

Goldenseal
Hydrastis canadensis

Goosegrass
(see Cleavers)

Goto Kola
Hydrocotyle asiatica

Gravel Root
Eupatorium purpureum

Great Burdock
(see Burdock)

Grindelia
Grindelia squarrosa

Groundsel
Senecio vulgaris

Gumweed
(see Grindelia)

H

Hawthorn
Crataegus monogyna

Heartsease
Viola tricolor

Heather
Calluna vulgaris

Hellebore, False
Adonis annua

Hemlock
Conium maculatum

Henna
Lawsonia alba

Hens and chicks
(see Houseleek)

Hibiscus, red
Hibiscus rosa-sinensis

Hills of Snow
(see Hydrangea, Root)

Holly
Ilex aquifolium

Honeysuckle
Lonicera caprifolium

Hops
Humulus lupulus

Horehound
Marrubium vulgare

Horseradish
Armoracia rusticana

Horsetail
Equisetum spp.

Houseleek
Sempervivum tectorum

Hydrangea, Root
Hydrangea arborescens

Hyssop
Hyssopus officinalis

I

Indian Tobacco
(see Lobelia)

Ipecac
Psychotpia Ipecacuanha

Iris
Iris versicolor

Italian Woodbine
(see Honeysuckle)

Ivy, Ground
Glecoma hederacea

J

Jasmine
Jasminum spp.

Joe-Pye weed
(see Gravel Root)

Juniper
Juniperus communis

K

Kava Kava
Piper methysticum

L

Lady's Mantle
Alchemilla vulgaris

Lady's Slipper
Cypripedium pubescens

Lavender
Lavandula officinalis

Lavender, Cotton
Santolina charmaecy parissus

Lavender, English
Lavandula angistofolia

Lemon
Citrus limon

Lemon Balm
Melissa officinalis

Lettuce
Lactuca spp.

Lily, White Water
Nymphaea odorata

Lime
Citrus aurantifolia

Linseed (Flax)
Linum usitatissimum

Liquorice
Glycyrrhiza glabra

Lobelia
Lobelia inflata

Loosestrife, Purple
Lythrum salicaria

Lovage
Levisticum officinale

Lungwort
Pulmonaria officinalis

Lupin
Lupinus spp.

M

Malefern
Dryopteris filix mas

Mandrake
Potophyllam peltatum

Marigold, Pot
Calendula officinalis

Marjoram, Sweet
Origanum marjorana

Marsh Marigold
(see cowslip)

Mayapple
(see Mandrake)

Maypop
(see Passion Flower)

Meadowsweet
Filipendula ulmaria

Mimosa
Inga laurina

Mint, Spear
Mentha spicata

Mistletoe
Viscum album

Monkshood
(see Aconite)

Moss, Icelandic
Cetraria islandica

Moss, Irish
Chondrus crispus

Moss, Sphagnum
Sphagnum cymbifolium

Motherwort
Leonurus cardiaca

Mugwort
Artemisia vulgaris

Mullein
Verbascum thapsus

Mustard, Black
Brassica nigra

Mustard, White
Sinapsis alba

Myrrh
Commiphora myrrha

N

Nasturtium
Tropaeolum majus

Nettles
Urtica diocia

Nutmeg
Myristica fragrans

O

Oak
Quercus spp.

Oats
Avena sativa

Olive
Olea europaea

Onion
Allium Cepa

Opium Poppy
(see Poppy White)

Orange, Bitter
Citrus aurantium

Orange, Sweet
Citrus sinensis

Orchid, Wild
Orchis mascul

Oregon Grape Root
Mahonia aquifolium

Oregon Holly Grape
(see Oregon Grape Root)

Origano
Origanum vulgare

Orrisroot
Iris florentina

P

Pansy
Viola tricolor

Parsley
Petroselinum crispum

Pasque Flower
(See Pulsatilla)

Partridge Berry
(see Squaw Vine)

Passion Flower
Passiflora incarnata

Pau d'Archo (Taheebo)
Tabebuia impetiginosa

Peach
Prumus Persica

Pellitory of the Wall
Parietaria officinalis

Pennyroyal
Mentha Pulegium

Peppermint
Mentha Piperita

Periwinkle, Greater
Vinca major

Pheasant's Eye
(see Hellebore, False)

Pilewort
Ranunculus Ficaria

Pine
Pinus spp.

Plantain
Plantago major

Pleurisy Root
Asclepias tuberosa

Poke Root
Phytolacca americana

Pomegranate
Punica granatum

Poppy, Red
Papaver rhoeas

Poppy, White
Papaver somniferum

Prickly Ash
Zanthoxylum americanum

Primrose
Primula vulgaris

Privet
Ligustrum vulgare

Psyllium
Plantago affra

Pulsatilla
Pulsatilla vulgaris

Purslane, Golden
Portulaca sativa

Purslane, Green
Portulaca oleracea

Q

Quassia, Bark
Quassia amara

Queen's Delight
(see Stillingia)

Quince
Cydonia oblonga

R

Raspberry
Rubus idaeus

Rest-harrow
Omonis spinosa

Rhubarb
Rheum palmatum

Rose
Rosa spp.

Rose Briar
(see Rosehip)

Rosehip
Rosa canina

Rosemary
Rosemarinus officinalis

Rue
Ruta graveolens

S

Sage
Salvia officinalis

St John's wort
Hypericum perforatum

Sandalwood, White
Santalum album

Sassafras
Sassafras albidum

Savory, Summer
Saturefa montano

Saw Palmetto
Serenoa serrulata

Scabious, Field
Knautia arvensis

Scullcap
Scutellaria spp.

Self-heal
Prunella vulgaris

Senna
Senna alexandrina

Shepherd's Purse
Capsella bursa-pastoris

Skunk Cabbage
Symplocarpus foetidus

Soap Wort
Saponaria officinalis

Solomon's Seal
Polygonatum multiflorum

Sorrel, French
Rumex scutatus

Sorrel, Garden
Rumex acetosa

Southernwood, Field
Artemisia campestris

Speedwell, Common
Veronica officinalis

Squaw Vine

Mitchella repens

Squill
Scilla spp.

Stillingia
Stillingia sylvatica

Stinking Benjamin
(see Beth Root)

Stone Root
Collinsonia canadensis

Strawberry
Fragraria vesca

Sumac, Smooth
Rhus glabra

Sundew
Drosera rotundifolia

Sunflower
Helianthus annuus

T

Tabasco Pepper
(see Cayenne)

Tansy
Tanacetum vulgare

Tea Tree
Melaleuca quinquenervia

Thuja
Thuja occidentalis

Thyme, Garden
Thymus vulgaris

Thyme, Wild
Thymus serpyllum

Toad Flax
Linaria vulgaris

Tobacco
Nicotiana tabacum

Tormentil
Potentilla erecta

Turmeric
Curcuma longa

U

Unicorn, False
Chamaelirium luteum

Unicorn, Root

Aletris farinosa

Uva-Ursi
Arctostaphylos uva-ursi

V

Valerian
Valeriana officinalis

Vervain, Blue
Verbena hastata

Vine, Grape
Vitis vinifera

Violet, Sweet
Viola odorata

W

Watercress
Nasturtium officinale

Water Horehound
(see Gypsyweed)

White Birch
(see Birch)

Wild Indigo
Baptisia tinctoria

Willow, White
Salix alba

Willow-herb
Epilobium angustifolium

Winter Green
Gaultheria procumbens

Witch Hazel
Hamamelis virginiana

Woodruff
Galium odoratum

Wormwood, Common
Artemisia absinthium

Whortleberry
(see Bilberry)

Y

Yam, Wild
Dioscorea villosa

Yarow
Achillea Millefolium

Yellow Lady's Slipper
(see Lady's Slipper)

APPENDIX 2

SOCIETIES

The National Association for Holistic Aromatherapy
P.O.Box 17622, Boulder, CO 80308-7622; (800) 566-6735, FAX (410) 564-6799.
Conferences and trade shows. Dues $35/year, include *Scentsitivity* newsletter.

For informational and research services:
The Herb Research Foundation
1007 Pearl Street, Suite 200, Boulder, CO 80302,
Telephone (800) 748-2617 or (303) 449-2265, FAX (303) 449-7849.
Dues $35/yr, include the magazine *Herbalgram*, and newsletter *Herb Research News*.

American Botanical Council
P.O.Box 201660, Austin, TX 78720; (512) 331-8868, FAX (512) 331-1924.
Quarterly magazine *Herbalgram*. Not-for-profit research and educational organization. Mail Order bookstore.

American Herb Association
P.O.Box 1673, Nevada City, CA 95959; FAX (916) 265-9552. Annual dues $20
include 4 newsletters/yr. Directory available.

The Herb Society of America, Inc.
9019 Kirtland Chardon Road, Mentor, OH 44060; (216) 256-0514. Membership
is through sponsorship of a current member. Annual dues $35 include the annual
The Herbalist and quarterly *HSA News*.

For professional herbalists:
Herb Growing & Marketing Network
P.O.Box 245, Silver Spring, PA 17575-0245; (717) 393-3295. Annual dues $45
include the annual *The Herbal Green Pages* and bimonthly *The Herbal Connection*. Both
can be obtained by separate subscription for $28.

Northeast Herbal Association, attn: Janice M. Dinsdale
P.O.Box 146, Marshfield, VT 05658; (802) 456-1402. Annual dues on a sliding
scale of $30-$100.

National conferences, member discounts, networking etc.:
International Herb Association

1202 Allanson Road, Mundelein, IL 60060; (707) 949-4372, FAX (708) 566-4580. Free brochure.

MAGAZINES

The Herb Companion
and
Herbs for Health
Interweave Press
201 East Fourth Street, Dept. A-CA, Loveland, CO 80537-5655; (800) 645-3675. Bimonthly $24/yr.

The Herb Quarterly
Long Mountain Press, Inc., P.O.Box 689, San Anselmo, CA 94960. $24/4 issues.

For advanced reading:
The Herb, Spice and Medicinal Plant Digest
University of Mass. Cooperative Extension, attn: Lyle Craker, Dept. of Soil Science, University of Mass., Amherst, MA 01003. $10/4 issues per year.

Newsletter on how to incorporate herbs into your life:
Herban Lifestyles
Stone Acre Press, 84 Carpenter Road, New Hartford, CT, 06057-3003. $18/4 issues per year.

A holistic newsletter for women:
Nature's Intent, WestCoast Wholistic Resources, 3792-H West 1st, Vancouver, B.C. Canada, V6R 1H4.

PRODUCTS

For dried herbs, beeswax, bath products, nut oils etc:
Gabrieana's
P.O.Box 215322, Sacramento, CA 95821. For orders: (800) 684-4372.

Seeds, plants, potpourri supplies, wreaths:
Heart's Ease
4101 Burton Drive, Cambria, CA 93428; (800) 266-4372.

Bulk organic herbs, spices, blends, potpourri, oils etc.:
San Francisco Herb Co., 250 14th Street, San Francisco, CA 94103.
For orders: (800) 227-4530. Free catalog.

Bulk herbs, year-round workshops, classes & special programs, books and garden
ornaments, potpourri, gifts and dried flowers:
Catnip Acres Herb Nursery
67 Christian Street, Oxford, CT 06478; (203) 888-5649. Online address:
http://www.catnipacresherbs.com

Fresh and dried herbs, potpourri, wreaths, classes, festivals, newsletter:
Betsy Williams/The Proper Season
155 Chestnut Street, Andover, MA 01810; (508) 470-0911, FAX (508) 470-1482.
Free brochure.

Bulk herbs, herbal supplies and books:
Rosie Moonbeam's Herb Cottage
1101 S. Logan Street, Denver, CO 80210; (800) 881-2086. Free catalog.

Herbal massage oils, soaps, potpourri:
Windy Hill Farm
3000 E. Colfax Avenue, No 105, Denver, CO 80206; (800) 484-6684, code 5104
or (303) 321-5104.

Flower essences, books and herb classes, natural skin care:
Herbal Essence, Inc.
P.O.Box 330411, Fort Worth, TX 76163; (817) 293-5410.

Herbal teas, essential oils, salves & extracts, organic herbs:
Mountain Rose Herbs
Box 2000H, Redway, CA 95560; (800) 879-3337. Catalog $1.00.

Essential oils, essences, dipsticks etc:
Gilbertie's, P.O.Box 118, Easton, CT 06612; (203) 452-0913.

Herbal remedies, simple and compound extracts, teas, body care products, oils and
salves, homeopathic kits. Workshops and classes. Retail and wholesale:
Avena Botanicals

219 Mill Street, Rockport, ME 04856 (207) 594-0695, FAX (207) 594-2975. Catalog $2.00.

Herbs, wreaths, potpourri, general supplies:
Oak Ridge Farms, P.O.Box 28, Dept. HC, Basking Ridge, NJ 07920. Catalog $2.00.

Natural Herbal products:
The Herbfarm
Tray HH, 32804 Iss-Fall City Road, Fall City, WA 98024; (800) 866-4372, FAX (206) 789-2279. Free catalog.

SUPPLIES

Jars, bottles, candlemaking supplies:
Mid-Continent Agrimarketing
8909 Lenexa Driva, Overland Park, KS 66214; (913) 492-1670. Free catalog.

Bottles, jars, droppers, vials seals etc:
Sunburst Bottle Company
5710 Auburn Blvd. #7, Sacramento, CA 95841; (916) 348-5576, FAX (916) 348-3803. Catalog $2.00.

Herbalware, including lip balm tubes, muslin bags, essential oils, atomizers:
Lavender Lane
7337 #1 Roseville Road, Sacramento, CA 95842; (916) 334-4400, FAX (916) 339-0842. Catalog $2.00.

Essentials & Such
4746 W. Jennifer Avenue, Suite 107-HC, Fresno, CA 93722-6422; (209) 277-4747, FAX (209) 277-9755. Free catalog.

Cape Bottle Co., 687 State Road, Plymouth, MA; 02360.
Phone/FAX (508) 224-7165

SEEDS & PLANTS

Numerous nurseries and garden centers across the country offer herb seeds and plants, many of them by mail order. All the large seedsmen also carry some herbs.

The following nurseries carry a large selection of herbs, many of which are hard to find elsewhere:

Deep Diversity
P.O.Box 15189, Santa Fe, NM 87506. Catalog $4.00.

Goodwin Creek Gardens
P.O.Box 83, Williams, OR 97544; (541) 846-7357. Catalog $1.00.

Nichols Garden Nursery
1190 SW Pacific, Albany, OR 97321; (503) 928-9280. Free catalog.

Richters Herbs
357 Hwy. 47, Goodwood, ONT, Canada LOC 1AO; (905) 640-6677. Free catalog.

Sandy Mush Herb Nursery
Dept. HBC, 316 Surrett Cove Road, Leicester, NC 28748-9622. Catalog $4.00, deductible from first order.

Sunnybrook Farms Nursery
9448 Mayfield Road, P.O.Box 6, Chesterland, OH 44026; (216) 729-7232. Catalog $2.00.

Tinmouth Channel Farm
Box 428B, Dept. HC, Tinmouth, VT 05773; (802) 446-2812. Catalog $2.00.

Well-Sweep Herb Farm
Dept. HC, 205 Mt. Bathel Road, Port Murray, NJ 07865; (908) 852-5390. Catalog $2.00.

Wrenwood of Berkley Springs
Rte.4, Box 361, Berkley Springs, WV 25411; (3-4) 258-3071. Catalog $2.00.

COURSES

Correspondence course covering Western and Chinese Herbology with oriental diagnoses and nutritional therapy:
East West Herb Course

Box 712, Santa Cruz, CA 95061; 800-717-5010.

Home Study Course:
Institute of Chinese Herbology
Admissions 2-H, 3871 Piedmont Avenue, #363, Oakland, CA 94611.
Telephone (510) 428-2061.

Home study programs leading to degrees in Natural Health and Holistic nutrition: The Clayton School of Natural Healing/The American Holistic College of Nutrition; (800) 659-8274 or (205) 930-4785.

Aromatherapy Studies course at home:
Jeanne Rose, 291 Carl St, San Francisco, CA 94117; FAX (415) 564-6799.

State Certified one and two year programs in Western Herbalism:
Rocky Mountain Center for Botanical Studies
P.O.Box 19254, Boulder, CO 80308-2254; (303) 442-6861.

Courses in aromatherapy, herbal medicine, homeopathy, nutrition, and flower essences etc.:
The Australasian College of Herbal Studies
P.O.Box 57, Lake Oswego, OR 97034;(800) 48 STUDY(78839),
FAX (503) 697-0615. Free prospectus.

Internships & apprenticeships, classes:
Dry Creek Herb Farm & Learning Center
13935 Dry Creek Road, Auburn, CA 95602; (916) 878-2441, FAX (916) 878-6772.
Catalog $2.00.

Herb gardens are a pleasure to visit as well as being educational. The Herb Society of America, Inc. is responsible for the Herb Garden at The National Arboretum in Washington, DC. They also publish a *Traveller's Guide to Herb Gardens*, ($6.00), listing herb gardens across the country. It can be obtained from The Herb Society of America, Inc., 9019 Kirtland Chardon Road, Mentor, OH 44060; (216) 256-0514.

INDEX